BILL BRUFORD
THE AUTOBIOGRAPHY

The practising drummer amid the romance of the road: Bristol, England, 1981

BILL BRUFORD
THE AUTOBIOGRAPHY

YES, KING CRIMSON, EARTHWORKS, AND MORE

BILL BRUFORD THE AUTOBIOGRAPHY

YES, KING CRIMSON, EARTHWORKS, AND MORE

A GENUINE JAWBONE JOURNAL
First edition 2009
Published in the UK and the USA by
Jawbone Press
2a Union Court,
20-22 Union Road,
London SW4 6JP,
England
www.jawbonepress.com

ISBN: 978-1-906002-23-7

EDITOR: Tony Bacon
DESIGN: Paul Cooper Design

Origination and print by Regent Publishing Services
Limited, China

4 5 6 7 8 15 14 13 12 11

Contents

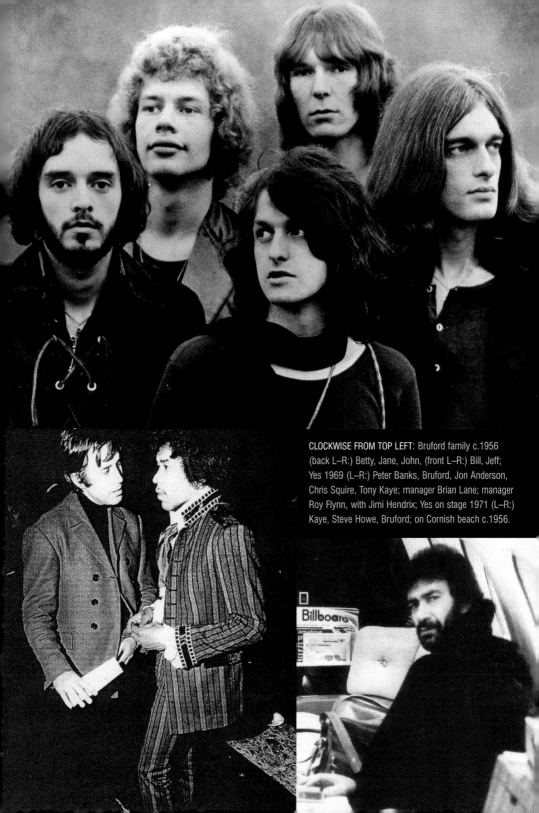

CLOCKWISE FROM TOP LEFT: Bruford family c.1956 (back L–R:) Betty, Jane, John, (front L–R:) Bill, Jeff; Yes 1969 (L–R:) Peter Banks, Bruford, Jon Anderson, Chris Squire, Tony Kaye; manager Brian Lane; manager Roy Flynn, with Jimi Hendrix; Yes on stage 1971 (L–R:) Kaye, Steve Howe, Bruford; on Cornish beach c.1956.

CLOCKWISE FROM TOP LEFT: Jamie Muir in action c.1972; UK (L–R:) Eddie Jobson, Allan Holdsworth, Bruford, John Wetton; backstage and trouserless, NYC '76 (L–R:) Genesis manager Tony Smith, Atlantic's Ahmet Ertegun, Bruford, Atlantic's Earl McGrath; EG Management directors Sam Alder (L) and Mark Fenwick; Genesis 1976 (L–R standing:) Mike Rutherford, Bruford, (L–R floor:) Phil Collins, Tony Banks, Steve Hackett; King Crimson in the studio c.1973 (L–R:) John Wetton, David Cross, Robert Fripp, Bruford.

MAIN PICTURE: Crimson soundcheck at the Greek Theatre, Los Angeles, 1981. OPPOSITE: Simmons drums publicity shot c.1981; *Feels Good To Me* sessions, Trident studio, 1977 (L–R:) Allan Holdsworth, Dave Stewart, Annette Peacock, Bruford, Jeff Berlin. ABOVE: Thinking about rehearsing, England 1980 (L–R:) drum tech Graham Davies, Bruford, manager Paddy Spinks, Adrian Belew. BELOW: *Fridays* ABC TV show, Hollywood 1981.

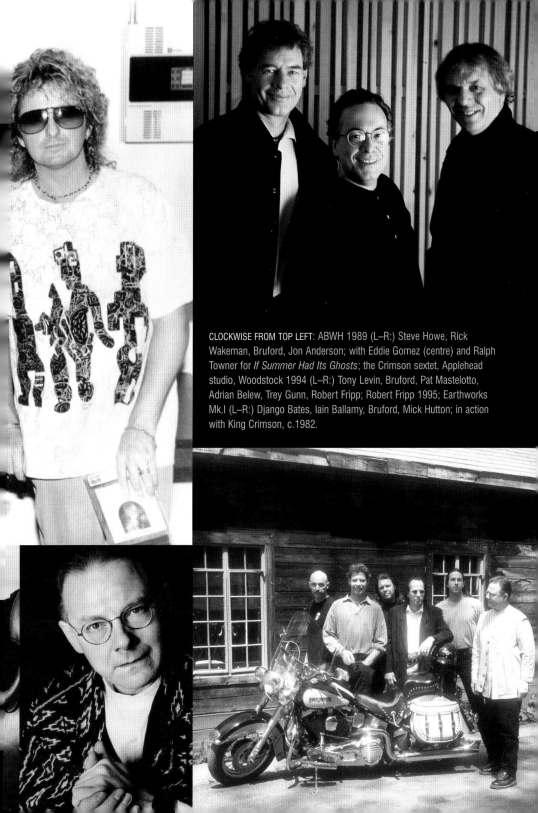

CLOCKWISE FROM TOP LEFT: ABWH 1989 (L–R:) Steve Howe, Rick Wakeman, Bruford, Jon Anderson; with Eddie Gomez (centre) and Ralph Towner for *If Summer Had Its Ghosts*; the Crimson sextet, Applehead studio, Woodstock 1994 (L–R:) Tony Levin, Bruford, Pat Mastelotto, Adrian Belew, Trey Gunn, Robert Fripp; Robert Fripp 1995; Earthworks Mk.I (L–R:) Django Bates, Iain Ballamy, Bruford, Mick Hutton; in action with King Crimson, c.1982.

MAIN PICTURE: World Drummers Ensemble, Amsterdam 2005 (L–R:) Chad Wackerman, Doudou N'Diaye Rose, Luis Conte, Bruford. INSETS L–R: Earthworks Mk.II 2003 (L–R:) Mark Hodgson, Patrick Clahar, Steve Hamilton, Bruford; Bruford Levin Upper Extremities (B.L.U.E.) Tokyo 1998 (L–R:) Chris Botti, David Torn, Bruford, Tony Levin; with Earthworks 2000; Earthworks Underground Orchestra 2005; improv with Michiel Borstlap, England 2008.

ABOVE: Earthworks Mk.III 2007
(L–R:) Laurence Cottle, Gwilym
Simcock, Tim Garland, Bruford.
RIGHT: with Carolyn in Capri,
Italy, 2007.

A NOTE FROM THE AUTHOR

In conversation at the school gates, the cocktail party, or down the pub, the subject of my occupation occasionally rears its head. When I reluctantly admit that I am a musician, the response, after slightly too long a period of reflection, is usually either: "Yes, but what do you do in the daytime?", which I love, or perhaps: "Yes, but what do you *really* do?" Few seem inclined to dig deeper, fearing rightly that the answer would be too far from the received notion of what it is to be a freelance player – have drum kit, will travel.

In this book, I've taken a series of these disarmingly simple and frequently asked questions, which so far I've spent much time and newsprint avoiding. Only now am I finally able to answer them, for myself as much as anyone, without fear or favour, and with as much honesty and accuracy as I can muster.

The music business seems to have only two stereotypes, rock god or has-been, and plenty of excellent musicians fit neither. This is the memoir of a modern instrumentalist who has found a middle way. I've toiled for 41 long and mostly happy years at the coal-face in the Industry of Human Happiness, and I can assure you that plenty of the work is done in the daytime.

Bill Bruford
Surrey, England, January 2009

1 SO HOW DID YOU GET STARTED?

Bruford to retire from active service.

Yes, King Crimson, and Earthworks drummer and bandleader Bill Bruford will no longer perform in public effective January 1 2009. After an exemplary 40-year career that has moved through progressive rock to electronic jazz and on to acoustic jazz, Bruford will hang up his sticks and concentrate on 'related activities'.

"It's been an exciting four decades, but now it's someone else's turn," said Bruford. "I'd like to thank my friends and colleagues and the greater listening public for giving me a more-than-fair hearing. My ambition was always to try to contribute to drumming and music in the broader sense – to try to imagine a better way of doing things today, or the sort of things we might expect drummers to be doing tomorrow. If I've managed to push things forward an inch or two over the years, then that is a source of satisfaction."

Bruford will continue to talk and write on the subject of his career and the percussion scene in general, and will archive and manage his voluminous back catalogue of recordings on Summerfold and Winterfold Records.

called Carolyn into my room for a second opinion. She said something about it not seeming much after all those years of graft and went back to the kitchen licking the spoon. This was the worst thing – there was no gold watch in this game. I should have liked one of those. Presented with that bauble, the mothballed colliery worker, the creaky security guard, and the dusty academic with the elbow patches on his Lovett tweed jacket could all put a line underneath their lives' work and move on. But that seems beyond us in the music business, which requires that, like Sir Cliff Richard and Donny Osmond, we are all Peter Pans, forbidden to grow old. I have to write a book before I can move on.

❏

It is 1965, and Ernest Marples has only recently opened the initial stretches of Britain's motorway network. The whole thing is a bit of a novelty. In a fabulously plummy voice, the UK government's Minister of Transport has spoken about "previously unheard-of speeds of up to 70 miles an hour". The Great British Public, attracted to these slabs of racetrack like moths to a flame, proceed to treat them as if they were no different to the tiny B3857 road to Worsley. They pull over and park on the slow carriageway. They enjoy picnics on them. They reverse up them, they go down the wrong side of them, and they fall asleep while driving on them. In these days before a central barrier, they even cross over and turn around to head in the opposite direction.

To this madness is added a small army of rock groups, in vehicles rented from a highly unsupervised and fledgling car-rental industry. Suddenly it's possible to get from Sheffield to London in time for last orders at the Speakeasy, a musicians' drinking club and home base to many of London's finest, if you pack up the gear quickly and put your foot down. And that'll save having to run out of the hotel in the morning without paying the bill.

By the summer of 1968, a long line of Ford Transit vans points north up London's Earls Court Road. It seems as if everyone, like me, is in a band – and the one I'm in is called Yes. Our transport arrangements are pretty standard. We used to travel with our equipment in our cool-enough long-wheelbase Transit called Big Red, but at the first sign of success, musicians and equipment had separated. The gear could then be driven ahead by a road manager, and – untold luxury, this – the band could drive itself, or, for the wildly successful, *be driven to the gig* and swan in elegantly for the soundcheck without having had to lift, hump, plug in or set up, or otherwise spoil your hair.

In Yes, we have the use of an over-powered Volvo sports car, unwisely loaned to the group by its owner and our manager, Roy Flynn. Left to our own devices, we somehow have to arrange pick-up times at several addresses around London, get to the beginning of the M1 motorway at Hendon before the rush-hour kicks in, and make it half way up England to Kidderminster in good time for the show.

Mindful of Ernie Marples's unheard-of speeds, we have naturally set the departure time hopelessly late. A punctual arrival would have been scarcely achievable even if all the participants had actually been ready to depart when the car pulls up outside their pads. It is now, always has been, and will always remain a matter of status among males as to who keeps whom waiting and for how long. If I can enter the room after you, I shall have kept the occupants waiting a shade longer than you, and shall have successfully demonstrated my superior rank. When gentlemen held the door open for ladies and ushered them into the room first, I had always concluded that that was as much to do with the male indicating his dominance over the female as anything to do with being polite.

In Yes, this game is played to a high level of brinkmanship. The end result is that the five musicians will become familiar with the high-pitched whine of the Volvo's intercooler as we scream into the outskirts of town anything up to an hour or two late. I no longer care that, again, I am not going to get a bite to eat before the show or that the rehearsal of new material has again been postponed. I no longer care that audiences are by now being kept waiting, that I never get to check the drums before walking on stage, or that there is now a thin trickle of sweat running down the back of my neck.

Oh no. What I really care about is running red lights. The first time it happens, my head is in a book and I pretend I haven't seen what I thought I had just seen. But the second time, the blood drains from my face and I cannot restrain myself.

"Christ, are you mad?" I scream. "It's red!"

"Really?" says the irritated driver, knuckles white on the steering wheel. "Looked green-ish to me."

"Bloody hell…" contributes a dozing keyboard player, woken into a cold sweat as the driver slams the brakes on at a T-junction. "Where's the fire? What time are we on?"

"Eight, I think," says the bass player. "Or is there a support group?"

"Micky said nine, I swear. But he didn't say anything about a support." Micky is the band's long-suffering road manager, now driving the equipment van. My palms are sticky. The Volvo ducks and weaves in heavy traffic on the Kidderminster ring road. I am going to die in this thing not because we are late – and this is very Yes – but because no one knows whether we are late or not.

Assuming we've actually survived the outward-bound journey, there is always the return to look forward to, and this has a number of blood-curdling variants. Inevitably, a majority will conclude that if we pack up the gear quickly and step on it, we can make the couple of hundred miles back to the Speakeasy in time for last orders at 2:00am. It always takes longer to pack up than you think. Dressing rooms have to be emptied of clothes and alcohol, strange-looking cigarettes have to be rolled and smoked, bits of gear forgotten, remembered, looked for, found, re-packed.

If we leave behind the lights of Kidderminster, or Accrington, or Boston around 11:00, we are doing well. Adrenalin-fuelled conversation will eventually give way to a lolling silence, while the Volvo howls down the motorway into the black night at around 90 or 100 miles an hour. Outside, parallel Morse-code streams under Cinturato tyres; inside, canned humanity nods, burps, snores. All except me.

I'm sitting shotgun, next to the driver. Because now the big danger is sleep, and my self-appointed function is to keep the driver awake. It has been a long day, a potent brandy, an energetic set, and some stately weed. I talk. I talk for England. I talk for my life. I demand answers from Jon Anderson, our singer and occasional chauffeur, his face lit by the glow of the dashboard, shoulders slumped, head dipping, dropping, drifting, nodding, dipping, dropping, drifting, nod …

"Jon!" I scream. "Wake up! Are you sure you're all right?" The car jerks back into the centre of the lane. It's begun to drift toward the siren song of the central reservation, and there is no crash-barrier. "Sure, man. No problem." Another ten minutes or so, and the eyelids lower again, the head lolls, the vehicle drifts, and the whole sorry cycle repeats itself. Incredibly, we usually do get to the Speakeasy for last orders. Our manager Roy also manages the club, so the steak sandwiches and the scotch and cokes come at a very favourable price. From there the individuals will usually cab it home with various female companions in tow.

But sometimes they don't. Martin Lamble, the gifted 19-year-old drummer with Fairport Convention, died when their rental Ford, the same one that Aynsley Dunbar's band had used the week before, crossed the central reservation and ploughed headlong into an oncoming lorry. They had lorries in those days. Martin never got his steak sandwich. The more I dwelt on this, the more I realised our transport arrangements couldn't continue the way they were. I told the band at the next meeting that I'd make my own travel arrangements. I hadn't thought this through, and it would be expensive, but it didn't seem to bother the other guys. They said: "See you there." The next gig was in Amsterdam.

It seemed a bit weird on the plane all on my own, and, way before the era of cheap flights, this was a pricey sort of jaunt. But I had face to save and a point to make. I said I'd travel solo, and by God I would. Maybe if I could get the band to pay, they'd notice the extra expense and agree, as a way of reducing costs, to drive a bit slower. I cab'd it in from the "aeropuerto" (all airports were so named, for some larky reason that I can't remember), checked into the small but mercifully clean two-star on the Leidseplein and, feeling unusually independent and sophisticated, settled down with a farmer's coffee to await the arrival of my colleagues.

After several hours of mulching around the area, I thought I'd better go back and wait by the phone in case they'd stopped to give me a call. Back in the room, I dug out practice-pad and sticks, and began my working day, in a routine that was to change little over the next 35 years.

I sat myself on a chair with the pad on another chair or the bed, preferably in front of a mirror to check the hand positions. I use a matched grip: both sticks should move identically, describing the same slim arc of travel, and left and right wrists and fingers should look alike. Then, through a long-honed series of rudimental warm-up exercises, sometimes with metronome, sometimes without, I worked on single-stroke rolls, paradiddles, and triplets, with and without various accent patterns. Then the various ornaments and embellishments, handed down through the dust of some American Civil War battlefield: the flams, drags, and ratamacues.

I was plugging into some deep well of rhythmic consciousness. Others had been here before; others were probably here right now; and others would be here in the future. This certainty made me feel connected. This routine and honourable labour had nothing to do with chart positions, styles of music, or record companies. It had existed since before all that and would exist long after all that had ceased to exist – the musician's endless struggle to master the instrument. As hotel rooms improved over time, I might be able to break this hour or two with tea. As practice-pads became even quieter, I no doubt irritated fewer occupants of the next-door rooms, but it was to be essentially the same ritual of connection throughout my working life.

I also knew the feeling and the result of over-practising, whereby after two hours or so of intense work I'd blown it completely for the evening's gig – wrists and fingers too tired to co-operate to my satisfaction. And I knew the opposite hazard, of too little warm-up time, where the blood had not circulated properly to wrists and fingers, and my left stroke in particular felt jerky, without fluidity, and sounded like it.

"But I'm sure no one noticed," would come the tender response when I brought either of these two difficulties to the attention of my girlfriend, Carolyn. "But *I* did," I would mutter on the first few hundred occasions, after which I didn't bother any more. There are two principal questions that I've been asked a thousand times by everyone, but particularly by those who I'm surprised don't know the answer. One of them floated to mind again, as I turned back to the practice-pad.

"But what, exactly, do you do during the *daytime*?"

Without much noticing, it had moved from dusk to dark outside, and we should be at the club by now, setting up. I cursed to myself and felt my stomach turn over. They should have been here hours ago. Finally, the phone emitted a Euro buzz from the bedside. "Bill? It's Chris." That was unnecessary; the drawling whine of Chris Squire, the bass player, was instantly recognisable if a bit faint. "Where the hell are you?" I asked.

"We're at a police station about 30 miles away. They are just taking down some details."

"About what?"

"Well, Jon had bit of a nod-off, and we left the road and went down this embankment kinda fast." My attention drifted with the detail. I didn't know whether to laugh at the stupidity, cry thanks for deliverance from potential disaster, or scream blue murder at their irresponsibility.

"As I said, good job it was grassy," the voice was saying. "We just rattled along at 45 degrees until the thing came to a halt. Messed up the front bumper, though, but no one was hurt." Idiots, I thought. Then I said, "How long will it take you to get to the club?"

"Thing is, Bill ..." I knew trouble was coming; it was always preceded by a Thing-is "... if you pop down the club now, you could give Micky a hand setting the gear up and soundchecking, and it would be all sorted by the time we turn up, and we should just about be able to make it."

This was the only man I was ever going to know who could impose upon me, give me a near heart-attack, force me to change my own plans, and then get me to set up his bass, all in the same sentence.

❏

Born in 1949 in Sevenoaks, Kent, in south-east England, I was raised the third child in the post-war-Britain household of a veterinary surgeon. John Bruford, my dad, had a large-animal vet's practice that, before the war, had stretched as far east in the county as Canterbury. By the time I arrived, he was mostly servicing the farms that nestled in the idyllic nooks and crannies of West Kent. He knew the lanes like the back of his hand, and, in the halcyon days before instant communications, would potter gently from farm to farm, cowshed to cowshed, listening to *Woman's Hour* on the radio in his Morris Oxford, just about getting through his rounds. This work-rate, it must be said, was not conducive to the generation of a large income. We lived the modestly threadbare but always comfortable existence typical of many an elbow-patched doctor, rector, teacher, or solicitor in the austerity of 50s England.

We talked little, my dad and I, but words didn't seem very important to fathers and sons of that generation. They usually got us into trouble or led to misunderstandings. He seemed a contented man, as well he should have been, being well looked after by my mother and our always elderly Irish live-in help. The permanently stooped and ever-twinkling Mrs Young seemed the oldest living creature upon which I had set my young eyes. Every birthday I asked her how old she was, and every birthday I got the same reply in her broad County Cork brogue. "A hundred and eight."

My father provided the income, looked after the local cattle, and received a decoration from the Queen for his work on tuberculosis in the post-war milk supply. But it was my mother Betty who tended to all the serious matters in life: the social position and health of the family; her children's moral and physical education; sport, games, and exercise; and travel, which was much promoted and perennially said to broaden the mind. The small frisson of excitement I still get as I turn the corner into Heathrow airport, long since unwarranted in today's unglamorous conditions, seems left over from an earlier age.

Failure to acknowledge a gift, or to write a thank-you letter after any social engagement, was a capital offence, worse even than 'showing off' or 'boasting'. Two spoons of cod-liver-oil a day, moderation in all things, eating a little bit of everything off your plate, and no stealing – these were the fixed beacons of my life that, I was assured, would guide me safely though all the choppy water I was likely to encounter. Half a century on and safely through much choppy water, I see little to add to this modest list as I attempt fatherly advice to my own children.

I roomed with my brother Jeff, a few years my senior and a cheerful soul, whom I rated as marginally less important than my older sister, Jane, only because she had a boyfriend of some importance. This fellow had come into possession of a pair of brushes for a snare drum. Uncertain what to do with them, he gave them to Jane, a gesture of some magnanimity, I suppose, but hardly a token of undying love. Equally uncertain, my sister asked around, and gave them to me, indicating that if you swished them around on a thick-card album-sleeve of the day, it'd sound just like the real thing.

The brushes weren't bad as far as they went, but I thought they'd be infinitely more useful if applied to the red-glitter drum kit I'd noticed lurking in the small ads in *The Sevenoaks Chronicle*. It seemed reasonably priced at 17 guineas. A brief negotiation with my father, the extraction of muttered promises of renewed effort at school, a short car ride with my mother to collect, and the little beauties were mine. Initially they lived in my bedroom, but after an anonymous note or two through the letter-box, I was ordered up another flight to the attic space.

It was there, in the must and the dark and the smell of old suitcases, that I first got to grips with the mysteries of the percussive arts.

❑

As a young boy, I'd beaten silent time with my fingers along with the windscreen wipers on my father's Morris Oxford. I'd shivered excitedly as I watched the rollers and the tides come and go on the longer rhythmic cycles to be found on Polzeath beach in Cornwall. As a teenager, I would synchronise my being with the clickety-clack of the fast train up to London from Sevenoaks to Charing Cross.

Rhythm seemed to be everywhere, but no one else seemed to notice it. And if it did raise its head, people pointed, looked the other way, and hurried on by. Instinctively, I knew it wasn't to be found in machinery but in the human heart – each one with its individual, measurable rhythmic pattern. With time and experience, I came to know how you could fine-tune rhythm and how you could deceive with it.

Early on as a young professional I loved to tinker about in the engine-room of rock groups. I always had a greasy rag handy, because setting up a drum set was a dirty job that required ratchets, spanners, the odd screwdriver, and some oil. Then I tinkered about in the engine-room of jazz groups – finer, more sophisticated mechanisms altogether. After that, I just tinkered about.

Later on, Yes had a manager named Brian Lane. A colourful man with a ready smile and a heavy beard – part East End barrow-boy, part con-man – he was the sort who would sell his own grandmother for an extra punnet of winkles, if they put winkles in punnets.

As is best with any manager, I'd studiously avoided the discussion of music or anything directly connected with it. One afternoon, fate had thrown us together on the tour bus, and, despite my best endeavours, the man seemed determined to indicate his knowledge of the subject. It clearly wasn't going to be a long conversation, and a discussion of drumming had only just got underway, when it occurred to me that this otherwise seemingly intelligent man beside me thought that the drummer in a band hit any drum or cymbal as hard as he liked pretty much at any time that took his fancy – mostly, or even preferably, at random.

Nowhere could this misguided soul detect any pattern, any repetition, any logic, any thought, any passion, or any skill in the drummer's efforts. He was the type who would fail to understand that success at football, cricket, indeed all sports, is largely dependent upon rhythm and its close cousin, split-second timing. Brian, from whom musical understanding was not going to be required, was later to be the rocket fuel that propelled my career to unimagined heights, but the subtleties of rhythm were well beyond his sphere of comprehension.

What, then, was this rhythm thing that seemed to fox Brian and to cause such mirth, such embarrassment, such covering of table legs? Was it a bang on a drum? No: no rhythm there; that's merely a single event in time. Was it the banging of two notes on a drum, one following the other? No, not really. It seemed to me that rhythm was the space *between* the two notes, and that was what counted. Rhythm was a hole, an emptiness, a negative, a place you put yourself. It was a nothing – the silent space between two musical events.

The wind and the waves also had their own rhythms, of course, but they were so large and blurred they made the heart leap in a different way. Plenty of great drummers had become experts at coming and going in waves upon the drum set, boiling masses of white foam crashing over the cymbals and drums and then retreating over the shingle into a lull before returning with renewed power.

Over four centuries, the West had developed and perfected the marvellous machine called tonal harmony and its cousin, counterpoint, but had allowed its rhythm to wither on the vine. The elemental power of rhythm atrophied in the face of the new invention, and in my corner of the world, rhythm was everywhere in retreat. The three-quarters of the world's population that, through ignorance or indifference, had failed to espouse the new system of harmony, continued as usual. For them, melody and rhythm remained the primary carriers of music.

THE AUTOBIOGRAPHY / 1

Africans, Indians, and Chinese developed sophisticated drumming cycles of enormous subtlety and complexity, but these systems were usually denigrated in the West as 'primitive' so that the sophisticated new invention of harmony should be given precedence.

Britain was living through the halcyon lazy summers before the Great War, when, seemingly out of the blue, Stravinsky turned up in Paris with *The Rite Of Spring* and scared the living daylights out of everybody with what they imagined 'pagan' rhythm sounded like. Rhythm was back in a big way. For British middle-class youth, it was time to uncover the table legs.

Britain hurriedly looked to America and began to import something it thought was jazz but immediately became confused. The gentleman's approach to rhythm lay with the swish of patent leathers and coat tails on the dance-floors of the Trocadero and Quaglino's. Popular music was dance music, and dance music was popular music. After World War II, the seductive rhythms of Afro-Caribbeans and Afro-Americans were suddenly sashaying down the gangplanks of ships. There was no turning back.

This was the rhythmic terrain that greeted the very young Bruford as he set about his mother's pots and pans with a couple of old wooden spoons. I listened, liked what I heard, and found it to be good. All of it.

I loved it when my mother rolled up the carpet and danced with my father, a graceful man whose quickstep must have made the girls' eyes flash at the West Kent Hunt Ball. He was Fred to her Ginger. I loved the smell of the wooden cupboards by our fireplace that housed a huge collection of mostly cracked 78rpm shellac discs by people like Charlie Kunz and Caruso. I loved the show tunes of *Oklahoma!*, *The King And I*, and *Salad Days*. But overnight they were eclipsed by Scotty Moore's guitar break on Elvis's 'Hound Dog'. How could a guitar sound like that? Where was Memphis? What was the Cumberland Gap? Who were the Puerto Ricans, and what were they doing on Leonard Bernstein's West Side? So many questions, and no one to ask.

❏

29

Upstairs in the attic, my efforts began to bear fruit as I played along to Kenny Ball's trumpet on 'Midnight In Moscow', determinedly swishing my new brushes around on my red-glitter snare drum and, for relief, picking out the melody on our tired and little-visited upright piano. It wasn't until I landed at boarding school, seven miles away in Tonbridge, that I fell upon grittier musical fare. I wasn't entirely sure my father knew where the place was, and I can remember him setting foot on the premises on only three occasions. Sent there to learn how to behave and be self-reliant, I was nonetheless grateful to be left alone and in peace to get on with my growing-up and my musical studies.

As an impressionable young teenager, I gravitated toward some older boys at the school who were jazz-hungry, and they had a pretty decent quartet. These guys weren't much interested in the British version of dixieland jazz purveyed by the stripy-vest brigade of Chris Barber, Kenny Ball, and Acker Bilk, you understand. They hung on the cutting edge – Miles, Monk, Gillespie, Parker. We checked out the Stones, and we quite liked The Beatles, but there just didn't seem to be enough action happening in the music. The drummer, Mike Swann, was leaving the school, so he taught me how to swing on the ride cymbal, said something about bebop, and told me I was his replacement.

My public debut came at 14. After a handful of lessons with Mike, I was sitting in with the hotel band on a skiing holiday in Saint-Cergue, Switzerland. Egged on by my friends, and with my mother's encouraging "you can do anything you put your mind to" ringing in my ears, I flailed away precociously to, if not roars of applause, then at least smiles of approval.

This was hip! This was a breeze! These people loved me! I did it some more. Back at school, Mike brought me down to earth with a bump, the first of several occasions on which I would require that particular service, and set me to work on the jazz drummer's bible of the day, Jim Chapin's *Advanced Techniques For The Modern Drummer*. I frequently wish I'd mastered a few more beginner's techniques, the bypassing of which was to fester within my playing for many years.

My academic diligence at school was rewarded with permission to go up to classical concerts in London's West End, back in the dormitory by 11:00 sharp, sir, promise. These 'classical concerts' were not usually in any concert hall but in some pub or club down the fabulously exciting back-streets of neon-lit Soho. The musicians were classic but certainly not classical: a minor semantic difference. There appeared to be no age restriction getting into these over-heated and cramped little jazz and blues places, or if there was I never encountered it.

Here I heard, by the age of 18, just about everyone I needed to hear: the Harlem stride pianist Willie 'The Lion' Smith; organists Jack McDuff and Jimmy Smith; British rhythm-and-blues stars John Mayall, Cyril Davies, Graham Bond, Long John Baldry, The Yardbirds; guitarists Eric Clapton and Johnny McLaughlin; Ornette Coleman; Jimi Hendrix jamming with Roland Kirk. The list was long, varied, and distinguished.

At Ronnie Scott's Old Place in Chinatown it was drummer Allan Ganley, tenorist Tubby Hayes, Ronnie's group, saxophonist Evan Parker, and a host of others. But British jazz was becoming rough work. In the late 60s, it adopted a hard-left political posture, indicated musically by the squeaky-bump improvisations of The Spontaneous Music Ensemble. It came to occupy much the same political ground as the Italian Communistas, who insisted all music should be free and then broke down the barriers outside the Palazzo Dello Sport in Rome – and helpfully let down the tyres on King Crimson's truck when we turned up to play for them in the early 70s. Presumably they thought the truck was free, too.

The good drummers were mostly jazz drummers, but they were fast becoming ex-jazz drummers. Peter Baker was about to become Ginger Baker of Cream; Charlie Watts was a Stone; Mitch Mitchell of Riot Squad fame was about to have an experience with Jimi. Any red-blooded rhythmatist who could handle his instrument well would have preferred to play with Hendrix rather than The Spontaneous Music Ensemble, and jazz in Britain sulked accordingly for a couple of decades until the arrival of a whole new corps of revitalisers with names like Django Bates and Iain Ballamy in the early 80s. When I started with Yes in 1968, I wasn't sure if it was going to be a rock, pop, or jazz group – and we didn't care, so long as it sounded as far removed from all three as possible.

Meanwhile, I drank it all in: the way these people walked, the way they talked, the way they sat, the way they held a cigarette, the way they played. I noticed what they wore and delighted in their eccentricities. I sweated and then shivered and sweated again, more with the excitement of the sheer visceral power of the music than the temperature in the room. It was the nearest thing to my childhood memories of the Cornish beaches, of the salty swirling rollers smashing against the rocks. The only thing I didn't notice were the other people. I was as oblivious to them as they were to me. When the music started, there *were* no other people.

Then the drizzly walk to Charing Cross station, the illicit No.6 cigarette, the endless clickety-clack of the old slam-door train as it lurched through the night, the walk up Tonbridge High Street, and, yawning, bed. Those clubs were my university. I wasn't quite sure what course I was on, but I was definitely learning a lot about something in a hurry. School finished, and armed with a place at the more tangible Leeds University as a fallback if I could make no headway in the Industry of Human Happiness, I struck out boldly on what is now called a gap-year, to see where my drums would take me.

❏

Early and brief discussions with my parents about what I might do with my life were not promising. My father had only two recommendations, the first being that any occupation under consideration should be something that made you happy. This was a revolutionary idea in post-war Britain, where a whole generation of men viewed any work that you were lucky enough to possess as an unpleasant duty, suffered only to support the family. What made me happy was intense concentration upon my red-glitter drum set, to the exclusion of almost everything else. My mother frowned upon this, believing that obsession and over-concentration on any one passion would surely bring ruin. Both were deeply suspicious of the notion of being a musician, deemed in the Bruford household, with some accuracy, to be a sophisticated but underpaid form of showing off.

I remember in the early days coming home proudly with my first record with Yes, but the music fell on deaf ears. Both parents winced at the clanking bass of Chris Squire, Tony Kaye's churning Hammond organ, the warblings of Jon Anderson, and the sheer aggression and drive underpinning the whole exercise. I also produced an early appearance in the local newspaper, which caused my father some consternation. For him, the only people who appeared in newspapers were attention-seekers, criminals, or those for whom something had gone badly wrong in life. Which one was I?

His attitude was broadly correct, if perhaps wanting in detail. This business of being a musician is not all it's cracked up to be, really. We Brufords, philistines to the last, had never met one – if you discount gnarly old Pilbeam, who had turned up at my sister's 21st birthday party in 1963 to play some foxtrots. He came in by the back door, with the caterers. When I announced my intention to join the profession full time, my father thought I wanted to be gnarly old Pilbeam.

❏

For centuries, musicians have necessarily tended to combine their musical activity with some other trade or profession, and a separate occupational group did not appear until the Victorian industrial revolution heralded the division of labour. What people like me do is relatively new. Two-thousand years of recorded history shows that while music itself is highly valued, the social position of those who perform it is rather less exalted. It's generally been a low-prestige job, accorded ambiguous and often dubious status.

In ancient Greece, musicians were scorned as merely manual

workers; in ancient Rome, female instrumentalists were ranked with the courtesans and prostitutes; and in other times and places they have been slaves. By the 13th century, the social roots were clearly evident of the distinction between popular and art music, between the scholarly music of the elite and the oral tradition of the people. The pop guys were always, and always will be, a dodgy lot.

Medieval jongleurs and minstrels were regularly under suspicion because their mobility, unusual occupation, and often scandalous behaviour put them on the margins of society. So the rock idea of Mrs Average having to lock up her daughters as The Rolling Stones, The Sex Pistols, or Arctic Monkeys come to town, is not new. In fact, the reverse is the case. This is such a well-imbued convention in popular music that perfectly pleasant but reluctant beginners have to work hard to adopt sufficient anti-social standing, or street-credibility, to give their efforts a suitably dangerous air.

Elite medieval or renaissance musicians were in the service of the royal court or the church, or both, under patronage. Mozart is traditionally cited as the paradigm for that most heroic and romantic of figures: the artist no longer prepared to tolerate the constraints and servitude of patronage. It was Mozart who sought to establish himself as the first freelance professional musician. Such a risky move was economically incomprehensible to his father Leopold, brought up in the old world, but Mozart continued, with relatively little success, dying poor but not in penury. He was a model for so many things, but particularly as the first to suffer while trying to reconcile artistic ideals with economic reality, God with Mammon, art with commerce – an unavoidable struggle for the creative musician in today's highly competitive market.

I was blissfully unaware of all this on January 1 1968, the day I had chosen to become a professional. Seemed like a propitious kind of day to me, a good day to start something. I had loftier, infinitely more romantic ambitions than hanging around chasing hits. I was going to be Max Roach, the American jazz drummer and MacArthur

Foundation award winner. Never mind the skin colour, cultural background, and level of musical ability. I'd been told by school and parents alike that I could be anything I wanted. Well, I wanted to be Max. Effortless, elegant, and economical: three adjectives you could readily apply to his work. To me, they sounded like something worth aiming for.

Many years later I was to meet Max backstage at a King Crimson show. Aged past 70 and as interested as ever, he'd come to check out the latest deal in electronic drums, to see if these toys could really do anything. My friend who brought him, Steve Apicella, said Max had managed to sleep through most of the music – which was a first for anyone within the first 30 rows of a King Crimson performance.

❑

After a couple of false starts and an eye-opening trip to Rome, I met Jon Anderson and our bassist Chris Squire courtesy of a small ad in the *Melody Maker*, a national music paper of the day. The students may have been a-rioting at the LSE, a-sitting-in at the Sorbonne, or a-burning effigies of Nixon at Kent State, but all that summer of '68, Jon, Chris, and I were engaged elsewhere.

We beavered away with guitarist Peter Banks and organist Tony Kaye in the basement of The Lucky Horseshoe coffee bar on London's Shaftesbury Avenue, and by September we were airing the results in a handful of small venues in and around town. My place at Leeds university had to be accepted or declined in October. Vacillating horribly between two possible futures, I eventually decided that there wasn't enough evidence that this music thing might sustain me, that 'straight' life should be given a final chance. I announced, rather sheepishly, that I wanted to quit the group to pursue an academic future.

The band was not unreasonably as astonished at this turn of events as it was to be at my permanent departure four years later. They picked themselves up and found a replacement who could just about do the job. Temporarily more concerned with the quality of my accommodation in a grimy back-to-back in Eldon Place in Leeds than anything to do with music, I was thrilled to hear they were coming up to play shortly after my arrival. I could bask, surely, in a little reflected glory.

I duly assembled my new friends, put the word out that this lot were worth a serious listen, and turned up at the show, both pleased and proud that the old firm was in town. Unfortunately, it turned out that the new boy on drums liked to hit the sauce on a regular basis, including this evening, and he wallowed along at the back of the music, about a beat behind everyone else. They sounded like they were dragging a sack of coals uphill. Even my tone-deaf student companions noticed, and they began to slope off to something more exciting.

Humiliated, I went backstage to commiserate, only to find that the problem was worse, or maybe better, than I could have imagined. The band had an offer to play London's Royal Albert Hall the following Tuesday on a career-making show supporting Cream at their farewell concert, and doing it with this clown was out of the question. They begged. I played hard to get for about 30 seconds. "Never turn down an opportunity" was the second of the two invaluable pieces of career-advice my father had offered.

❏

The subject of money, its presence or absence, had been rarely mentioned in the Bruford house, except on the occasions when our increasingly upmarket neighbourhood began to be populated with those who clearly had too much of it. Our neighbour on the right was a civil servant with something called an index-linked pension, a new-fangled machine that meant you had all the money you were ever going to need forever. I was reminded by my mother, who noted these things more keenly than my father, that this was something not given to a professional man like him. A few others of her acquaintance she tartly dismissed as being "rather too pleased with themselves", this being one of very few sins – one rung below 'boasting' in fact – that would occasion serious disapproval from this generally warm-hearted and welcoming woman.

In our later teenage years, however, it emerged that there were insufficient funds to provide further education for all three Bruford children. My brother Jeff, hard-working to a fault but diagnosed as non-academic, would not be in need of an expensive university place. That left my immensely capable older sister Jane and me, but the available funds were unlikely to stretch to more than one set of fees. Until even the 60s, it was commonly thought that a girl would have less need of a degree because she would surely be married shortly, so Jane's continuing education was probably sacrificed on the altar of bright little Billy's future.

What was it that finally caused me to take leave of my senses, surrender my valuable place at Leeds, and lurch unwisely toward a precarious future in the music industry? Was it the lure of the Albert Hall offer, or the disinclination to say no, or the overbearing confidence instilled in the arrogant young student, or all of these? I had ignored the signs and looked the other way for years. I had pretended I couldn't possibly be a musician and persevered with this double existence for my entire adolescence. Enough, already.

The innumerable hours spent covering the 198 miles from Leeds to London and back in a VW Beetle, the magnificence of the red-velveted venue, the show itself, the swift rejection of my application for a sabbatical year from the university ("best wishes for the new work to which you will be turning …"), the breathless phone call home from the call box outside the Brotherton Library ("leaving the university, dad; I know you and mum will be a bit upset but …"), all sped past in a blur.

Bright little Billy's sudden rejection of the academic path brought an understandable and tearful sobbing on my shoulder from my sister, with wailings and lamentations about what this would do to mum and dad. Happily, mum and dad, in an admirably pragmatic British-middle-class sort of way, perked up no end when I turned up two or three years later with some gold albums. I couldn't fail to notice that the notion of a career in music, bathed suddenly in this warm, golden light, was accepted as quickly as the unhappy rejection of the much valued university place was forgotten.

Finally, I packed my bags and drove south from Leeds for the last time, green around the gills but utterly committed to my new occupation. Never was there a keener recruit. I hadn't written the word musician in my passport yet – that would take a while. It seemed to me you had to earn it. You could call yourself what you liked, but it didn't mean anything until it was written in your passport.

2 WHY DID YOU LEAVE YES?

There had been a couple of one-night stands, but Yes was my other first girlfriend, the first to whom I had committed, and as such I shall never forget her. For four years, the insufferably arrogant and astonishingly ignorant young drummer from Sevenoaks tripped and smashed his way around in the engine-room of this Yes machine, pulling levers to see if they worked, turning knobs and dials to see if he could get a reaction. My adolescence at Tonbridge School had left me with too much self-confidence – an unshakeable belief that I was some kind of Übermensch, ready to change the world. An unstoppable Taurean bull in a china shop. Had I motto, it might have been: Just do it.

In Yes, I learned that you couldn't take a song publishing agreement to a divorce lawyer and that it's wiser to read any contract before you sign it. I learned that you can have a totally different mix of instruments in your recording studio headphones to the man standing next to you, and I learned what happens if you down too many scotch and cokes on an empty stomach. I began to get an idea that music was a substance that might react poorly to brute force, that could not be bludgeoned into submission no matter how great the enthusiasm you brought to the task, and about which there may be several contradictory opinions, all equally valid.

By the end of my first year with the group I'd already managed to leave and rejoin. I may have got that from Robert Wyatt, the much-loved drummer from a contemporary group, Soft Machine. When he left that band, the music press screamed "WYATT LEAVES SOFT MACHINE!" with the appropriate degree of hysteria. After about a week, another headline trumpeted "WYATT REJOINS SOFT MACHINE!" with a secondary line in smaller print: "Drummer can find no other group he'd rather play with." In two clean steps, Robert had managed not only to lever himself twice onto the front page but also to bathe the Softs in reflected glory.

Yes had played chic little clubs in London, countless universities and colleges up and down the country, and had visited the Royal Albert Hall twice. By the end of my second year, we'd established a residency at the Marquee, the very place in London's West End where I had gone to see my original heroes. We'd reached as far as Ireland, Germany, and Belgium – there was always a lot of Belgium – and driven the 891 miles to Montreux in Switzerland in one long haul, seven up in the six-seater Big Red, the seventh bottom having to make itself comfortable on an upturned milk-crate.

I'd heard my performances on radio and record, and I hadn't got a clue where the money was going. By 1971, I was making an acceptable £25 a week, and we were becoming a headlining group, slowly building an audience – still possible to do in those days. But we'd seen altogether too much of Birmingham Town Hall, and we were all tiring of the Blue Boar motorway services. Two albums had been received either coolly or with complete indifference, and any real success seemed to be as far away as it had the day we started.

More precisely, success appeared to live about 3,000 miles away in North America, but we were lost as to the right direction. We had started to operate a cold revolving-door policy, of which Josef Stalin would have been proud, replacing manager Roy Flynn, guitarist Peter Banks, and keyboard player Tony Kaye in short order, as better, sleeker versions appeared on the scene.

The captain was starting to throw the sailors off the deck, and onlookers could only conclude that the ship, if not exactly sinking, was going round in circles. After the triumphant evening with Cream at the Royal Albert Hall, great things had been predicted for us. But two-and-a-half years and a couple of albums later, we were down to our last £50 and desperate.

❏

In the UK in the early 60s, the public perception of musicians, insofar as the public noticed them at all, was that they were either in an orchestra, a dance band, or a skiffle group. Or possibly one of those 'beat group' johnnies from Liverpool who wanted to get famous as fast as possible. If none of those templates appealed, then you could always be a music teacher, one of the much-reviled squad of mostly female harridans who made the lives of their pupils a misery with scales and graded exams.

The options on offer were miserable, and I didn't care for any of them. I saw the whole thing differently. I was all for suffering for my art, especially as I had yet to try some of that. It was the old romantic notion that Mozart had got us into. I didn't care about classical music – not enough drum action there for my taste – but I was in shock from A.B. Spellman's *Four Lives In The Bebop Business*, one of the books the jazz guys at school had given me, presumably by way of initiation.

Here was courage and heroism of the highest order. Here were musicians inventing – nightly, on the bandstand – a musical language at the highest technical and aesthetic level. No one had ever played like Charlie Parker or Dizzy Gillespie before, let alone to general indifference if not outright hostility. Turned out they redirected the course of popular music, but they certainly didn't get much thanks for it. When folks don't like what you do, they can stay away in droves.

My mother's opinion of 'show-offs' probably helped steer me toward the notion of success rather than fame. Having achieved a level of respect from my peers, and hardly any fame at all, I'm pretty happy with that. The only time I was famous, for the obligatory 15 minutes, was for a negative – for leaving Yes, the group I had helped form. Not famous for having co-founded it, you understand, but famous for having left it.

Fame didn't, and doesn't, look any fun at all to me. All that being hounded out of supermarkets when all you want to do is restock the fridge. Drummer and singer Phil Collins was a barrel of laughs when Genesis was on the verge of the Big Time. When I caught up with him several million CD sales further down the road, the twinkle seemed to have disappeared from his eyes. With the first of several subsequent divorces under his belt, exiled from his own country for tax reasons, and shouldering the complexities that come with having an income approximately equivalent to the gross national product of a small African nation, it was perhaps to be expected. But no, fame didn't seem like my kind of thing at all.

Success, on the other hand? Now ya talkin'. Even at a young age I had plenty of views on that. Success meant being able to leave the party when you wanted to. It implied having something interesting to contribute, like Roach and Parker, and having that contribution acknowledged by your peers. Having them run with that idea, take it some place. Success meant being listened to, making a difference. It meant leaving your patch different to the way you found it. I figured that was what the listener was paying me to do.

With experience, I came to believe there was a dignity to be had as an instrumentalist who pushes things forward. What if you did this and I did that? What if we looked at this another way? Ideas were to be tried out without fear or favour, irrespective of what the public might or might not want. What the public wants is what the public had yesterday, or so runs the facetious opinion among musicians – so not much succour coming from that direction. British jazz commentator John Fordham put it well. I wanted to belong to a "unique community, in which ideas are freely shared; fashion, fame, and wealth are secondary; dogma is suspect and tolerance prized; and life is lived vividly – and humorously – in the present".[1] I wanted to be a jazz musician.

These ideas may be easier to articulate now than when I was a raw recruit, but they were in my DNA from the get-go. I believed intuitively that the non-classical instrumentalist – someone like me – could be more than a mere functionary. We could be explorers, smashers of icons, boundary crossers, slaughterers of sacred cows. For the bold, those prepared to cross the Bridge of Inhibition, there was useful work to be done on the instrument, any instrument, and particularly the drums.

The classical world, about which I knew little, appeared to revolve around the composer, the conductor, and the soloist. The Big Three. Everybody else, it seemed, lived in fear of losing his job. A fluffed note in an exposed position – horn players could lose a lot of sleep over that particular nightmare. Or, if you were rank and file in one of the older and better-endowed European orchestras, and had a job for life, you were in fear of dying from boredom. As a mature musician, I remember describing my work schedule to my indulged colleagues in the percussion section of the Amsterdam Concertgebouw Orchestra. I explained to them, gently, that I played the music I liked. Quizzical expressions. With whom I liked. Mild incomprehension. When I liked. Incredulity. Where I liked. Slack jaws and disbelief. This from guys with a dedicated Boeing 747, police outriders to escort them to the world's finest concert halls, and a staff of social directors, psychologists, and physiotherapists that would make a Dallas Cowboy blush.

In the commercial world, about which I came to know rather more, the three big cats in the jungle were the singer, the songwriter, and the producer. During my time, the first two often became the same person, and at time of writing, everyone does everything – not necessarily an improvement. But certainly no one cared what the drummer thought.

There was a brief post-Beatles aberration from the norm, during the late 60s and up to about 1976, that involved so much money flowing into the industry it couldn't be spent fast enough. If The Beatles had been to India and used a sitar, you could too. They write their own songs? Cool! You can too, and drive a ton more money your way. In the 70s, all manner of stray musicians were turning up in studios. Now we can produce ourselves, let's get an orchestra! (Deep Purple.) Or some jazz guys! (Mahavishnu Orchestra.) Or some jazz guys with an orchestra! (Mahavishnu Orchestra with orchestra.)

The crew had mutinied and taken over the ship. For a short moment, for a few crazed years, people even cared what the drummer thought. We all wanted to do it differently from the other guy. Hell, everybody had a record deal, and everybody was selling records. The only smart thing about me was that, in the warm post-Beatles sunshine, that was the time I picked to be a musician.

❏

"So whad'ya need?" The voice comes from my left, its owner an enthusiastic and bright-eyed record company assistant. Solid son of a professional Englishman, I'm unaccustomed to ever needing anything much, and obviously look perplexed enough at this idea to warrant a second try. "Whad'ya need? What am I gonna getcha? Champagne?"

We've just arrived at JFK for Yes's long-anticipated first American tour, and the party splits into two limos. Jon Anderson and I end up in this one, together with this over-attentive record company minder and Brian, the arrhythmic manager. I've never seen, let alone been in, a vehicle as preposterous as this before, nor have I ever walked into the stultifying sauna that is an August Manhattan evening, nor have I ever seen a billboard that size opposite the terminal exit which loudly instructs: "1-800 LOSE FAT." Within minutes of setting foot on United States soil, therefore, I've acquired a fair introduction to the long-running and deep psychosis of this great nation, and at 20 years of age, I'm about to get my first lesson in the general workings of its economy and the specific workings of its record industry.

"It's un-American not to consume," says Brian. He lets that hang in the air for a bit before elaborating. "It's a capitalist, service economy. You're supposed to need something," he patiently explains, "and then you pay for that need to be satisfied. If you don't need anything just now, hang around for a bit; you'll need something very soon. If you don't buy, the market won't work. It's all about the artificial creation and sustaining of perceived needs, which can only ever be partially satisfied; or rather, the satisfaction of one only leads to the creation of another."

"Got some aspirin, Brian?" whines Jon. "My head is splitting."

"Sure, buddy." The minder leaps into action before the manager can respond, pleased to be helpfully American at last. Finally these guys need something.

Brian produces a *Cash Box*, finds the Hot Hundred Albums, and waves the magazine around. There we are: our *Fragile* album is Number 5 on the list, below Neil Young's *Harvest*, *America* by America, Paul Simon's *Paul Simon*, and Harry Nilsson's *Nilsson Schmilsson*. We have a hit, and all I'm thinking is how small the word Yes looks in the magazine.

But I'm getting the hang of this capitalism thing. I reach forward for the cold fizzy stuff in an ice bucket by the TV. "Well, since you insist, I could try a little of this by way of celebration." How thoughtful of the label to provide so generously – you'd never get this in tight little old England. Jon's headache is about to get worse. We clink glasses, and just as I raise mine to my lips, Brian, staring out of the window with a long-suffering, been-there, done-it-all-before look, mutters into his beard: "Been in the country five minutes, and he's drinking the royalties away."

"I thought this was on the house," I say, feeling a bit dim. "Nah – nothing you get from a record company's free," says Brian. "There are no gifts. It's all your money. It all gets charged back to you, and if you spend it all on the band, none of it ends up in your pocket." Sound advice indeed. I drink his very good health.

❏

I immediately loved North America, despite, or because of, the fact that in 1968, habits and conventions there were a greater mystery to a middle-class English boy than those of, say, the French. Famously, the British are separated from Americans by a common language, but the canyon between the two cultures was all the more grand for being unexpected.

In England, it could take years to make a friend. In the USA, Hank was your friend in five minutes and for ten minutes, and you were then expected to remember this tenuous association were you to meet Hank again two years later, because Hank certainly would. Americans put names to faces.

In post-war austerity Britain, we were taught to eat everything on our plates. "Think of the starving Africans," I was told a thousand times. I was astonished to find in the USA that the reverse pertained: it was polite to leave half of everything on your plate, amid protestations as to the size of the portions. Evidently, my American friends needed a constant reminder that at least there, in that vast and beautiful land, the milk and honey still flowed.

The local promoter was hugely efficient, enthusiastic, and concerned to make the evening go well – not least because he'd probably be out of pocket if it didn't. Some North American talent-buyers remain princes in their local fiefdoms, territories they fought for and won in rock's 70s heyday, sustained in power by nothing more exciting than being the best at what they do. Today, in a homogenised market dominated by a few big players, many promoters have succumbed to the national bacillus of the likes of Clear Channel and promote music they don't like for people who don't really want it. Sullen and squeezed to the margin, the small local promoter is no longer offering cold cuts in the dressing room, and the place turns into a dance club with glitter ball at midnight to pay the rent. "I want that gear out of here by 11:30 latest, so we can let the new people in."

Travel was easy; no need for upturned milk-crates in this shiny land. A band like Yes would put all its instruments in the belly of a small commuter jet – Mellotron, drums, guitars, the lot – and travel by discounted DUSA tickets (Discover the USA), which got you a long list of cities for a cheap price. The road manager was sent ahead to the airport to check in the bags and collect boarding passes for the musicians, without further identification, so they could arrive minutes before the gate closed and stroll onto the plane as if it were a private jet. From kerbside to take-off was regularly timed at under ten minutes, but Chris Squire still managed to keep the plane waiting.

Americans "can do", or at least could do. In 1968, unusual phrases such as "Yep," "Sure," and "No problem" could be heard under blue American skies as frequently as "Not a chance, mate," "I shouldn't think so," or "I wouldn't if I were you, guv" were heard in the grey mist of a London morning. Forty years later, it seems that Americans still "can do", but with tangibly less confidence. And in a reversal of roles, Europeans are, gratifyingly, beginning to entertain the notion that they might also be able to do.

In 1968, the Italian promoter had failed to build the stage because he had neglected to obtain the 'permit' from the Communist town mayor; the Spanish promoter had forgotten to promote the gig, because attendance figures were irrelevant to him as he already had his budget from the city; and the French promoter, if he showed up at all, was unable to unlock the dressing-room door because the guy who had the key had just left town for a month on holiday. And, naturally, getting paid was a three-act play, usually in Italian.

Four decades later, much has changed. The European promoter tends to regard you, the musician, as his guest for the evening. He'll meet you at the airport, provide local transport, pay for the hotel and feed you decently, or even spectacularly if he is Italian. He now has both dressing-room key and a stage. Throw in the single European currency, cheap flights, and no requirement for work visas, and it's easy to see how for the British musician a four-night run in Madrid or Barcelona is increasingly easier on the nerves and the pocket than four nights in New York or Los Angeles.

Chances are you can now call around European promoters' offices at 9:00am and reach a helpful assistant who speaks acceptable English and knows what the problem is – impossible 40 years ago. The European promoter flatters himself that he is in the company of artists whom he will parade to his friends at dinner; his North American counterpart wastes no time explaining that you are part of the hired help for the evening, only there to boost bar sales, and ranked slightly below the waitresses, upon whom he will lavish considerably more attention.

Europe 1968 – impossible, unreliable, complicated, carnet-demanding, communist in part, and culturally diverse to the point of confusion (is it Monday? is it Belgium?) – has turned steadily into the sleeker, single-currency, single-border, art-sponsored, jazz-loving, train-loving, super-continent of today. The once welcoming, warm-hearted, generous, hugely efficient, big-sky North America, on the other hand, has understandably become the questioning, paranoid, closed-borders, visa-loving, gotta-make-a-buck, probably bullshitting North America of today.

Sure, back then both had baton-rounds and smoke curling up from the Sorbonne or Kent State, Grosvenor Square or Mayor Daley's Chicago, and both used to have good coffee. Today, however, outside of Starbucks, you're going to have to go to Europe for a good cup. The decline and fall of great nations may be monitored in the diminishing strength of the coffee: when it reaches the consistency of ditch-water, the end may be nigh.

Dirty tricks remain on both continents. They are just easier to understand with the common language in the States. Given that the US club owner's profit lies in the bar sales, you won't be surprised when I tell you a particularly nasty one that centres on the time the band is due to play and the air-conditioning arrangements.

It's 1990, and my group Earthworks is working well in California. We've just driven down from San Francisco for our next one-nighter at a place in Redondo Beach, in the Los Angeles area. The club tell us we're on at 10:30, after a support group, but, unknown to me, they've

told the locals that the show starts at 8:00. We take a leisurely dinner at
the hotel as the house fills up rapidly with an expectant crowd. It's a
warm October evening on the Coast, and when we turn up, the
temperature inside the packed room is like a sauna. It's like the Black
Hole of Calcutta. The people are four deep trying to get to the bar for
drinks and, having been kept waiting for some music for two-and-a-
half hours, are beginning to turn ugly.

The promoter's man tells us the support group has mysteriously
failed to appear, the air-conditioning is – very unusual this – on the
blink, and we take the stage to a slow handclap from a perspiring and
openly hostile crowd. It takes every bit of my modest stage patter to get
them, and the band, back on side, and we finish the gig acceptably to
the sound of merrily-ringing bar tills. The promoter thought we were
"great". I could have killed him.

Like an elephant, the promoter never forgets. Make him five bucks,
and he'll love you forever. Lose him the same amount, and you'll never
darken his door again. It's all about the money, which means it's all
about food and beverage sales. Forced to cancel part of a tour due to
family illness, I called around the West Coast buyers whom we were
scheduled to visit next, to apologise and explain. All were unhappy,
understandably. It turned out that I was unable to reschedule these
dates for a very long time, and when negotiations finally began, most
had a note that flagged up against my name, with a complete
breakdown, to the cent, of the promotion money I had indirectly
caused them to waste eight years earlier. Naturally, negotiations began
there.

❑

Back in the UK in the summer of 1971, Yes was teetering on the edge
of bankruptcy. But Brian Lane, the group's recently arrived and shiny
saviour, was rapidly solving this predicament. Money was the aviation
fuel that made this man's life fun. He understood how to manipulate
it, how to generate it, how the business worked: mostly on the twin

drivers of fear and greed. He had graduated with high distinction from the University of East London with a first-class honours degree in Fear & Greed, and his confidence threw our own individual and collective ineptitude into sharp relief.

There had been squabbles between the band members from the beginning, of course, usually attributable to caffeine, testosterone, or tiredness. Differing attitudes to money, hitherto unstated and only dimly perceived, were crystallising into an awkwardness that could no longer be easily overlooked.

On so many fronts, the disagreements ran to the very core of our relationship. But this was hardening into armed resistance to the other man's position. I, ever the frugal Puritan, always had a little money, even when there wasn't any, because I could always imagine the day when money would buy me freedom, when money would hermetically seal me from the demands of manager, agent, or record company. Money would enable me to stick two fingers up to them and play the music that I wanted and with whom I wanted.

And the way you got money was by starting right now. Peter Banks, on the other hand, could see no point in such forward-thinking abstention. Ludicrous. Either we were all going to make a fortune, in which case all was won and money would never again be a problem, or we were going to die trying, in which case all was lost and money would never again be a problem. But in the meantime, could I spare a fiver till Friday?

❏

In the early days, we would stop the van about ten miles down the road and split up the dosh from that evening's gig. Somebody may have said we should put something aside for petrol, but that was absolutely as far as any kind of forward planning went. The gigs always cost more money to do than we would get in fees after the agent had had his cut, so Jon was on the permanent lookout for money and gigs. And he was good. I can see him now, sitting on the bottom of the stairs in the band's London flat, at 50A Munster Road in Fulham, bullying some hapless dance-hall owner in Bromsgrove into giving us a booking, or scrounging another £100 off Jack Barrie, an early benefactor of the band and proprietor of the Soho drinking club La Chasse, where the embryonic Yes had first met.

My understanding of how these things worked was less than minimal: it was zero. I had no idea where the money, precious little of it that there was, was coming from or going to. So long as someone found me the £25 a week I presumed we were all taking, I didn't ask any questions. Eventually, after one too many tedious and avoidable arguments about cashflow in a lay-by after the gig, I suggested we have a band bank account, with a chequebook, from which regular weekly wages would be paid into personal bank accounts. And maybe some annual accounts, I added, for good measure.

I'll never quite forget the look of incomprehension as this idea wafted around Big Red like a bad smell. Everybody thought it was the stupidest thing they had ever heard – *Give it to a bank?* And on reflection, I think I was the only one with a bank account anyway.

The background to this was an expanding record industry, tripling in size every year through much of the 70s. Everybody was working, everybody was on the make, everybody was robbing everybody else blind, but it didn't seem to matter much, because there was going to be more money around next year than last.

Eventually, even Yes understood that a bank account and an accountant might be helpful, and David Moss of Bryce Hamner, with smart offices on Albemarle Street off Piccadilly, was appointed to set the band and its tax affairs on a sound footing. This was confirmed when a £16,000 tax bill with my name on it arrived at breakfast one morning. In 1972, that was a large sum of money, even if you had played on *Fragile*, and I've been cautious about brown envelopes at breakfast ever since.

The unfortunate Mr Moss was given the job of imposing some financial discipline and setting and assigning a monthly allowance to all members. The problem was, some members went through money a whole lot faster than others. Following the success of the group's first big hit, *Fragile*, the unrealistic assumption was that we could draw any amount of money we wanted. Fists would be slammed on David's desk until he finally gave in to demands for yet more funds, as if to a lapsed alcoholic demanding a drink. Despite a desperate rearguard resistance, the profligate were allowed to overdraw to the detriment of the frugal, and for his pains David was rewarded with a heart attack and premature retirement. The band was never good at cashflow, and I understand not much has changed today. Many distinguished rock and jazz musicians, unable to kick the cash habit, usually have a line of creditors who need paying and so have to continue to sing for their supper, whether they want to or not.

My impression of managers had so far been sketchy. Yes's first manager, the charming, suave, Volvo-owning Roy Flynn, was all ties and jackets with a silk handkerchief flopping out of the top pocket. When not up in town managing the Speak, or lending us his car, he lived in south-west London with his beautiful blonde girlfriend Suzanne, a relationship for which I thoughtfully provided accompaniment with salvoes of steadily improving drumming from the basement below.

Roy worked the London club social network well, and he found us gigs at most of the chic places of the day and, better still, at the Royal Albert Hall, supporting Cream. It was for that concert that I had driven down from Leeds University, following the humiliation of Yes's visit a couple of months earlier. I'd never been in a building of this size and opulence, let alone played in one.

I set up my small black Olympic drum kit on the vast stage, in front of Ginger Baker's Ludwig double-bass-drum behemoth, and stared up at the gods, transfixed. Our set starts bravely with a bravura rendition of Leonard Bernstein's 'Something's Coming', from *West Side Story*. A fanfare of ominous chords leads to a fancy drum break, recently made famous by Buddy Rich. Rich would later say kind things about my efforts, but given the provenance of that particular passage of music, and the fact that I was sharing the stage that evening with someone widely considered to be one of the best drummers in the world, the word 'ambitious' comes to mind.

The ominous chords sound great … sudden pause … and 5,000 pairs of ears turn to the weedy-looking kit being driven by a skinny 19-year-old, to see if he can improve upon Mr Rich's not inconsiderable efforts in this area. The occasion proves too much – I drop a stick. I can assure you, the sound of a drumstick clattering and rattling down over a bass drum to the hard wooden floor of a silent and packed Albert Hall is absolutely the loudest sound I shall ever hear.

Roy had got us as far as the Cream farewell concert and a poor deal with Atlantic Records, but there we were left to swing in the breeze. The other major signing in 1969 by the UK arm of Atlantic was Led Zeppelin. They had rocketed off to success in America, and everywhere we looked, others flourished. King Crimson had an enormous first outing with their 'observation', *In The Court Of The Crimson King*, and were shortly to play Hyde Park with The Rolling Stones. The Nice were writing suites and flirting with orchestras, Cream was breaking up, and Genesis were getting together. But for the next couple of years, Yes managed only to tread water, run red lights, and lose money at gigs in Kidderminster that cost us more to do than we were paid.

The situation couldn't last and somebody's head had to roll, and it was Roy's. It was messy. He was an emotional man who, rightly, felt hard done by. In the Wild West that was the music industry at the time, there were precious few rules, and those that did exist were being made up on the hoof. We musicians understood nothing at all about recording or publishing contracts, or the rights an artist may have in several aspects of his work, or even how much we were paying key functionaries like booking agents or tour managers. And we understood even less about how to fire a manager.

Hemdale was an expanding entertainment-industry firm run by John Daly on the back of actor David Hemmings's huge success with the classic 60s movie *Blow Up*. Their partner Harvey Freed had recently adopted a double persona, and in Yes we knew him in his second incarnation as Brian Lane – the fellow with the champagne in the limo. Harvey/Brian assumed the reins of the struggling Yes, brokered a deal with the outgoing Flynn, and immediately promised great things as our new manager.

In my wide-eyed innocence, I couldn't understand the source of Brian's confidence. He explained that he was a plugger and got artists' records played on the radio. He'd had recent successes with Jimi Hendrix's 'Hey Joe' and Pink Floyd's 'Arnold Layne', and could offer Yes a similar service. In fact, he'd decided to adopt the name Arnold Layne (A. Layne) as a nom de guerre, but removed it one step by calling himself Brian Lane (B. Lane). I thought this rather colourful.

In Brian's mind, the public was an ignorant beast that couldn't be trusted with something as important as selecting the nation's popular music. Better we all left it to Brian, who only had to make the right connections, give Hendrix or Pink Floyd a shove, and then they would be away on long fruitful careers, which everybody knew they should have had anyway. We were next in line. If we could just appear in the album charts, we'd be up and running. We just needed a helping hand. Everyone knew Yes was going to be a great band eventually. So why not give a good record a little help?

❏

The popular music industry was born on the wrong side of the tracks. With an infancy in vaudeville and a doubtful adolescence in music hall and burlesque, it was now coming of age in Britain under the watchful eye of men like Sharon Osbourne's father Don Arden, with loud suits, questionable business practices, and connections to London's East End. Corruption was endemic and its general prevalence not worthy of mention until the 50s when the US Congress legislated against the practice of payment by record companies for the broadcast of recordings on music radio, otherwise known as payola. Brian evidently saw song-plugging and payola as a branch of the social services – practically a charitable activity. That kind of imaginative leap was what your manager needed in 1971 and probably still does today.

B. Lane was good at spotting opportunities, and he was about to be presented with a big, fat, golden one. There happened to be a postal strike in Britain around the time that *The Yes Album* was released, and the two mainstream charts – the ones that had some semblance of veracity – had to be suspended. This played nicely into the hands of a young music entrepreneur called Richard Branson, who, again with a useful leap of imagination, saw that a 'chart', then as now, comprises whatever the compiler chooses to put into it. Brian and Richard got together, compared notes, and *The Yes Album* duly appeared in the following week's Virgin Chart. Once there, everything else followed, and it all became plain sailing. It wasn't rocket science, but it meant the world to us, and those few days began a lengthy 40-year career for the group and its young drummer.

Once a couple of key lieutenants have decided that the ship isn't sinking after all and in fact its sails are beginning to fill with wind, the speed with which people clamber back on board is quite alarming. Sit down: you're rocking the boat. Plans were instantly afoot to get to North America, now suddenly back in the frame. The band's growing reputation crossed the Atlantic, and on June 24 1971 we played our first date on that continent, at the Edmonton Gardens arena in Alberta, Canada, supporting Jethro Tull.

My last year with the band rushed by in a blur of half-empty stadiums of the kind that traditionally greet warm-up acts, the brilliant blue and vast skies of North America, back in the studio for *Fragile*, and more relentless touring. My first professional date with anybody was on January 12 1968, and the 500th gig shot past in August 1971, so we must have been putting in some miles.

But it wasn't until Yes's 1972 single 'Roundabout' – my first and last bona fide hit – that success really kicked in. You could laze by the pool on top of the Sheraton Manhattan and hear it on WNEW-FM every 45 minutes. My world was all 'heavy rotation' and *Billboard* placings interlaced with enormous salads and suntans. Much more of that and I would have turned into a rock star.

Back in the UK, the rehearsing and recording of our next and fifth album was inevitably going to be a lengthy affair. Even if we hadn't heard that Simon & Garfunkel had taken the better part of three months to complete *Bridge Over Troubled Water*, thereby ensuring we would have to take a minimum of three-and-a-half months, the way we went about our painfully democratic music-making would guarantee a long ride.

Bands were competing on excess in all areas, from studio time consumed to the power of your PA systems, from the lengths of guitar solos to the length of your bar bill, from the number of trucks on the road to the number of guitars on stage. In that general spirit, we decided it would be 'fun' to have one track last the whole side of a long-playing vinyl album, which meant about 20 minutes. This was, understandably, an unheard-of feat; perfect, then, for our little ensemble. Rehearsals eventually moved from the Una Billings School of Dance in Shepherds Bush, west London, to Advision recording studios in Gosfield Street, in the centre of town. And still we couldn't play the first couple of minutes all the way through.

I behaved badly, larking about, bored. I would have killed for a decision on anything, but multi-track recording and the deft editing work of our engineer Eddie Offord ensured that all decisions could be postponed, seemingly indefinitely. Alternative takes and optional instrumentations began to sprout like mould around the edge of the control room, on short bits of brown two-inch recording tape. The piece was being assembled in ten, twelve, sixteen-bar sections. Nobody appeared to have the slightest idea as to the form it should be taking, but everybody and his aunt had an idea as to the form it should not be taking.

Days rolled into weeks. Occasionally things would brighten up when we stripped down the mics and the board, broke down the gear, loaded it into Big Red, and scorched up the motorway for a couple of weekend dates, reconvening the following Monday to continue where we had left off. Such a cavalier attitude to the consistency of the sound on the record would these days be considered heretical, but nobody worried about that.

The sessions ran late. There was a cheap black velour settee at the back of the control room, much prized by those of a quicker metabolism than the cold-water Chris Squire, who moved slowly and could thus outlast everyone else in the room. My memory as I slipped into a fitful hour or two's sleep at about 3:00am was of Chris, back towards me, poring over a couple of knobs on the desk, and jerking awake a couple of hours later to find him in the same place, still considering the relative position of the two knobs.

The cleaning lady became part of the routine of the day. Since we were there all night, she had to sort of clean around us, and would frequently be asked for her opinion on this or that, since none of us were in any fit state to decide. On one occasion, we all agreed absolutely, beyond doubt, that we should go with Edit Section 1[b] v.2 sec: 7. Eddie, thrilled with such an unusual display of unanimity, turned confidently to the wall where he expected to find the right strip of tape. The blood drained from his face. It wasn't there.

What do you mean it's not there? Where the hell is it? We rummaged fruitlessly in the studio until someone pointed out that the last person in the immediate vicinity had been the cleaning lady. As dawn broke on another grey London day, band and engineer trooped out into Gosfield Street to the dustbins, to scavenge through the studio detritus in a desperate hunt for the missing section. And there it was! With not too much muck on it!

Triumphantly, we shuttled back in, Eddie sewed it back into the music, good as new, and that became the Master. A damn close-run thing. The angels were looking over us: *Close To The Edge* was completed and was a huge hit, but, more importantly, it remains a classic of the genre. I don't understand how we managed it, but somehow we got lucky. To this day it seems to have the perfect form, and form is everything. Maybe it was karma for all the grief we had been through during the first three or four years. I loved the record, hated making it, and was immediately certain I would never try to do that again.

❏

Why would I want to leave this organisation on the brink of its international success? It is the obligation of every artist to exercise his or her higher sensibilities for as much of the time as possible, and with Yes I knew I could go no further. Repetition follows popular success like night follows day. Drummer Alan White was already available as a suitable replacement and – essential for me – would ensure the continuation of the group. If I didn't want to troll around the world's stadiums playing *Close To The Edge*, now was the time to say so.

And there was a very appealing alternative. I'd been stalking Robert Fripp of the sensational King Crimson for a while, and he had finally conceded to the badgering of this over-praised ingénue. He waited until, like a ripening tomato, I just fell off the vine. King Crimson, a darker and more mysterious organisation altogether, would offer another level in musical education for this drummer, so eager for knowledge and so protective of his sensibilities.

Brian Lane could turn sharply, as he did on me when I announced my decision a few weeks later in the warm afterglow of the completion of *Close To The Edge*. There was much talk of settling accounts. "You can't just get up and leave the restaurant without paying the bill," was Brian's imaginative analysis of the situation. Incredibly, and as testament to my ignorance, I paid handsomely to leave the group that I had co-founded. To the incoming Alan White, I donated a handsome set of brand-new silver flightcases for his drums and half of my royalties to what was to become the platinum-selling album. To the band, I donated a substantial cash handout, for what Brian was pleased to call 'material damage', meaning he had had to call the US booking agency and reschedule some concerts.

There may have been times in my career when I should indeed have heeded Squire's advice to slow down a bit, but I had more money today than yesterday, so what the heck. Yes had opened my eyes and ears to the size of the musical problem, to the distance that would have to be travelled before I could achieve any kind of maturity. I'd only played with a handful of people in my short four-and-a-half years as a musician, and I knew that what I was after was not to be found in my current position, despite the rocket-fuelled start to my career that the band had given me. I loved Yes, but I thirsted to learn more, and I was ready to change the world with King Crimson.

3 WHO MANAGED THE MANAGER?

Mark Fenwick and David Enthoven of EG Management were managers number three and four, and they were from an altogether different breed. They were a class act. Rumour has it that the tall, languorous Enthoven had mortgaged his house to get King Crimson underway. He and Mark, scion of the famous Fenwick family of Fenwick's of Bond Street, were wealthy and well educated.

Both men were emblematic of the racy early 70s, when dabbling in the nascent rock music industry was a little like investing in the dotcom revolution of the 90s or gambling online today. Mark and David appeared elegant and charming, a thousand miles away from the East End barrow-boy mentality of Brian Lane. Everything was done on a handshake, I was told, as I left their cool offices on the even cooler King's Road, Chelsea.

Among their early clients were King Crimson, T.Rex, and Emerson Lake & Palmer. Fenwick eventually became absorbed in Roxy Music's affairs, and having parted with Enthoven, who went on to manage Robbie Williams, teamed up with Sam Alder, a businessman from the Isle of Man with an accountancy background. It was Sam who had hands-on control of my day-to-day affairs for about 20 years through the 70s and 80s. It was to Sam that King Crimson turned for guidance and strategy as the tours and albums rolled past, and by whom it was confirmed, had I ever doubted it, that it is accountants who rule the world.

Being in my first King Crimson was probably a bumpier and definitely a shorter ride than I anticipated. We managed only one studio album, *Larks' Tongues In Aspic*, before our delightful and moustachioed percussionist Jamie Muir left the group under a cloud of confusion and disinformation. He never said goodbye, and I don't believe we have met since. I liked Jamie a lot, even though he was, shall we say, unkind in his assessments of the talents of the arrogant and over-praised young drummer from Yes. He taught me to try to see life from the far side of the cymbals: drummers can be very myopic. He also pointed out – and I consider this my first and best drum lesson – that I exist to serve the music, the music does not exist to serve me.

By the time we reached our second album, *Starless And Bible Black*, we were dangerously low on material. We were reduced to taking improvised live tracks, removing the applause and extraneous audience noise as much as possible, and passing them off as studio tracks. 'We'll Let You Know', 'Trio', and 'The Mincer' were all born of desperation. It was rumoured that the record company paid a lower royalty rate on live music – hence the subterfuge – but I never got to the bottom of that.

❏

King Crimson was now a quartet, consisting of myself, Robert Fripp, bassist and singer John Wetton, who'd come from Family, and violinist David Cross, who'd come from a group called Waves. Two years of heavy touring that started in 1973, and the 'duck or go with it' muscularity of the rhythm section, were understandably taking a toll on David. A violinist's intonation depends on what he can hear around him, and Cross lived in an increasingly difficult world of heavy distortion, fuzz bass, and two road-weary Mellotrons, an early specimen of wheezing string-machine, persistently out of tune within itself and with any other Mellotron within earshot. And we had two on stage.

As Crimson biographer Sid Smith accurately put it: "Fripp ... accepts that Cross was placed in an increasingly impossible position, which saw a musical and personal distance develop between the violinist and the rest of the group as he failed to meet the strength and volume of the rhythm section."[1]

As we edged toward the last concert of what was effectively a four-month leg of European and American roadwork, John Wetton started to lobby for a more dynamic and confident replacement. I demurred, and Robert, on balance, agreed that David should go but that we would wait until after a last and very important outdoor gig at Wollman Rink in New York City's Central Park before we told him.

In my few short years as a musician, I'd already failed to say goodbye to a manager, a guitarist, a keyboard player, a percussionist, and a violinist, and this was beginning to look like carelessness. It seems there are no goodbyes in the music business, no matter how intensely you may have shared a musical relationship. When bits drop off groups, it's always painful.

A week after the Wollman Rink show, we were back as a trio in Olympic studios in Barnes, west London. I was steeling myself for another round of excruciating, teeth-pullingly difficult music-making as we surveyed the mountain that was to be our third album together. Why did it have to be this difficult? In part, because we were not drawing on a shared heritage of music-making, and our overblown sense of importance encouraged us to believe we should be reinventing music, or at least this genre of it, with every album.

The absence of a shared sense of *what music was* meant, for example, that we were unable to play anything at all outside the band's immediate repertoire. There was no body of classics that we could limber up with. If a jazz quartet can think of nothing else to play, it plays a blues, the DNA of the genre. Before you know it, the pianist is re-harmonising the chords, the saxophonist has departed from the melody for a little instant composition of his own, based on these new harmonies he's hearing, and they're off. None of this was applicable to the progressive rockers.

None of the groups played each other's compositions. The bands never added or swapped personnel informally. The group culture of the day required that you slit wrists, mingled blood, and till death or success us do part. I would have preferred a looser culture, where musicians brought things to bands, stayed for a while, and moved on. A culture in which, for a tour, or an album, King Crimson might play the music of Led Zeppelin, and vice versa; a culture in which Roger Waters of Pink Floyd might bring some new blood to Yes, or Chris Squire could be seconded to The Nice for a European tour.

As the only musician to have played in four of the premier progressive rock groups of the day – Yes, King Crimson, Genesis, and UK – it would seem, rightly, that I had subconsciously adopted just that strategy. In my foolish desire to play the music differently every night, and what seemed to outsiders like my constant group-hopping, I was exhibiting all the characteristics of the jazz musician I was to become a couple of decades later. I just didn't know it.

My diary confirms that I was at Olympic for 15 days in the summer of 1974 making *Red* with John and Robert, but it could have been 15 months. Robert neglected to tell us that, a few days before the sessions, he had undergone a spiritual awakening comparable to the one that Jamie Muir had undergone two years earlier, and which it now transpired was the reason for Muir's sudden and unexplained departure from the group.

Presumably it was in relationship to this that Our Fearless Leader decided to withhold his opinion on all proceedings in the studio, so a minor chord was as good, or not, as a major chord, and Take 4 was as good or as lousy as Take 5. This was spectacularly unhelpful. All this spiritual awakening certainly wasn't making the music any easier to produce, and what with the input of gurus and seers such as Paramhansa Yogananda and J.G. Bennett, it is indeed a miracle that any of these records were made at all. Robert would doubtless argue the opposite, that without such input the records would not have been made. Until the punks, not known for their spiritual empathy, arrived in 1976, it seemed you had a better chance of a spiritual awakening in these bands than getting a decent cup of coffee.

Red was eventually completed by John Wetton and engineer George Chkiantz. Meanwhile, I amused myself with my new toy, a cymbal I found in the rehearsal-room trash can, deposited there by the group before us. It was turned up on one side in an effort to get it to fit in the bin, like an Australian bush hat, and it had seen rather better days. It was a 'foreign made' Zilco Standard cymbal imported into the UK by Arbiter Co Ltd – and before you ask, I have no idea what happened to Zilco. Its maltreatment had bequeathed it this fabulous trashy sound with a very short, fast decay. It looked so sad; I took pity on it and we fell in love. I used it on 'One More Red Nightmare' and during the following year or so before it split. And the end came swiftly after that.

Listening back to old efforts is a bit like looking back through the family photo album: you're mostly just embarrassed not only by the terrible jeans you wore but also by the fact that you didn't appear to know they were terrible. But I love *Red*. It was my third attempt at recording with the band, and despite the confused and genuinely upsetting circumstances surrounding its creation, the record has a coherence and a gritty consistency that has translated well across several decades of rock and an influence beyond the pain of its making.

❏

Fripp will confirm that after some two years of steady roadwork between 1973 and 1974, we never saw any tour accounts. More astonishing than that, to my mind, is that we never thought to ask for any. Our weekly stipend by this time had probably gone up to £50, with a lot of talk about tour losses, tour support, and per diems, but accounts there were none.

The general idea was that the manager "took care of everything", including, if you were foolish enough, your domestic running costs: heating, electricity, property taxes, and so forth. He thus controlled all aspects of your financial existence, both income and expenditure, and all information was coming from one source. In those days, he could also be your manager, record company, and publisher, in a three-way conflict-of-interest that these days would raise a lot of legal eyebrows.

And you thought we were smart? How any bunch of reasonably intelligent people could let this happen is beyond belief. A few years later I was running my own outfit, Bruford, and we were on a gruelling two-month van tour in the USA in the heatwave summer of 1980. Back in the UK, Sam from EG called my wife Carolyn – herself at a low ebb with two small children and a rambling house in need of much renovation – to tell her we couldn't continue. The band was too expensive, he said, and the hole was only getting deeper.

He was probably right. We were freighting around a Hammond organ, drums, and a shed-load of equipment, and the costs must have been heavy, but I had no way of confirming or denying this. This sort of information appeared to be classified. But not to worry, said Sam with his next breath, because he had persuaded Robert to reform King Crimson, and the gig was mine if I wanted it. Refuse and starve. Once the musician had so thoughtfully volunteered to put himself in the dark, it was a managerial breeze to keep him there. The puppeteer had only to pull the strings. I was eventually presented with an impressive bill for my touring with Bruford, duly repaid from the record and publishing royalties.

I was headed toward jazz, which, on the whole, doesn't have managers. It's a high-end cottage industry rather than mass market – it's Jaguar to General Motors. In the absence of volume sales, it looks to niche market and to cut costs – and 20 per cent of your gross income to pay for a manager really is a major cost, especially when the expenditure is only putting another tier of bureaucracy between you and the customer.

Sam had been a good teacher. Like most things in the music industry, you can do it yourself if you can find the time. Self-managing jazz musicians these days multi-task with any number of hats on – booking agent, composer, recording engineer, travel agent, road manager, publicist, producer – but it hurts. So enjoy the immediate sunshine of being 20 per cent better off when you part company with your manager, because you are very soon going to realise what you paid him for.

Jazz works on a person-to-person level and is broadly frequented by people who love the music and still have hearts. With low-volume sales, there is insufficient blood in the water to attract the sharks, so you are going to be sailing your own ship, and probably single-handed. Messrs Flynn, Freed/Lane, Enthoven, Fenwick, and Alder had been high-maintenance and expensive people, and a good representational cross-section of the management species. They could make you if they were good; they could break you if they were hopeless; and they could just sit expensively in the middle and get in the way. By the time I had arrived at my jazz group Earthworks in 1986, they were barely managing to do that.

❏

As the industry grew from its amateurish adolescence through the 70s into an accountancy-driven business exercise in the 80s, its operational tactics matured, and it soon developed a reflex need for control. It sought to control the producer (relatively easy and inexpensive), the consumer (more tricky and more expensive), and the relationship between the two.

The analogy of the horse race may be helpful here. The idea broadly was that if a record company had ten artists or 'horses' at the start of the race to success, the one that came in first would pay for the nine losers and still return a handsome profit. In such a scenario, there were clearly several things that the record company might do to influence the outcome. It could breed, rear, and train horse and jockey the way it wanted, to ensure an enthusiastic departure from the gate. A sleek, glistening, perfectly groomed Whitney Houston, niece of rhythm & blues diva Cissy Houston – good bloodstock! – owned and trained by Clive Davis, the Machiavellian head of Arista Records as the owner, comes to mind. The record company could own all the horses and jockeys, and here one might think of Simon Cowell, who seems to own several of the *Pop Idol* successes and perhaps even the songs that they sing on his TV shows. In fact, the term a 'stable of artists' was and maybe still is in common use. The label could own and control the 'race track', the means of distribution, retail outlets, and the like.

The company's preferred weapon to help achieve this – one that all musicians will recognise – was separation, and it came in three particular forms, starting with the separation of the artist from the audience. In medieval Europe, the relationship was between the performer and the listener, in real time. There was no method of capturing the performance and replaying it for solitary listening after the event. The event or ritual was the performance; the performance was the event or ritual. In the West, the church was the original controller and commissioner of most music and art, but the ritual use of music diminished as we industrialised.

A growing middle class with leisure time needed, first, someone to organise the musical event, and then someone to make and distribute artefacts of the event in the form of, originally, sheet music and, latterly, recordings. Once the record company had established itself in this position of power, it abrogated unto itself the function of expert. It separated listener from performer, the better to go between them to extract a profit.

Eventually, at the height of the record boom in the 70s, no band seemed able to perform without tour support, effectively the record company's permission and financial backing to go on tour. So no listener could hear the band without the record company's say-so: a complete and highly effective separation. Currently, artist and groups are encouraged to spend as much as possible on video, in the same way as they were encouraged to spend on elaborate stage production in the 70s. Both expenditures had the same result of placing the band in debt, and thus in an inferior position, to the record company, now well placed to control the relationship between it and the artist, and the artist and audience.

The successful grooming of a star often demanded his isolation and separation from the world with which he was familiar – family, friends, location, diet – the better to rebuild him in the new world into which he was being projected. This was a second aspect of the technique of separation.

The tabloids love the recurring story of the embarrassing mother-from-hell who is produced to horrify the sleek star. She's always just done something terrible, and we are invited to note the distance travelled by the star, a distance often measured in haircuts and cosmetic surgery, since his modest early days in a two-up-two-down in South Wales – and I'm not only thinking of Welsh rhythm & blues singer Tom Jones here. Jones's guitarist Bill Parkinson was on the wrong end of manager Gordon Mills's ruthless separation of the singer from his backing band, The Squires, around 1968. Clearly his mates from the early days wouldn't be continuing with him on his meteoric journey to Las Vegas.[2]

Generally, it's the drummer who goes first, replaced in the recording studio by a session musician because "your time is shaky, man". Like the wretched stack-heeled, bouffant'd, and powdered drummer from 80s heavy rock group Cinderella, he may or may not be invited back on tour, only to be praised for his performance on the subsequent platinum-seller that everyone thinks he's on, but he's not. Bass players and keyboard players are equally dispensable and are swiftly replaced by hired guns. The core relationship between the 'star' and his writing buddy is the last to go – it needs to be handled with some care. This may be the oldest relationship in the band, dating back to its very inception. Bowie may initially have felt unable to cope without sidekick Mick Ronson, Bryan Ferry without Phil Manzanera and Brian Eno, Tom Jones without The Squires, Cliff Richard without The Shadows – but, sooner or later, they'll all be ditched.

Separation took its third and final form in the parting of the artist from control of his own artistic and business affairs. As suggested earlier, as the artist grows in stature, everything would be "taken care of" to use the common expression. In other words, he'd be systematically removed from everyday control of events, thus putting himself nicely into manipulative hands. And generally the system worked. Stars were reliably produced – although it was not a system known for its aftercare when the services of the celebrity were no longer required – and records were reasonably reliably sold. Horses ran down the track, and, generally, the one winner paid for the losers, with money left over.

There is an interesting side theory that centres on the role of the stock-analyst and his influence on the popular music of the day. Back in the 60s, record companies were seldom quoted on the stock market and so had no one for whom to make money apart from themselves. Oh, simple days! Yes made two or three albums in about three years of an expanding market before anyone at the label politely suggested we actually try to get a hit. There was time for the act to develop, improve.

Now, goes the theory, the publicly-quoted company is highly pressured to turn a profit on any given investment much faster, before the shareholder loses interest. The stock-analyst may rate the label down, advising his clients against investment, if there isn't the smell of a hit in the very near future. If your prime filly is Whitney Houston, and she's staying out too late at night with Bobby Brown, behaving erratically, and generally refusing to run, the share-price can dive. This in turn makes it harder to raise money for future artist development, starting a whole negative cycle. So much is bet on the stars to deliver that the strain can show physically, on face and body, evidence the tragic face of Michael Jackson, among others. A society gets the music it is willing to pay for or, to put it perhaps more accurately, the music it deserves.

❏

It's noon on a blustery March Friday in 1973. Carolyn Antonia Clifton and I have just been married, between King Crimson tours, in a small ceremony at St. Mary's Church, Kippington Road, Sevenoaks, by the splendidly named vicar, Barzillai Beckerleg. His ancestors are surely Cornish, or Puritan, or both. My American girl looks beautiful in a cream Ossie Clark creation, and, at 23, we are both painfully young.

Generally I'm not good with big occasions, and despite its low-key appearance, this is the event of my life so far. I dig deep to fool the participants that I am all casual charm, but my insides are churning at the enormity of what I have just said in public to friends and family and in the eyes of God. I can't bear the thought that I might let down her, myself, or my family by failing to adhere to these promises. I've been married 30 minutes and already I'm consumed with what-ifs.

It'll take the better part of 30 years before I begin to calm down about this and accept that we might, really, be a steady item. I will eventually come to consider my marriage as one of the four pillars of my existence, one of the principal supports preventing me from complete collapse into the abyss. I will come to find all aspects of life so bizarre that I will be in strong need of a witness to events – someone I can turn to and say: "Did that really happen, or did we make it up? Maybe we imagined it." Doesn't everyone need to have his or her life witnessed?

A five-minute walk takes the motley congregation, clutching hats and laughing, back to my parent's house. I don't remember much, other than that it was a small, efficient, and modest affair, mostly for my mother's benefit. In the post-Summer Of Love backwash, early-70s weddings were evolving into smaller, more discreet affairs, which might actually be enjoyed by the participants and upon which the participants, who might well be paying, were not of a mind to lavish much money. The earlier heresies of eloping to a Caribbean island, or not inviting your parents, or running away to a registry office as far away from anywhere as possible, had long since been breached by braver souls than us. We, too, similarly favoured the minimum of fuss and the maximum of restraint.

There is a small buffet lunch, the inevitable pushy photographer, a speech from the best man that embarrasses no one, some champagne and the cake, and within about three hours Carolyn and I are in the family saloon car and heading, with some relief, back up to our London flat in Harcourt Terrace, Fulham, for an altogether different kind of party. The transport is on loan from my father, on strict condition that it is to be garaged overnight. The vehicle thus protected from what he perceives to be life on the mean streets of Fulham, my father feels he has an odds-on chance of seeing it again in one piece.

That evening our flat is a rowdy place with an assembled throng of music-industry types, some of whom I know – Jon Anderson of Yes, Jamie Muir of King Crimson, shortly to leave the industry and repair to a monastery in Scotland, John Wetton of Family, King Crimson, and shortly the enormously popular Asia – and plenty of whom I don't. Already unfaithful, I am in love with Herbie Hancock's *Crossings*, and since it's my party and I'll cry if I want to, we play that, or something like it, all night long.

Jamie and Jon spend much of the evening in deep conversation in the corner by the sash window opening onto the little garden. Jamie, supporting a fine pair of waxed mustachios that would have made Salvador Dali proud, is the percussionist in the new King Crimson that we had both joined the previous year. Older than me and with considerable experience in the European improvised-music scene, he possesses an intimidating sense of enquiry and a warm smile. Jon, who has admirably and speedily forgiven me for leaving the band we formed together, and which has now happily absorbed a satisfactory replacement in drummer Alan White, is all ears.

Evangelical in his advocacy of Paramhansa Yogananda's *Autobiography Of A Yogi*, Jamie is about to put a kink in the course of progressive rock. Following the enormous success of *Close To The Edge*, Jon's radar is up and scanning for subject matter. He has been looking for inspiration from a wide range of esoteric literature from Herman Hesse to Carlos Castenada, but this sounds like something special. Sure enough, the much-anticipated Yes double-album *Tales From Topographic Oceans*, with typically elliptical lyrics loosely based on the Shastric teachings alluded to by Yogananda, will be released nine months after the wedding party to, shall we say, mixed reviews and substantial sales.

If my services as a drummer are replaceable, I know now for certain that my services as someone who thinks up album titles are indispensable. I had proposed the group's fourth album be called *Fragile* because I thought we were breakable, and the band's art director, Roger Dean, brilliantly parlayed that idea up to the prescient image of the fragile planet earth, with implications of a delicate and breakable eco-system. I had suggested the fifth album be called *Close To The Edge* because I continued to feel we were on the verge of implosion.

Not great titles, but surely better than the muddled *Tales*. Can oceans *be* topographic? Are they all topographic, or is the term applicable to specific oceans? If so, to which oceans do these tales refer? Are these tales from *some* topographic oceans or *all* topographic oceans? And yet surely infinitely better than the appalling and yet-to-be-conceived *Tormato*.

The four-song, four-sided *Tales* came to be seen by some commentators as An Album Too Far for Yes and the one that put them way irretrievably too far on the wrong side of the imminent punk explosion. Thus it was that a wayward King Crimson percussionist unwittingly sowed the seeds of a downturn in the Yes camp in a corner of my flat on my wedding night, March 2 1973.

4 HOW DO YOU GET THAT FANTASTIC SOUND?

"**W**e're going back to England tomorrow," said the Braided Waif. "You could come with us." At last, music to my ears. It was an unseasonably hot Roman night in the pre-Yes spring of 1968, and I'd already made the most elementary of all pre-school mistakes in this, the opening weeks of my future. In my enthusiasm for the first overseas gig I'd been offered, I'd accepted a one-way air ticket to Rome from an Italian–English guitarist called Ronnie, who was proposing an open-ended summer playing clubs in that most romantic of cities. First mooted back in the UK, this proposition, to more experienced ears, would have leaked like a sieve, but this beginner was only hearing what he wanted to hear.

The accommodation in Rome consisted of three-in-a-room above a garage mechanic's work bay on a noisy street in the Trastevere district. He was an enthusiastic mechanic, who, unusually for a Roman, started remarkably early. His work consisted mostly of hitting things – transmissions, exhausts – very loudly.

The only thing I remember about the Piper Club is that it stayed open late. The owner paid us only on occasion, and then only after the lightweight Ronnie had created a sufficient scene. We supported a psychedelic lot from London who took their name from two Louisiana blues men, Pink Anderson and Floyd 'Dipper Boy' Council. I didn't think they would go far at all. Our music wasn't much good either, with the sole exception of an appropriate version of 'Manic Depression', originally by Jimi Hendrix.

The whole trip had collapsed in a welter of mutual recrimination, sulking, and blame, as these things had a habit of doing. Sitting nursing my favourite scotch and coke, bought with my last few liras during what was to be, thank God, my last night in the club, I'd overheard this hippy-dippy American couple discussing their travel options in a language in which, at least, I was fluent. I scraped together enough for a round of drinks, and after perhaps an hour of a shamelessly exaggerated sob story, I'd extracted this offer of transport from the under-nourished, tie-dyed, and wide-eyed Jodie, whom I immediately and privately re-christened the Braided Waif. No, my drums wouldn't be a problem. They had a VW camper van – of course, this being 1968 – and the drums would probably fit in the back OK.

This was great news. I'd been toying with the idea of selling my drums and buying an air ticket, a drastic manoeuvre now happily abandoned. We left town the following day: Jodie, partner Jay, and myself rammed in the back between bass drum and traps case. Jay seemed to follow Jodie's lead on most things. He was happy to do the first driving shift while the Waif navigated out of town and we headed north. Tall and laconic, Jay had one of those droopy, sandy-coloured moustaches – which made him look like Custer or maybe Wild Bill Hickok – and, of course, a bandana.

The van puttered north, noisily, all day, the two lovebirds in the front talking animatedly and, irritatingly, just below audible level. I fancied some of it was about me, a fancy in part confirmed by the occasional look thrown back over the seat in my direction. We'd loaded with some provisions, to which, being skint, I'd hardly contributed, but which Waif and Custer seemed inclined at first to share. Engrossed in each other, they barely said a thing at the rest-stops to the kid in the back.

By mid evening we were in the Alps. I pulled on extra clothing against the distinctly chilly air, and I thought their attitude had become tangibly unfriendly. My mind was leaping forward wildly to mass-murder road movies when Jay, who had barely addressed a comment to me on the journey so far, pulled the van over to the side of the road and turned round in his seat to face me. "I guess this is where you get out," he drawled.

"What?" I said.

"Well, this is our home, buddy." His hand waved around the van's interior. "I mean, me and the little lady gonna want some privacy, right?" Giggles from the little lady.

"Where do I go?" I said lamely, not expecting an answer. Of course, this was bound to happen. I could and should have seen it coming. A night on doorsteps in the Alps, which can be nippier than you think, even in late May – and no money for a hotel.

"Ain't my problem. We'll meet you over there by the bus station at eight in the morning. G'night." The door slammed shut behind me, and blinds were pulled down. More giggles from the Braided Waif.

It was shaping up to be a long cold night. I smoked my few remaining cigarettes too quickly and ambled aimlessly up and down the streets. Well before midnight, the last bar was shut and the last shutter barred. An interminable eight hours to go. I'd make a thorough and logical survey of all parts of the town, from riverbank to town square, church to main street, and I resolved to avoid looking at my watch more than four times an hour. If I divided time into 15-minute blocks – only 32 of those – that sounded more survivable.

Walking slowly, hands thrust deep into my light summer jacket, shoulders hunched, I stretched out the survey for a couple of hours. These alpine towns were clean in an antiseptic kind of way and, at two in the morning, deserted. A cat, caught in the act of trying to raid the trash, shot across the street in front of me as the trash-can lid clattered noisily to the ground. An upstairs bedroom curtain twitched in response, and I was aware of being studied. Earlier, at turning-out time, there had been a noisy bunch of lads, recognisable in any town, mouthing off the usual expletives, recognisable in any language. They didn't look much older than me, but it was probably worth crossing to the other side of the street as a precautionary measure.

The pile of rags in the corner of a shop doorway suddenly upped and moved as I approached, limping off toward the river in a shambolic shuffle, bits of cardboard and string attached. The pile of rags had thoughtfully left a couple of empty bottles of something that smelled like high-octane aviation fuel, some empty boxes of matches, a powerful smell of urine, and, best of all, a sizeable stash of newsprint. I wasn't much good at being a bum, but I was learning fast. I recognised the warming qualities of newspaper, and it took no more than a few seconds to occupy this recently vacated palace, sheltered on three sides. Exhausted and frozen, I curled into the newspapers, got my head down, and reflected on the abortive trip to Rome.

We'd begun in such high spirits at Heathrow. A lot of drinking on the plane. Lunch in the bright sunlight at 30,000 feet. And it had ended in this butcher's shop doorway in Visp. If it hadn't been for the bloody drums, and the inevitable excess-baggage charges, I could probably have borrowed enough from the other guys in the band to do a one-way ticket home. But the drums had killed that idea. Bloody albatross around your neck, they were. Should've played the flute. I wondered what it would be like to have enough dosh to have someone set up and carry the bloody things for me. I dozed some more, and my last conscious thought was wondering if it would always be this glamorous.

❏

Must be a big improvement being a flautist, or a blues harmonica player, or a pianist, although, come to think of it, they had other problems. Carting drums around, finding instruments to do the job, being responsible for the damn things – the Rome trip warned me that this was going to be a lifelong leitmotif through my musical existence.

In the early days, musical instrument rental was all but non-existent, so you had to bring your own drums if you wanted to play at all. Then, when we made some money, we started to waste it by shipping drums all over the world at unheard-of expense. When drummer Pat Mastelotto joined King Crimson in 1996, well past our sell-by date, he put a few drums in heavy cases to fly them up from Austin, Texas, to Woodstock, New York, and produced a bill frighteningly near $6,000. It was gently explained to him that those days were gone. Now, good equipment rental is everywhere, so you tend to avoid shipping costs and get the promoter to provide.

No matter how much you try to guard against it, equipment failure is an occupational hazard that you have to script into life. Shortly after my 40th birthday, in June 1991, the Yes Reunion tour pulls into Manhattan for an intimate little soirée with 20,000 others in a sports arena called Madison Square Garden. It's 23 years since I started in the business, and I'm reliably informed that this is the Big Time. I agree. My suite at the Plaza is certainly more comfortable than a butcher's shop doorway in Visp, but the Big Time comes with strings. The music has so far been sufficiently dull and repetitive that I've had to look elsewhere for daily entertainment, and there has indeed been plenty available in the internal bickerings, the backstage back-stabbings, the remarkable logistical hitches, and even more remarkable solutions to those hitches, and that's not to mention the romances, feuds, and other excitements in the accounting, legal, catering, and merchandising departments – all the good honest stuff you would associate with any travelling circus.

Of some interest to me, and much flagged in the percussion press, is the unusual nature of the percussion set-up I'm touting on this tour. Audiences at these big places tend to listen with their eyes. Until and unless you can associate a particular sound with a particular source or action, it's all but impossible to decipher who's doing what on stage. My answer to this is to erect a wall of electronic percussion pads, most of which I have to physically reach for, even stretch for. The resulting choreography will, I hope, prove an entertaining alternative to the more usual arrangement of drums as furnished by my opposite number,

Alan White, 20 paces away on the other side of the circular stage. It is a sophisticated and expensive set that, had *The Guinness Book Of Records* been advised, would certainly have won the Most Expensive Drum Set Ever Staged category. It necessitates the deployment of two huge, early Apple Mac-style computers with tracker balls and nine-inch TV screens, whose function is to create, edit, store, and assign samples to pads and alter them at the click of a footswitch. These units don't come cheap, at about $15,000 a go. Notoriously unreliable, they are run in tandem, one as backup to the other.

The show proceeds smoothly, in its lumbering, over-inflated kind of way. Leaving the stage at half time – the soccer player's designation seems entirely appropriate in the sports stadium – I mention to my assistant, Props, that there is a minor buzz in the monitors, of interest only because the system is usually so clean it sounds like you're listening to the band on your home stereo.

I think no more about it, sling the proffered towel around my neck, and repair to my dressing room for my usual tea. Eventually, all manner of bells and knocks on the door indicate that half time has run its course, and the stage manager leads Alan and me back to the tunnel. This is in fact no tunnel at all, but a barricaded gangway from the dressing rooms that cuts across the floor of the arena to the enormous revolving stage in the centre of this gargantuan building. We are scheduled to start the second half of the proceedings with an elaborately-arranged drum duet.

We enter the tunnel, and a battery of Super Trooper follow-spots picks us up. I feel like a heavyweight boxer; the crowd roars its enthusiasm. Off to my right I can just about make out a completely matter-of-fact voice, blithely announcing with about as much excitement as a speaking clock: "They can't go on. Bill's drums ain't workin'."

My blood freezes, and I momentarily falter. "What the hell do you mean?" I shout back over the deafening background din.

"Can't get 'em started. They're powered down." Props, my loyal and hitherto utterly reliable drum tech, is a man of few words. Turns out he has decided, in the last five minutes of the break, and probably because he had nothing better to do, to trace down the buzz so off-handedly mentioned earlier, which necessitated powering down both computers. He tried to get them back up again quickly – too quickly – and has precipitated some malfunction.

There is no turning back. I have covered at least half the distance to the stage. England expects every man to do his duty … . Bloody hell, this is going to be a carnage. On the far side of the stage squats Alan's powerful set of Ludwig drums and ancillary electronics, polished, gleaming, the Formula One of rock'n'roll drum sets. If you just tickle them they go off like howitzers, 20-inch cannon shells through an 80,000-watt stereo PA system.

Closer to me, as I rise up on to the stage, are my own 18 electronic pads, mute, silenced by two blank computer screens. They won't be going off at all, through any PA. The only armament I can bring to bear is a snare drum and two cymbals, scarcely sufficient for a dinner-dance at the Pump Room, let alone amusing these baying hounds. These people want action, and they want it now. About 5,000 of them are drummers from New York, New Jersey, and half the states in the Union. They've heard about this legendary drum set-up, and they want to know, right now, what kind of bang you get for 30,000 bucks.

An image involving Christians, lions, and an amphitheatre drifts across my field of vision. Artificial smoke, like an early morning fog, floats low across the vast empty stage, to give the blinding lights something to bite into, and we two protagonists face each other across no-man's land. This is turning into the battle of the Somme. I can feel the heat of the lights, can hear the baying throats, but can see no one except Alan reaching for a heavy pair of sticks to deliver his first percussive onslaught.

Two thoughts flash across my mind, equally absurd. The first is that, somehow, I can't be seen. Maybe if I can't see them, they can't see me. They won't be able to actually see my pain, my humiliation. Ludicrous, given the strength of these infernal lights. My second thought is of 'The Downfall Of Paris', an appropriate but asinine rudimental exercise for the snare drum. Maybe if I play that extremely loudly, no one will notice. Again, unfeasibly optimistic. This is going to be the longest five minutes of my life, and there is no getting out of it.

❏

It seemed that equipment – its provision, malfunctions, and shipping charges – was going to be an ongoing low-level headache through most of my time in the trenches. I still have a recurring nightmare, which comes with very few variations. The room is always full, and the audience is becoming restless. I am holding up proceedings – something is wrong with the drums. They are slowly melting, or turning into chocolate. The people in the crowd look hugely disappointed as they slowly turn away and begin to file out of the building, while I implore: "Wait! Wait! Just a few more minutes!"

Give a musician the latest electronic or even mechanical gizmo, and tell him what it can do, and, invariably, if he is a creative sort of character, he'll say: "Yes, but can it do *this*?" Whatever the design parameter, the worthwhile player always wants to exceed it. So it was with the computer brains at Madison Square Garden. They were loaded down with too many megabytes of samples, and then asked to do histrionic things with MIDI code, a kind of language in which electronic instruments communicate with each other. Sometimes they all communicated at the same time, like a clutch of old hens, and the computers gave up.

Yet this natural inquisitiveness as to what might be possible on a drum kit was leading me to fruitful avenues for research and was ultimately to be much of what I was about. Could it play tunes as well? What if you got rid of all the toms, and substituted oil barrels instead? What if you put a baking tray in the bass drum and chains all over the toms: could you 'prepare' a drum kit in the same way that Cage and Nancarrow and Cowell had 'prepared' the piano with thumbtacks and other paraphernalia? Jamie Muir had done just that in his *Larks'*

Tongues In Aspic period to produce the divine clattering on the album's title track.

I was brought up in the days before the heavy marketing of matching sets of glossy drums, when a 'kit' was whatever you thought appropriate to the job. My kits had always sprouted unusual noise-making tendrils. Following Muir's departure from King Crimson, I assigned myself his percussion function and grew two side racks and a rear rack of steel plates, ratchets, blocks, gongs, suspended triangles, and a thunder-sheet.

In my own first band, Bruford, the racks remained but the drums were augmented and much coloured by the clanging sound of Rototoms. These are tuneable drums without shells that can be tuned quickly by rotating the head, which sits in a threaded metal ring; rotation raises or lowers the tension-hoop relative to the rim, which increases or decreases the pitch of the drum. For much of the last two decades of the last century I was in the analogue and then digital world of electronic percussion, only to exit from that into a particularly unusual configuration of the acoustic set. In the area of timbre – the quality of sounds – it seemed that I'd found a small space from which I might contribute.

An additional benefit to altering the parameters of the ballpark like this was that you couldn't be judged by the normal rules of the game. If your drum kit had no hi-hat or cymbals, and the snare drum was draped in chains, and the electronic toms sounded like plastic bottles, you could hardly be found lacking when you didn't sound like the masters. You could invent your own rules, and you'd be the only guy on the pitch. Brilliant.

But this approach, like that of all innovators, came at a price. There were the exhausting hours foraging up dead-end streets. If you wanted something to sound unique, you had better be ready for mechanical and electronic failure, horrific cartage costs, and mysterious power failures. Enjoy the drifting oscillators, the endlessly fraught soundchecks, the desperate phone calls in the dead of night to

Japanese R&D departments so the unit could once again have life breathed into it before tomorrow's show.

My drum set at Madison Square Garden was, for all its faults (and not working is a fairly substantial fault), an amazing bit of kit. It was the product of the fevered imagination of one Dave Simmons, a British keyboard player and designer of electronic musical instruments. By the late 70s, Dave could reasonably claim to be the father of electronic drums. No British 80s synth-pop band could be seen without a set of hexagonal yellow Simmons pads.

Crimson loved new tools with which to work, and our 1980 album *Discipline* was groaning under the weight of Roland synth-guitars, Emmett Chapman's Stick – a ten-string instrument held vertically, with additional treble strings, and tapped rather than plucked – and, of course, Simmons drums. At the height of their popularity, the 135-strong workforce at Simmons HQ couldn't ship them out fast enough. The company expanded into a new facility, but manufacturing quality began to suffer. Production was frequently interrupted with larky outings for the whole workforce to the racetrack for the day. With the introduction of each new model, quality control appeared to worsen. The wait-time for a set in the USA had stretched to about three months, and there was every chance you could open the box when it finally arrived and find the unit all in bits. Americans in particular have a short fuse with this kind of treatment. Sales started to decline on the back of an appalling word-of-mouth reputation for poor reliability.

I was so heavily featured in the company's advertising and marketing as a high-profile endorser of the product that people thought I worked for Simmons. At gigs, there would be a local drummer with an evil stare clutching a broken box with wires coming out, looking like he was ready to kill someone. And I was in the firing line. The fun trips on the corporate jet declined, and the company was in crisis when it moved into production of its last desperate do-or-die flagship instrument, the SDX. Dave had the lunatic stare and whacky manner of the great British inventors, the men who are about to go where no man should. On balance you warmed to him, wanted to support his ideas, and forgave him when it didn't quite work. That was, until you were dying at the hands of two silent SDXs at Madison Square Garden. Then you just wanted to kill him.

Even when electronic instruments had finally taken their toll and I'd thrown up my hands, somewhere in the mid 90s, admitted defeat, and bayed loudly to the moon for an instrument I knew would actually work at 8:00 the following night, I couldn't quite leave my equipment alone. Having finally reverted to the 'standard' acoustic set, I was unable to resist setting them up in an unusual way.

Adopting the style of a classical timpanist, I decided to arrange the drums flat in a semi-circle around me, out of pitch order, snare drum in the middle. A couple of cymbals on both left and right, and I had a symmetrical kit that was mirrored on both left and right. Simple, elegant, effective, and this particular configuration would ensure that unusual combinations of drums would 'fall' under the sticks, hopefully making my phrasing sound … well, a little different. There was only one fly in the ointment. To make this outfit work, I would also need a custom hi-hat on a remote cable. No big problem: the wonderful Tama Drums could be relied upon to produce something, but I would have to take it everywhere I went. At worst, a minor inconvenience, I thought. Until I arrived in Moscow.

❏

Everything is half an hour late in Moscow. You agree 8:00 and that, it is immediately understood, means 8:30. The Spanish have an unwarranted and outdated reputation for this sort of thing, but since the Germans arrived in Madrid to build VWs as Skodas, something had to change. The Germans have yet to bring similar change to Moscow, but we live in hope.

It is 2004, my birthday was on May 17th, and now a couple of days later I am to play my first concert with my current jazz group, Earthworks, in that great city. I am cobbling together my recently reconfigured drumset with mostly the right bits of kit that our Russian host, Sasha Cheparukhin of Green Wave Music, has managed to produce.

My eye, as usual, is on the clock. There is never enough time for this, and my blood freezes as I realise I've forgotten to bring a critical component from the UK for this remote hi-hat. Our tour manager, the adroitly named Mr Kalashnikov, is calming and says he'll go and find the part from the nearest Tama outlet. Traffic is heavy: it'll take half an hour. I immediately translate this to one hour, which means he should arrive back shortly before the doors are opened, allowing enough time to fit and test the part.

One hour passes. A further half-hour passes, and the audience is let into the raked auditorium. Another 30 minutes – we are already due on stage – and the audience is by now visibly restless. Ten minutes later the part arrives, and I explain the difference between 30 minutes and 130 minutes quite carefully. Unfortunately, I am the only soul in the dressing room who knows how to fit this thing onto the wretched drum kit, which I am by now deeply regretting I had decided to reconfigure.

I part the curtains and, hoping no one will notice, advance to the drums to a deafening roar of recognition. The remedial work needs to take place at floor level. Reluctantly, I bend down to the hi-hat positioned right at the front of the kit, and with my back to the crowd. I descend to my knees with a small screwdriver, my replacement part, and my nose two inches from the ground. My posterior juts out proudly, up into the air, facing the audience. A less dignified posture would be hard to imagine. A drop of sweat blinds my left eye, and as I screw it up to avoid more of the same, I hear 500 pairs of Russian lungs roaring 'Happy Birthday To You' in really passable English.

❏

Musician and listener both have had to absorb the implications of new technology with alarming and increasing frequency. Technology has affected everything about listening: the *when* – namely, after the event;

the *where* – away from the event; the *how* – with whomever we please, or alone; and the *what* – particularly in terms of detail.

The technology of music simply refers to the methods by which sounds are produced and then reproduced. Looked at in this way, sociologist Simon Frith suggests that "the history of music can be divided into three stages, each organised around a different technology of musical storage and retrieval. In the first (or 'folk') stage, music is stored in the body … and can only be retrieved through performance. Music is either marked off from the everyday as ritual and ceremonial, or is so totally integrated into everyday social practices (work song, for example, or lullabies) as to be part of their meaning.

"In the second (or 'art') stage, music is stored through notation," Frith continues. "It can still only be retrieved in performance, but it also has now a sort of ideal or imaginary existence (against which any individual performance can be measured – and found wanting). … In classical music, the musical mind is elevated … over the musical body. In the final (or 'pop') stage, music is stored on phonogram, disc, or tape and retrieved mechanically, digitally, electronically."[1]

When recording began, the reproductions were of very poor quality, unable to faithfully track low frequencies, disfigured by surface noise and crackles, and infinitely worse than the live experience. After swift improvement, and starting first in the classical world, came the idea of the perfect recording achieved through multiple takes and editing. Into the relationship of three people – composer, performer, and listener – stepped a fourth, the recording engineer, and debate raged, and continues to rage, about the authenticity and purpose of a recording. For whom is this artefact being made, and what is it trying to achieve?

Modern software programs such as Pro Tools, designed to furnish the maximum of control over all aspects of a recording, are occasionally urged upon me, the jazz-group leader, so that the performance can be edited, tweaked, improved, cosmetically enhanced. But the way I wish to use the recording process is to document a quartet performance in real time, recorded that day. Another day, it will be different, certainly, and it may be better or worse, but that's irrelevant. Another take is possible, but microscopic adjustments to pitch and time within the chosen take miss the point. Life and music are all dirty and imperfect, and so will a living breathing jazz performance also be dirty and imperfect. In this world, the world of performance music, Pro-Tooling can only offer an antiseptic sort of cleanliness or perfection, which is not always required.

For others the priority in a studio may be different, and the way the studio is used is indicative of the philosophy of the user. The avant-gardist Brian Eno, for example, was the first I heard talking about using the studio as an instrument. He didn't play a conventional musical instrument, so he'd play the studio instead.

Furthermore, the different sections of the potential audience for the recording might want different things from it. Kenneth Goldstein, a folk record producer in the 50s and 60s, had to "figure out what my responsibilities were, first to the public, which is a record that is good to listen to, easy to listen to, straight through; second to the folklorist, an actual representation, an ethnographic record, if you will; and third to the singer, which is the best that he bloody well can do, which is what the singer wants to present to the world."[2] Simon Frith comments that Goldstein "saw his role in this respect as like that of the high-street studio photographer, not snapping candid shots, but going to whatever technological trouble it took to capture people's sense of themselves".[3] Personally, I want the candid shot.

Frith's suggestion, then, is that the history of music can be divided into three stages, each organised around a different technology of storage or retrieval – ear; notation; recording – and that each of those can be associated with a particular social mode.

First, he posits the 'folk' society, a rather unspecified repository of all pre-bourgeois forms, roughly up to the mid 18th century. This 'folk' mode implies that the relationships between music and musician, musician and community, musical content and collective expression are direct, non-contradictory, and non-alienated, 'pure' if you like. There is as yet no music industry to muddy the waters. Music is played by ear, composition and performance are the same, anyone can take part, and music is not yet 'objectified' into works for sale.

Second comes the bourgeois society, the growing middle class of merchants and shopkeepers – the people who owned the four million pianos in Britain at the dawn of the 20th century. The first enormous technological invention, notation, came as a negation of the folk mode. You can read something of its impact in Howard Goodall's book *Big Bangs*.[4]

Notation emphasised the eye, not the ear, it encouraged the calculation of complex scores, and it objectified the work, storing it in a tangible form, as personal property, a commodity that may later be offered for sale. It gave us the phenomenon of the highly skilled classical musician for whom the music only exists on paper, and who is therefore unable to play a note without it. It led to the division of labour between composer and performer, to individualisation and specialisation, and production *for* a market rather than *by* a community. All very suitable characteristics in a bourgeois society.

Finally, says Frith, the potentially socialist society is built around the latest method of storage and retrieval, recording, in which the potential of electronic media is seen as only coming to full fruition in an egalitarian, classless setting. Drummer, writer, and theorist Chris Cutler takes this further when he suggests that the recording stage is a "negation of a negation" that blurs the distinction between performer and composer and re-emphasises sound and improvisation rather than formal notational and compositional skills.[5]

In this way, all the main characteristics of recording echo the folk mode, although of course now any sound is available, and for the present these characteristics are contained within the stifling constraints of the music industry's need to buy and sell – subject to any havoc the internet is currently wreaking on the way that may be done.

Cutler's argument is neat, but maybe a bit too neat. Cultures and outlooks dominated by these three modes – oral, literary and print, and electronic – are indeed distinctive. But let's not forget the struggles and tensions and compromises between the characteristics of the different modes, between varying practices in the same mode, and between musical form and content.

For example, the young post-war pop performer often started out with printed song copies of the popular tunes of the day but slowly transformed them and his style away from the literate mode and into the rock world of aural, un-notated transmission. Conversely, the young Lennon and McCartney of The Beatles took mostly orally worked-out ideas to their producer George Martin, who then might transform them through literate methods by adding string parts.

Within the oral tradition alone there can be big differences, for example between the orally-produced blues of a solitary rural Southern black musician such as Blind Lemon Jefferson and the equally orally-produced collective 'gospel' song of black Southern churches. There are clear musical and sociological contrasts, such as secular/religious, solo/choral, free-rhythm/strong-pulse, personal/group.

Almost all music lies somewhere between the notated/oral extremes. At one end are the extreme notation-believers in the Austro-German tradition, from J.S. Bach through to Schoenberg; at the other are the extreme oral traditionalists: the current folk practitioners of global music. The rockers and jazzers lie somewhere in the middle, using notation as and when it suits.

Technology has always changed and continues to change the context in which the efforts of musicians are heard. Equally, it has consistently replaced or 'improved' the tools the musician has to work with, affording him a broader palette of sound. In King Crimson, the band I had left Yes to join, we were all well aware of the new developments in recording and performance techniques. As a group of musicians of like mind, innovation was in our collective bloodstream. But Crimson, the perfect vehicle for further work in this area, was proving to be alarmingly unreliable.

5 WHY WOULD YOU WANT TO FORM YOUR OWN GROUP?

King Crimson was to develop a habit of "ceasing to exist", as our leader would have it, during my 25 years as the drummer. This was a recurring irritation that you could set your watch by, as we began to settle into a pattern of three or four years on, seven years off. It dissolved in front of my very eyes for the first time in 1974. Ejected, as it were, into the street, I busied myself with a little amateur research into the music-making procedures of others.

I suppose I was thinking that there must be a better way. I did some supposedly anonymous studio work, only to find that the album appeared "featuring ex-Yes Bill Bruford" or was billed in such a way as to give the impression that this appalling music was, in some way, my idea.

A few toothpaste commercials came and went. By November of '74 I found myself in the group Gong, as a brief replacement for drummer Laurie Allen, who had been banned from a couple of European countries – pre-union, of course – for crossing borders with illegal substances. Gong is an Anglo-French ensemble led by an ageing Australian hippie, Daevid Allen. The organisation is still very much with us, wallowing along in the same completist nostalgia backwash that keeps afloat almost any group over 30 years old.

We had a chaotic and argumentative lifestyle that I espoused as readily as the Summer Of Love, the flared loon-pants, and the psychedelia of the early Yes days – which is to say, not readily at all. Searching Gong for alternative methods of communal music-making was like searching a children's playground for paths to higher enlightenment – not immediately fruitful – although Allen would doubtless have insisted that such a place was exactly where enlightenment was to be found.

The group was signed to Virgin Records, the proprietor of which had already had an enormous hand in sealing my fate back in 1971 with *The Yes Album*. Richard Branson has an air of the perpetual schoolboy about him: earnest, inquisitive, and enquiring. One evening at the hotel bar – he'd appeared on our tour to see how Gong was progressing – he quizzed me steadily on what it was I thought could make the music better, the band better, anything better. My answers were listened to in depth and at length: very flattering to the new boy who was at best only a hired gun. I rather suspect others have succumbed to Richard's soft interrogation techniques in the years since.

From sessions and tours with Annette Peacock, Roy Harper, Pavlov's Dog, and Phil Manzanera of Roxy Music fame, among several others, I received precious little useful information about how best to proceed. I was badly adrift in the industry, thrashing about without a paddle and getting low on water, when a lifeline was thrown from a passing vessel. On the end of it were two people who were to give me hope, direction, and focus, in no particular order.

Dave Stewart had been through the progressive-rock mill with Egg and Hatfield And The North, this latter ensemble shrewdly taking its name from a large blue road-sign that had to be passed by everyone driving on the M1 motorway north out of London. Unmistakeable and huge, this was free roadside advertising of quality, and I thought the man that pounced on that must have something going for him.

I found Dave forming a new ensemble called National Health, which was broadly to perform written instrumental music, based around two keyboard players, that was patently neither classical music nor jazz and so, by default, must be rock music, he reasoned. But it was brainy stuff, with titles like 'Borogroves', 'Paracelsus', and 'Agrippa', and the girls at Trent Polytechnic in Nottingham would excuse themselves as we launched bravely into the 'Lethargy Shuffle', heads down, brows furrowed, all concentration. I was right at home. I don't quite remember either joining or leaving the group, but I did take with me Dave's phone number, which I would keep until my research was over and I felt ready to strike out on my own.

The other person on the end of the life-rope was Phil Collins, who went on to have global success as *the* Phil Collins. Our first meeting had been several years earlier, when, taking a night off from the group he was in at the time, Flaming Youth, he came down to the Town Hall in Barnstaple, Devon, with Yes, to set up my drums. He was a very good drum technician, so there is plenty of work in that area for him if this singing thing doesn't work out. We'd stayed in touch and, some time in late 1975, he was knocking around in Brand X, a fusion group alongside his regular gig with Genesis. It didn't seem to be directed at much other than having a good time and delivering some blazing playing as light relief to the participants' day jobs. I appended myself as percussionist to his drumming, and we did a couple of dates around London.

During one of these, Phil was explaining that things weren't proceeding smoothly in Genesis. Peter Gabriel had left, or was about to leave, and Phil was auditioning for a suitable replacement. They'd looked at dozens of hopefuls, but Phil reckoned he could do better than all of them anyway. Either he or I made the next step to the obvious solution: why didn't he become Genesis's singer and I play drums for a while behind him until he was settled in?

Phil and I were admirers of each other's style, and he knew enough about me to know that the nightmare scenario for a drummer-turned-singer – namely that the music might collapse around his ears like a house of cards – was unlikely to happen. Three months later, in March 1976, I was on stage with the band at the Arena in London, Ontario, playing the first date on a tour that would earn me the unheard-of remuneration of £500 a week, and during which the house of cards did not, indeed, collapse.

I was, on the whole, a lousy hired gun. Accustomed to arguing my corner in Yes or Crimson, and being as a consequence emotionally involved in the music from the first note onward, there was simply too little for me to do. I dutifully learnt the music, which I didn't particularly like or dislike – I just knew it was nothing to do with me. This was an alien feeling, which I had found barely acceptable in the anodyne recording studio, but which troubled me more on stage. I had no motivation other than that of earning a living. I felt bogus and fraudulent, and began to behave badly.

I sniped ineffectually from the sidelines, offered my opinion too frequently, and generally forgot to hold my tongue. The group remained unfailingly polite and generous to Carolyn and me, which only made me feel worse. I must have been trying to provoke my own dismissal, but the tour ended in the nick of time in the cavernous Bingley Hall in Staffordshire, with the presentation of a gold album that I hadn't earned, and certainly didn't deserve, for a record I wasn't on. By the time I got back to London, I couldn't wait to get started with the rest of my life. Enough research, already.

Phil and I kept in touch, and he no doubt found my replacement, the American drummer Chester Thompson, a good deal more agreeable and much better behaved. In the next few years, Mike Rutherford and Tony Banks both started families and moved out of London to the bucolic landscape of Sussex and Surrey. We had become family friends and were socially, if not artistically, of like mind, so Carolyn and I, with our two youngest children still babes in arms, started to look for a house in the same area. Phil lived only a few miles away when we, the Brufords, finally settled down in the village of Ewhurst in 1980, and that autumn he and I would have the occasional pint in his local, the Queen Vic, if only to get away from the paintbrushes, prams, and nappies.

One such evening we drank up and went back to his place to hear his first solo record. I wasn't sure I knew he'd made a solo record. I'd been flat out producing children and records in equal measure and was in recovery from two long albums at Trident Studios in London's Soho: my own first record, *Feels Good To Me*, and then the first by the sleeker, more marketable new group, UK.

Phil sat me down and played what was to be *Face Value*, although I don't believe he'd settled on that as a title. Maybe I expected a jazz-rockish Brand X with vocals; maybe I expected some more quaintly English Genesis, with lawn mowers and garden gates; but whatever I expected, it wasn't what I got. What I got was a remarkably assured leap into the big-time world of serious, dramatic, gut-wrenching soul music. The songs didn't fidget – a common problem in the twitchy world of progressive rock. They did what they had to do extremely effectively and no more. They were the vehicles for the tension of someone who was about to spill his guts out all over the floor, with a passion and intensity rarely known outside black soul music and within which this would resonate well.

This wasn't a 'drummer's album', with all the condescension that that term implies. This was blue-eyed soul at its best, and knowing as I did very little about music that had the ingredients to cross over, to cross boundaries, to cross genders, to touch people from Azerbaijan to Zaire, I nevertheless had the vague feeling that this was going to make him extremely popular. Just how popular, I think neither of us could have guessed.

❏

In my early years, I had been a ferocious student of my instrument. I spent hours in practice, either on the full set if I could find a place, or on phone books and pillows if not. I shall be forever grateful to Yes's first manager Roy Flynn, who put his Putney basement at my disposal, morning, noon, and night. A little later, I was to build several soundproofed music rooms in London flats and houses – and we're not talking about a few egg cartons on the wall, we're talking a full room within a room, raised floor, lowered ceiling, double doors, triple-glazed, air-conditioning, the works. I needed to practise as a fish needed to swim, and hours drifted past locked in Roy's basement, grappling with the complexities of paradiddle inversions.

Most rock guys cobble together whatever chops you need in an afternoon or two and then hurriedly return to weightier matters, such as the parlous state of your wardrobe for tomorrow night's show. I knew that popular music was a simple music based on three chords and there was little call for a fourth or fifth chord, but that didn't bother me. I knew rock was part charisma, part crowd control. Rock was a party at which the singer was the host, a circus at which he was the ringmaster. It was an event at which music played a part, but not the only part. God, if you want 100 per cent music, go and fall asleep on the leather armchairs in front of Hindemith or Berlioz at the Royal Festival Hall. But as backup – and I'm always backed up – I reckoned I needed some technical armament in case the three chords couldn't sustain me.

I've always been an ideas man. If you have ideas, you need an outlet, or sooner or later you're going to blow up. Depending on others to provide the outlet can be more unnerving than just doing the job yourself, so I guess I was inevitably going to be a bandleader, whether I wanted it or not. Initially, the ideas were about what to do on a drum kit, then what to do in the engine room of a group, and finally what to do with the whole group. Robert Fripp had said something about picking only one in ten of them, because they came so quickly off the assembly line.

Behind the profligacy, however, I suspect there lay a terror that the ideas would run out and I might have to play someone else's idea, and be found wanting. I always knew very quickly how the music should go – preferably my way, over my rhythmic figures – so I would know what to play, rather than have to react to someone else's direction and open myself to the possibility of not knowing what to do.

The solution was staring me in the face: to write my own material and run my own band to play it. But that evidenced the same need to control, born of insecurity in my own musical completeness. For the mature player, having nothing to play probably means it's best to play nothing, but I have always lacked such trust in my musical self. Lack of confidence while taking yourself too seriously – an indictable offence indeed – was to prove my Achilles heel as the years rolled past. Guilty as charged.

Running a band is the punishment you suffer for wishing to define the musical environment in which your efforts are heard. While 'control' is not a popular word, I can see no other way by which A Man With An Idea might bring it to the public's attention. People who make an impression generally do so as a Chief, not an Indian. I would start by cold-calling the players I liked and respected, on the basis that if I hired people who knew more about music than I did – and there were plenty of *them* around – then some of it might rub off. But I knew if I called these people over for a rehearsal, I'd feel obliged to provide them with some music, so I made an effort to have something ready.

An alternative and tougher policy revolved around the idea that if you lock four or five interesting players in a recording studio and get out of the way, what you get will never be less than interesting, if they don't kill each other first. Miles Davis's groups seemed to be assembled along similar lines, as, I suspect, was the *Larks' Tongues In Aspic* King Crimson of 1974. Contemplating the idea of having my own group, as I sat in the Genesis transport for hours in 1976 planning my future, filled me with excitement and terror in equal measure. If it was going to happen, I had to start by finding some players.

❑

I would never do it again now, crossing the Atlantic cold, but it's the sort of thing you do when you're on a mission. I have had people do it to me on occasion. They contact me, tell me they sound just like guitarists Robert Fripp or Allan Holdsworth, or saxophonist Iain

Ballamy, and say they would like to come for an audition. Just why would I want one of them? I've already done that. But my 'no' is not readily accepted as an answer, and they fly in from the States, usually from one of those music schools in Boston or New York City, sit in my room for about ten minutes, and sound just like Robert or Allan or Iain. I say no, thanks, and put them back on the plane. Avoiding the lemmings – it's an occupational hazard if you're hiring.

I was looking for a bass player, but in 1977 my country didn't make the kind I had in mind. Allan Holdsworth had agreed to join my band on guitar, but I was looking for an agile counterpoint to him, and if you knew Allan's playing, the counterpoint would indeed have to be agile. The British players, with their solid root and fifth fixation, were passable, but I wanted an electric player with the harmonic knowledge of a jazz musician and the sonic wallop of a rock guy.

Keyboardist Patrick Moraz, who at the time was in or close to Yes, had found just the man, and played me his work on Patrick's new album. His name was Jeff Berlin, and I had to have him. Moraz had an address for him on Long Island, New York. I cold-called a slightly surprised bass player, made the necessary arrangements to visit, and turned up at Heathrow with Patrick's album and a couple of scratchy ideas for new music for my band in my suitcase. If this guy had sent me away with a flea in my ear I wouldn't have been surprised.

The Berlins were a big Jewish family living in big Jewish harmony in Great Neck, Long Island. The first thing I noticed was the food. I'd only been in the house about 20 minutes before the biggest plate of pasta in the world appeared, and Jeff and I couldn't escape to a downstairs music room until the whole lot had been demolished. It occurred to me after a while that the family might have mistakenly thought I was a rock star, but one with a disappointingly low-key demeanour. Maybe they couldn't quite understand why I had left Yes, evidently to seek out their son, whom I didn't know, and ask him to be in a band with me, based 3,000 miles away. Seemed perfectly straightforward to me – just another day at the office, in fact – but I can now, with hindsight, understand the gently questioning atmosphere around the dinner table.

Berlin maintained he was a fan of Cream bassist Jack Bruce and vibraphonist Gary Burton, in no particular order, and that he studied bass from trombone etudes. Blinded by his technical ability, I called a halt to an informal audition after ten minutes. His facility was simply unknown in my country. You had to work for months to master three-octave and four-octave arpeggios like that, and no self-respecting British electric bass player could afford that amount of time. He would be too busy looking cool and working on the style thing. The famous American work ethic sets our friends over there quite apart from us Brits over here – we prefer the cult of the talented amateur: Winston Churchill, The Beatles, tennis-player Tim Henman. A couple of years earlier, Daevid Allen, the poet and Beat, had sneered at me for being a 'professional' during my short stay in his chronically haphazard Gong. I knew what he meant, but he should have realised that I knew full well that this music thing was about a whole lot more than the paycheque. Why else would I have volunteered for his dysfunctional outfit?

In general, the Brits do the minimum work necessary on their instruments to execute something approximating The Idea, whereas the Americans sweat and drill, study and practise under what they see as a professional work ethic. If it doesn't hurt, it isn't going to do much good – no gain without pain. This in part explains the longevity of that nation's love of the UK progressive rockers. American audiences could see clear evidence of the expenditure of effort, resulting in the acquisition of a tangible skill. We knew how to play, and they liked that. And once America has decided it likes you, it won't give up easily on that notion.

Conversely, the next lot in from the UK, the punks, clearly had expended nothing but a lot of caterwauling that required the wrong kind of effort, and middle America didn't like that. On our side of the water we had ideas; on their side they had the ability to execute them, which made for a great, if argumentative, 1980 King Crimson, with two

Brits and two Americanos. I still prefer a good idea poorly executed than a bright, shiny, technically brilliant bauble with a hollow centre. I just didn't see why you couldn't have great ideas well executed, and in Jeff I was looking at the bass player for the job.

I stayed a couple of nights at his house, and we went into New York City to do a couple of demos for producer Jimmy Iovine at the Power Station, but I was marking time, and I wanted to get back to the UK to get to grips with putting the band together. I agreed to meet Jeff on our side of the water in a few weeks, but already I knew hiring an American was going to be an expensive option. Plane tickets alone could kill us off. Guitarist Jeff Beck had tried an intercontinental power trio a few years earlier, with bassist Tim Bogert and drummer Carmine Appice, but had lamented in a magazine interview that logistics and travel rendered the whole thing implausible. I must have been mad. But corruption at Heathrow, good old Heathrow, was to come to the rescue.

In those days, the airport was dubbed Thiefrow by the tabloid newspapers as a mark of grudging respect for its sheer brigandry. This was the same sort of respect they would accord a villain-with-a-heart-of-gold, a questionable honour they might confer upon someone like Great Train Robber Ronnie Biggs. Theft from suitcases was so prevalent it no longer attracted comment; heaven only knows what went on in the huge bonded hangars and freight depots on the commercial side.

We could only afford for Jeff Berlin to fly on a cheap standby ticket, the drawback being that you could never guarantee he'd be on a flight. Not a preferred arrangement for a band making gigs after connecting flights. But our tour manager, Chris Kettle, had found a contact. If you knocked on a grey door to the rear back left of baggage check-in with £20 in hand, stated the flight your stand-by was on, and didn't ask any more questions, Jeff could mysteriously become 'confirmed stand-by' and we could set our clocks by his arrival. Perfect. My band Bruford only survived as long as it did courtesy of the man behind the grey door at Heathrow.

Jeff's contribution to the band was enormous, and his talent so big it was ultimately uncontainable. Bass is a difficult instrument to keep fully occupied, and Jeff was turning into the kind of player you needed to keep fully occupied. His quiet moments had the air of marking time until his next blinding solo. Like a dog on a leash, he prowled the front of the stage looking for something to do. The chordal parts in our music were normally reserved for guitar or keyboard, but he would learn and play variations on those as well. As a solo performer later on in life he would be an act complete unto himself.

It's something of a mystery as to why musicians gravitate toward particular instruments, and it probably has as much to do with fantasy and timing as anything scientific. I have no real idea why I took up the drums, although there were a couple of pointers. My sister's gift to me of the pair of brushes came with a suggestion that I watch *Jazz 625*, the weekly primetime BBC TV jazz show, to see how they were used.

That led to the seduction of my innocent heart by the brilliant American drummers paraded before me, chief among whom was Art Blakey. Majestically in control, he coloured, whipped, sustained, and drove the music like an expert driving a four-in-hand. The music went nowhere without him, and it went where he said it would go. I was hooked. If Jeff Berlin had been a generation younger, he would surely have played the fiddle; a generation older, the electric guitar, at which, incidentally, he was equally astonishing. But on bass, it was difficult trying to contain him.

❏

So much of the work in these collective groups involved nudging, cajoling, steering the thing toward a perceived nirvana where all components functioned beautifully, as they were supposed to. Then you had to hold the damn thing there long enough to make a great album or two, and maybe a tour if you were lucky, before the whole pack of cards disintegrated in the wind.

The first four records from Yes were all practice runs for the fifth –

the killer – *Close To The Edge*. Personally I had no further need to do any more after that. King Crimson's tortuous existence in the 70s brought it finally to *Red*, a prescient album that exerted a powerful pull on Kurt Cobain and others of the upcoming Seattle grunge movement. Then Crimson stopped. With Bruford, the album was *One Of A Kind*. All-instrumental, it possessed the kind of focused vision that allowed for no ifs or buts. With the unnerving confidence of youth, it had This Is What We Do And This Is How We Do It stamped all over it.

The records before and after tend to be journeying to, and then away from, these moments in the sunshine. If you are lucky enough to participate in a strong co-operative endeavour such as any one of those albums, you can use the momentum to project yourself forward into uncharted waters.

I grudgingly admit that, more by accident than design, I have managed to contribute to the making of a handful of records and even fewer tours that really did seem to have legs, that changed me and others as musicians and people, and after which I did not view music or my position in it in the same way as I had before. With Yes's *Fragile* and *Close To The Edge*, and King Crimson's *Discipline* album and tour in the 80s, we knew we were on to something, but didn't quite know what. Later, there was the same feeling on the jazz side with the first Earthworks CD. In common with *Discipline*, this music also displayed new technology in an unusual setting, unusual or innovative instrumentation, and a deliberate obfuscation of musical references. As with the early Yes, I didn't care whether it was rock or jazz, so long as it wasn't overtly either.

Guitarist Allan Holdsworth, like bassist Jeff Berlin, was clearly developing something on his instrument that involved huge leaps forward. There was the liquid hammering-on technique in the left hand, by which perhaps only one in three or four notes are struck, with the rest hammered on, by just hitting the fingers on the frets. There were the spectacular leaps in intervals – Allan had given me Nicolas Slonimsky's *Thesaurus Of Scales And Melodic Patterns* as a Christmas gift, and he was by now a leading authority in the arcane world of palindromic canons, sesquitone progressions, and the like. Allan brought forward this heavy armament, more commonly found in classical composition, as source material for improvisation in rock and jazz groups. There was the whammy bar, more commonly known as the tremolo arm, which invested his work with so much passion. Just as it seemed the notes could go no further, the phrase would spin off into the ether with the crying vocal inflection caused by momentarily altering the pitch of all the guitar strings. There was his sound – a beautiful, passionate thing not always readily available. Many was the night you could find Allan, soldering iron in hand, five minutes before the audience was let into the hall, wiring together three complaining amplifiers, their guts spilling out onto the stage, solder and screws everywhere. For him, as with all good musicians, the notes and the sound are inseparable, and the pursuit of the perfect sound – defined here as the one you hear in your head, the one that won't go away – becomes a lifetime obsession.

In a good group, everyone's sound and style is in a permanent state of redefinition, relevant to and refracted through everyone else's redefinitions. If he's going to play like that, I'll have to rethink my contribution, which means a third man's going to have to start again with his. With luck, and the wind in the right direction, you come up with a collective shriek that sounds like no other band, and which no other band, quite probably, would wish to sound like. It's your little patch of the musical cosmos. In John Coltrane's classic 60s quartets, pianist McCoy Tyner developed a formidable block-chord technique as the only way he was going to exert influence on the music if drummer Elvin Jones and leader Coltrane, both busy revolutionising their instruments, were going to play like that. Necessity remains the mother of invention.

You could be forgiven for thinking that this formidable musical weaponry at Allan's fingertips, deployed with such imagination and skill – and recognised as such by Eddie Van Halen, Al Di Meola, and a whole platoon of leading guitarists around the world – would bring its owner a measure of satisfaction, if not peace. But you'd be wrong. By the time I'd nudged Allan into the group UK in the late 70s, he was more or less permanently unhappy. Terminally saddled with a bleak analysis of his own shortcomings, inconsolable about how poor the music seemed to him, wracked with guilt at the possibility of considerable success, Allan eventually threw in the towel, conceded defeat, and moved to California to run a series of groups in which he would refine his ideas about guitar playing, free from the necessity of filtering them through a group decision-making process.

Like all these things, it's all worth it to me if I can hear ten minutes of something beautiful that would not otherwise have existed but for our efforts. Allan's powerful solo on 'In The Dead Of Night'; his multi-tracked chords on 'Mental Medication'; his acoustic introduction to 'Nevermore'; the passionate playing on the end of 'Sahara Of Snow'; these little gems are all testaments to a musician with whom I consider it a privilege to have worked.

Dave Stewart, the fourth and final member of Bruford, if you discount the fleeting visitation from our singer Annette Peacock, was a different animal to Jeff or Allan. Studious, careful, and with a highly advanced sense of humour, he was the perfect counterfoil for Allan's single-note bravura and deepening identity crisis. Dave came equipped, in the early pre-synthesizer days, with Hammond organ and some combination of electric piano and Clavinet, all of which complained bitterly at being fed through a ring-modulator. He was deep into the texture of the sound, or the cloth it was woven from, if you prefer. The sounds in his head were hard to realise pre-synthesis, but when the Sequential Circuits Prophet 5 appeared toward the end of the 70s, it was the answer to his prayers, and he took to synths like a duck to water. I loved them too, because shipping a Hammond organ around on tour was crippling us financially, and synthesizers were a whole lot smaller and cheaper.

Dave and I prepared the music, booked the rehearsal room, and lugged the bloody Hammond and drums up and down stairs into rehearsal rooms in Clerkenwell and Kingston. He didn't drive, so together we planned the group's future in my old three-litre BMW in the constant traffic jam between our two houses in south-west London as I delivered him to and fro.

The car was a last desperate throwback to my rock-star beginnings. With my first decent paycheque safely in the bank – in the music industry you haven't been paid until the funds clear into your account, and you're never on tour until the plane has its wheels up – I marched into MLG Motors on Chiswick High Road and bought the bottle-green black-vinyl-top motor that I had been secretly lusting after for weeks. Above the passenger sun-visor it had an Apple Corps sticker, no doubt left there by the valeting people to confirm its provenance, namely that its previous owner was indeed ex-Beatle George Harrison. The car had a great 8-track sound system and lousy engine cooling. During our deliberations, Dave and I would frequently overheat in the stationary traffic on the Upper Richmond Road and have to pull the beauty over, raise her bonnet, and let her cool down as the traffic crawled past.

More important to me than overheating BMWs, however, was the fact that Dave was my writing partner. Groups need to get their material from somewhere, and if you are putting yourself up as leader, the assumption is generally that you will lead the band musically as well functionally. This hasn't always been the case, and drummer-led outfits in the past – by Buddy Rich, Gene Krupa, Art Blakey, Elvin Jones – functioned well with a variety of musical directors, arrangers, and orchestrators, only occasionally playing original material that the leader was not necessarily expected to provide.

Quite why, by the time we had arrived at the late 70s, I felt the need to provide original material for large parts of our albums, I'm not sure, but my guess would be that the urge to write was made from one part inspiration, one part obligation, and one part insecurity. If you write the music, you control the environment in which your own performance will be heard. I would be able to write into the compositions all sorts of unlikely things that the drums might do, and dictate the rhythmic terrain on which they might do it. My forte, or such forte as I may possess, has lain in that direction rather than that of the chameleon-like interpreter of other people's music – another skill entirely, and currently well exemplified by the brilliant studio drummer Steve Gadd.

Steve is a veteran of thousands of sessions, during which he can assess and provide exactly what is required to lift the music, in countless different styles. He is the interpreter without parallel. From the lilt of Paul Simon, to the blues of Eric Clapton, the jazz of Chick Corea, or the laidback vocal style of James Taylor, Steve does detail in one take. His encyclopedic knowledge of the appropriateness of a given rhythmic feel is born from his voluminous experience. No matter how dismal your little offering, if you have Steve Gadd on it, it'll shine.

But you probably don't want one of his few solo albums. Solo albums are about many things, but they are not generally about the art of the interpreter. They are about the manic gesture of the unstable, about the wild, broad stroke of the visionary, and they are made by people who can only play it one way – not because they are incompetent, but because they *must*. A good album, solo or otherwise, should always be much more about questions than answers. It'll be messy, unruly, and probably won't have brushed its hair. It needs the production of an ego, rather than the sublimation of one. It must be about one thing, not many things – it must be about the way the artist hears it. God was right to make it hard to get a record deal. The label was the censor that protected the public from having to suffer the sketches, the almost, the nearly right – all those demos. You took the music out on the road, you literally road-tested it to destruction, and if you still had something at the end of a long test-market process during which all possible options and avenues were tried, adopted, or abandoned, then you made the album. All groups were a work in progress to that *Close To The Edge*, that *Red*, that *One Of A Kind*, that

Discipline, after which you didn't care and would anyway probably want to move on.

Unsurprisingly, I was good with rhythm, acceptable with melody, and needed help with harmony. Dave Stewart corrected schoolboy errors, put tanned harmonic flesh on skinny rhythmic propositions, smoothed out bumps, and made the unmusical musical. Steve Hamilton, the brilliant Scottish pianist in the second edition of Earthworks, was to do much the same thing for and with me 20 years later, but I'd learned a thing or two by then.

6 DO YOU STILL LIKE PROGRESSIVE ROCK?

Among other things, I'd learned, as all musicians must learn, that the relationship between talent and popular success is oblique, at best. Popular success is evidence of little more than the talent to be successful. If I have talent, will I be successful? I have gold and platinum records on my walls. Am I talented? Who says you or I are, or are not, talented? Talent is something that musicians are held to possess, is talked about as being real. In the music academy, it is something that is recognised by someone else, often the teacher or music critic, and ascribed to the student.

Talent may never actually be in your possession at all. And there is a tension here that every musician will recognise, between tradition and creation, between the firm sense of musical tradition that has to be preserved, documented, refined, and elaborated, and is personified by someone like trumpeter Wynton Marsalis, as distinct from the equally firm belief in the value of creativity and the importance of the new, fresh, and original. Perhaps talent is the difference between playing the notes 'correctly' and playing music, between technical skill and musical skill. Perhaps musical talent is no more or less than the ability to be recognised as musically talented.

This dovetails closely with discussions of art and craft, and possible distinctions between the two. Some have posited the idea that a craftsman knows what he is doing: when a carpenter sets out to build a chair, he's pretty sure he'll get a functioning chair at the end of the process. An artist, by contrast, doesn't know what he's going to get. When Van Gogh painted a chair, it only approximated the 'correct' dimensions of an actual chair, because his artistic sensibilities informed him, for whatever reason, that his chair was more expressive that way.

Artists tend to express a loss of control – "the chair just came out that way", "I think it's a chair", "it's as if the tune wrote itself", "I'm just the vessel through which the music passes" – whereas the craftsman feels in control and knows when he is finished. In many ways, the artist is less employable, because he can only do it one way, his way; not because he is being obtuse or difficult, but because it must be done that way, otherwise he cannot sleep at night. The romantic notion is that he is dominated and consumed by his art.

In pop instrumentalists' terms, the studio musician is perhaps the quintessential craftsman, master of all styles and completely anonymous in their delivery. Ask for a guitar solo in the style of Jimi Hendrix, and that's what you'll get. Hendrix himself, however, was perhaps closer to the artist, doing it a certain way that was shot through with his personality, wholly individual, unlike the next man, because he sees and hears it differently. Some say the craftsman uses the materials he's given to produce a known end-product – a chair, a sellable record, an immaculate version of another man's composition – whereas the artist provides his own materials and puts them together, or rearranges them, as an act of faith, and probably without knowing the outcome of that rearrangement.

Typically, the artistic process involves looking at the raw materials from a different angle. CBS producer Mitch Miller saw the recording studio in the 50s as an efficient place to produce big-selling pop records: exactly what it was designed for. By our definition, he would seem to be a craftsman. But Phil Spector, and George Martin with The Beatles, saw the studio respectively as a place to produce walls of sound in mono or to reposition the listening point through the creative use of stereo. Brian Eno saw it as a musical instrument in itself – an artistic leap of faith.

Perhaps Spector, Martin, Hendrix, and Eno were more 'talented' or 'artistic' than Miller or the session guitarist. In religious ideology, the artist would be considered closer to God, in possession of knowledge or talent unavailable to the common man. How did Mozart actually acquire the knowledge he must have acquired by the age of ten in order to write and perform such masterpieces? There was not enough time to have come by so much knowledge had it been drummed into him at birth, which it wasn't, so what exactly was the origin of his talent?

The talent required to produce a hit record may lie closer to a craft than an art. We all know that the musical ability required is marginal to the far greater requirement for stamina, timing, and media organisation, all of which may be needed in depth. First, you'll need an analysis of topics currently under discussion at a national tabloid level – drugs, bad boys, alcohol and cars, God Save The Queen – and the selection of one that breaks, or at least nudges at, one of the dwindling supply of remaining taboos. Then the necessary three-minute bump-and-grind, complete with ear-candy – a sound, a motif, to make you sit up and listen. And finally, the bringing of this oeuvre to market, the endless manoeuvrings and contortions necessary to secure the substantial investment needed to bring it to public attention.

This is not easy, but the skill required for a successful outcome has little to do with music itself. In this regard, I don't think there has been much change in the hundred-year period between Marie Lloyd's 1916 hit 'A Little Of What You Fancy', Cole Porter's 1936 song 'I've Got You Under My Skin', the 80s hits of The Pet Shop Boys, and on up to today's stars. All were and are essentially playing the same game.

In a broader sense, this leads to what we feel the role of an individual artist might be, as distinct from the craftsman–entertainer. David Tame, in his book *The Secret Power Of Music*, would insist that a musician's work shapes the consciousness of the individual, and thus of society, whether the participants like it or not.[1] There is the useful analogy of society as The Great Whale, lumbering along, guided by its highly sensitive pilot fish that scope out what lies ahead. Perhaps we are asking our artists to literally imagine the future for us, to show us what might be.

Most practitioners tend to fall instinctively into either the artist or craftsman camp. On the one hand lies the Romantic ideal of the artist in his garret, driven by demons that won't let him sleep at night because he has imagined the future and must express it or he'll explode. He works continually to public indifference or open ridicule, scraping by with enough money from some tedious related labour, perhaps in the face of increasing illness – Beethoven and his deafness; Stravinsky hearing open laughter during the premiere of *The Rite Of Spring* in Paris; Gauguin; Van Gogh – before he too succumbs, to be buried in a pauper's grave, like Mozart is supposed to have been, or cut off in his prime, like Jimi Hendrix, Scott LaFaro, Charlie Parker, Janis Joplin, or Michael Hutchence. With a haste bordering on the indecent, a deluge of boxed sets, retrospective exhibitions, and concerts rains down, but too late, too late.

On the other hand, we have the industry craftsman – mercenary, canny, certainly going for success well within his lifetime, looking for that spark that will capture the public imagination, scouring modern society for that hook line, that topic, that slant, that will make him millions. A useful businessman, he lives by trying to guess what the public wants and then supplying it, be he Irving Berlin with 'Alexander's Ragtime Band', Paul Whiteman, who was sure that jazz could be a big thing if only he could get the jazz out of it, a songwriter in the Brill Building in Manhattan in the late 40s, putting words in the mouths of appealing young (white) men all called Bobby, or perhaps Mitch Miller with his late-50s American pop, or producers Trevor Horn or Simon Cowell.

Artist and craftsman co-exist nominally within the music industry, but they are as unalike as chalk from cheese, as art from money, as God from Mammon. The position you choose to take on this particular scale – God at one end, money at the other – will depend on many things, but in part on how much you want to affect or reach people, and how many, and what sort of people you want to affect or reach. It may be a distinction between affecting a lot of people very superficially (perhaps with a disposable hit single with a shelf-life of about ten minutes) and giving a small group of people (perhaps your colleagues or other taste-makers) the experience of a lifetime that they will never forget and that will cause them to alter their perspectives, in turn causing others to alter their perspectives, like ripples on a pond. The problem with Entertainment is that it's like juggling eggs. The man who can juggle two eggs has an audience until someone comes along who can juggle three eggs. The problem with Art is that it'll probably kill you. So take your pick!

Neither artist nor craftsman tends to make much effort to understand the other, and each has developed whole vocabularies to express their 'otherness': pretentious and self-indulgent on one hand; mercenary and mundane on the other. T.S. Eliot, clearly an artist, failed to understand the mediocrity required to connect with the mass, and in 1929 wrote: "Of course one can go 'too far' and except in directions in which we can go too far there is no interest in going at all; and only those who will risk going 'too far' can possibly find out just how far one can go."[2]

Certainly, the artistic path will demand change. If you don't like change, don't go down it. For the people coming into King Crimson, a group with its eye on something other than chart positions, there was a maxim: that we were required to change the way we did things. Whatever we had been doing before we entered the group, we were required to do it differently inside the group, and when we left, we would hopefully have a wholly different view of music, its functions, and the way we functioned within it. In the milieu in which I worked, we used music, and specifically the groups we were in, as vehicles for change. To introduce us to change, the artist must himself change. As

Miles Davis told *The Washington Post* in 1969: "I have to change. It's like a curse."[3] It comes with the patch.

❑

By these definitions, the late-70s group called UK comprised two artists and two craftsmen. Allan Holdsworth, who had worked with me in my first group Bruford, and I fell intuitively into the camp that hopes somebody is going to like it, but it's going to be done anyway. My colleague from King Crimson, singer and bassist John Wetton, and the keyboardist and violinist Eddie Jobson, fresh from the University of Frank Zappa, made up the other half of the group. They, equally instinctively, fell into the definition of craftsmen, on a mission to provide a known product for, they would like to hope, an extremely grateful customer.

The difference between Eddie and Allan was, I thought, succinctly drawn when, one day, Eddie asked Allan, one of the best improvisers in the world, for whom improvising was meat and drink, to perform the same solos nightly that he had performed on the preceding album, presumably in the interest of product consistency. Allan's mind utterly failed to compute the origin of this request, so bizarre did it seem. I understood the motivations of both men perfectly well, and I also knew that any group with a fault line greater than San Andreas was bound to crack eventually. With luck, the precarious balance would produce something worthwhile while it pertained, but sooner or later the group was going to disappear through a hole in the Earth's crust.

From the end of a short stint with Dave Stewart's National Health in November 1976 to the beginning of UK's first tour in March 1978, I had played no public performances. Carolyn and I were busily engaged on two different fronts: she giving birth to our first-born, Alex; I giving birth to my first album, *Feels Good To Me*, rapidly followed by UK's eponymous first album.

I seemed to live in Trident Studios for much of the period, cruising up to London's Soho in my gently overheating BMW, gathering strength for the pleading and bribery that would just about get me a space in the nearest NCP car park. We badly needed a second phone line in the small kitchen at home, but I was possessed, a man on a mission who knew no fear and would brook no fearfulness in others. Even when I produced an incorrectly transposed flugelhorn part for the wonderful Kenny Wheeler, the ground stubbornly refused to open up and swallow me. Even when I asked Allan for a couple of small rhythmic support figures, and he left the studio in a huff, I remained unfazed, and had John Goodsall from Brand X in there in a jiffy providing just the thing we needed.

The drumming was easy, mostly because I hardly gave it a thought. There was too much else going on. My album wrapped in September, and by November I was back in with Eddie, John, and an increasingly doubtful Allan for more of the same, only bigger, shinier, faster. For the rest of us, it was one of those periods when self-confidence was high. We knew we were more than capable of fulfilling the growing expectations around us. The writing was solid; the vocals had John's velvet, smoky-throat texture in spades. Eddie was doing well with the latest (and as yet little-heard) CS-80 polyphonic synthesizer by Yamaha. Allan delivered a knock-out blow on the first cut, 'In The Dead Of Night': 94 seconds of liquid passion married to a blinding technical facility that was to go down in the annals of rock guitar history. All the hallmarks of his brilliant playing were there in this solo: poise, pace, melody, the Slonimsky interval-jumps, the whammy-bar, and all over a killer groove. You could hear the reaction across the water in the USA from Eddie Van Halen, John McLaughlin, Al Di Meola, and all the other great guitar players of the day. Allan was obviously a jazz player, and this 'jazz' solo was about to get huge exposure on radio as Polydor Records went to town on promotion.

UK launched out on tour in the spring and summer of 1978 to excellent reviews and a rare case of substantial record-company support. Double-page ads in *Billboard* magazine started to appear in the USA, and at every stop we were met by the local radio and promotion men. This was the top-dollar treatment. It grabbed you by the pants and rocketed you uphill at a nerve-wracking speed. All you could do was go for the ride and enjoy it while it lasted. No need to make any calls: it was a seller's market, and everyone and his aunt was down in the lobby wanting a word with the 'supergroup' from England. Radio picked us up, and while the band wasn't quite hit material, we sold a respectable few hundred-thousand units of that record.

So it wasn't lack of success that caused the cracks to appear: rather it was too much success. First you must survive failure, then you must survive success. John, finally released from the complaining and difficult Robert Fripp, felt that the big goal was within range. Only now, the drag on proceedings was the drummer and another complaining guitarist. John had become deafeningly loud on stage, an approach that he explained to me was necessary because he could no longer trust the sound-mixer. Paranoid, moi? As with Crimson violinist David Cross five years earlier, John's volume pushed Allan into the hedgerow.

As so often the case, things came to a head in progressive rock's home city, Philadelphia. Philly's rock fans had espoused the progressive cause early in the day and been the music's most vociferous champions on radio and in print. Many of our tours began there, or ended there, or had special events there. The loudest sound I have ever heard was the deafening roar of 20,000 throats voicing approval for Anderson Bruford Wakeman Howe as we returned to the Spectrum ice-hockey arena in 1989 in what was taken by many to be the 'original' Yes. I was to play my last date with King Crimson at the Mann Center in 1996. Earthworks played jazz places big and small in Philadelphia for years, and we all loved the Theater Of The Living Arts down on South Street. Earlier in that summer of 1978, UK had played the Tower Theater supporting guitar-star Al Di Meola, who was much taken, in a sulky sort of way, with Allan's obvious prowess. Philadelphia had a way of pulling out the best and worst in us, and on August 8 1978 it did both.

The occasion was the last date of UK's tour, a free concert down by the water at Penn's Landing. The radio stations had gone to town on this, and despite the fact that there were no other name artists on the bill, some 50,000 people turned up. We put on an overblown, overplayed, over-everything'd kind of show. A three-alarm fire broke out in a nearby apartment block, so the fractious and hysterical atmosphere was accompanied by the sound of fire appliances arriving from all over the city.

Last dates of tours need to be negotiated with care. In the alcohol-fuelled excitement of the Last Big Gig, people are given to saying or doing things that they might come to regret on the plane home the next day. After the show, the limos pulled out over the fire-hoses and threaded their way carefully through the milling crowd to the occasional thump of approval on the roof.

John Wetton and I were sharing a car and driving back to Manhattan. He said he didn't want to work with Allan Holdsworth any more, and did I want to go with Allan or remain with them? Patently, John and Eddie Jobson were about to take the group to a mainstream in which neither I nor Allan would care to swim. I said I'd go with Allan. We struggled through a few more dates in the autumn, but for me, UK was over. John eventually went on to the platinum-selling Asia, and Allan and I went back to London to begin work on my second album, *One Of A Kind*.

UK was a short fiery furnace that scorched the participants and seared them into deciding what kind of musicians they were and, by extension, what kind of men they wanted to be. At the end of it, at least, some of us had a clearer understanding of who we were and what we wanted.

❏

Without The Beatles, or someone else who had done what The Beatles did, it is fair to assume that there would have been no progressive rock. The music emerged out of the psychedelic and pastoral folk styles of the late 60s and had a golden age from the early to mid 70s. Psychedelic bands such as Pink Floyd, The Moody Blues, Procol Harum, and The Nice, themselves all in transition, laid the foundations between 1966 and 1970. The release of King Crimson's album *In The Court Of The Crimson King* in 1969 signalled the emergence of the mature progressive rock style that reached its commercial and artistic zenith between 1970 and 1975 in the music of such bands as Jethro Tull, Yes, Genesis, ELP, Gentle Giant, Van der Graaf Generator, and Curved Air.

Demographically, progressive rock was a music from south-east England, overwhelmingly made by nice middle-class English boys like me. The musicians' backgrounds were strictly white-collar, and their parents were often downright distinguished. Never working-class, it was rather the vital expression of a bohemian, middle-class intelligentsia.

Art schools, colleges, and universities contributed mightily, but if you want to understand why the style grew and flourished in England rather than the USA, look no further than that powerful cultural agent, the Anglican Church. Many of the primary participants were initially moved by church attendance as youths: John Wetton of King Crimson; Peter Gabriel of Genesis; Chris Squire of Yes; Peter Hammill of Van der Graaf; all had formative experiences in the music of the church. Many of the bands had Hammond organists who were often church or college trained. Soft Machine's Mike Ratledge, Rick Wakeman, and one of the few foreign musicians, the Swiss keyboard player Patrick Moraz, all trained at or played in church.

Like many other musical advances, prog was accompanied by, or mediated through, or initiated by one or several parallel technological developments. The long-player vinyl record was ripe and ready to host the long song form of the progressives. Multi-track stereo recording encouraged increased production values. Both these were introduced into an era of rapidly rising living standards in the developed West, with more and more hi-fi systems being sold to an ever expanding middle-class to while away its new-found leisure hours. The technological wind was set fair for we progressives.

Added to this was a confidence in things English and an increasing advocacy of the romantic and pastoral, representing the softer or more feminine side of progressive rock. Following American group The Band's well publicised back-to-the-roots experiment, in which they communally reintroduced themselves to the American folk heritage by actually leading a more rural existence, British bands adopted this practical extension of pastoralism and decamped in their droves in order to, in the parlance of the day, 'get it together in the country'.

Gentle Giant put down roots in a farm near Portsmouth; Genesis decamped to Dorking, safely away from London. The band I was in moved lock stock and barrel to a farm in South Molton, Devon, to write and rehearse our breakthrough record *The Yes Album*, and the farm remains to this day the property of my friend, guitarist Steve Howe, who is probably there as I write. Song titles became self-consciously British – such as 'Grantchester Meadows' by Pink Floyd – and tended to involve things like tea parties. Peter Gabriel and Genesis sang about lawnmowers in 'I Know What I Like (In Your Wardrobe)', and we exhorted our singers to sing in English, not American.

The contrast between technical and pastoral, present and past, male and female produced a tension in the music that was ideally suited to the long songs. Typically, a blistering intro of some sort would give way to a rather fey, dreamy vocal delivery over some twinkling backing. This would wind its often tortured way through a number of extensions, second subjects, and codicils before a return, probably in a different metre or with a different orchestration, of the overtly masculine bravura main theme.

On the one hand there was a highly competitive arms race whereby every band wanted a newer, bigger PA, better lights, louder amps, the latest mark of Hammond organ, and if the other lot had just recorded with a symphony orchestra, then we had better do that too. Newer instruments meant a better sound; additional classical musicians meant bigger voicings, a bigger sound.

On the other hand there lay the remains of a Romantic pastoralism of the die-hard hippies, where all was softness and light, where the feminine was equated with the 'natural', where if Traffic had gone to a farm in the country to write an album then so did you. This was well illustrated by The Incredible String Band, a two-men two-women group that had scored hugely at the Newport Folk Festival and whose third album, *The Hangman's Beautiful Daughter*, rode high on the British charts.

The Holy Grail of all this seemed to be the production of a unified art work in which music, visual motifs, and verbal expression are inextricably linked to produce a single coherent artistic vision. This was not a new idea. The term Gesamtkunstwerk, or 'unified art work', was used to indicate the same thing in connection with the 19th-century composer Richard Wagner. This idea, implicitly or explicitly, seemed to be what the progressives were after. It embodied the counter-cultural ideal of protesting the soulless bureaucracy that was squeezing any trace of spiritual life out of Western culture, while simultaneously suggesting an ideal society in which technology and nature, past and future, matriarchal and patriarchal social values could be harmoniously interwoven. If the Gesamtkunstwerk was a real or imaginary goal, how close did we progressive rockers come?

The band I had helped to form, Yes, had come from early Beatles covers to the fragility of the earth on *Fragile* (1971) to *Close To The Edge* (1972), loosely based on Herman Hesse's *Siddhartha*, and to 1974's huge *Tales From Topographic Oceans*, structured around the teachings of Paramhansa Yogananda in his *Autobiography Of A Yogi*. The band seemed about ready to explode with the 'Gates Of Delirium', said to be loosely based on Tolstoy's *War And Peace*.

Now, I like a good meaty theme as much as the next man, but this was getting ridiculous. I'd got off the bus by this point, constitutionally unable to cope with any more of this, and perhaps in sympathy with the growing undercurrent that inevitably was gathering strength in opposition to the prevailing cosmic climate. After an opening bout with the Mighty Crim, it was therefore ironic to find myself back in the cosmic swirl with Genesis, playing 'Supper's Ready'. This was a psychedelic recounting of the New Testament's *Book Of Revelation* that presents the New Jerusalem as the model of the perfect, fulfilled society, only won, of course, after an epic struggle between Good and Evil.

If the progressives approached the Wagnerian concept of the Gesamtkunstwerk at all, it was only intuitively and obliquely. Certainly no one sat around at rehearsals and suggested we alter things so that they would better fit the shape of the Gesamtkunstwerk. Like most musicians, the plan was to get started and keep going, to survive failure, and then – much harder – to survive success. With critical hindsight, it may be apparent that there was a remarkable drift in the musical, visual, and verbal (but, notably, no dance) aspects to a unified theme or art work, but generally the chief protagonists didn't know where we were going with this – we were only able to look back on where we had been.

I think we were pleasantly surprised although hard-pressed to explain why this particularly British music found such a welcoming audience in the USA. From roughly 1966 to 1971, the musicians and audience were essentially similar in age and class-origins: the solidly middle-class socio-economic background ensured both parties were singing from the same high-cultural song sheet. By 1972, most of the major players that had broken in the States were touring in stadiums to the accompaniment of astonishing record sales, and the music had grown from a sub-cultural to a mainstream style.

The music flourished particularly in the Northeast and Midwest, both regions with a strong WASP population. The young white audience found a resonance in the nationalism of the music and a kind of surrogate ethnic identity at a time when the question of what it meant to be a white person in America was coming under scrutiny. In the Southeast, however, with its strong indigenous culture of roots and country music, progressive rock fared much less well.

The AOR radio format (album-oriented rock, or adult-oriented rock) that many FM stations adopted in the early to mid 70s replaced the freeform 'underground' FM stations with a solid diet of progressive, metal, hard rock, and singer-songwriters, ensuring that the stadiums were filled when the bands came to town. The groups usually ploughed back the enormous gross receipts from these concerts into their ever-more-elaborate stage shows, each act vying to outdo the other. The rooms got bigger, the music got slower, the better to translate in a hockey arena (Pink Floyd's fastest tempo was about the speed of a medium-slow jazz ballad), and the visuals became ever more expensive and stunning. And the audiences kept coming, at least for a while.

Critically, progressive rock was more or less loathed as much then as it is today, but that, of course, says as much about the critics as it does about the genre itself. Lester Bangs, classically portrayed by director Cameron Crowe in the movie *Almost Famous*, said of ELP: "These guys amount to war criminals."[4] To many critics, especially at the leading American magazines *Rolling Stone* and *Creem*, progressive rock's aesthetic stance was anathema, nothing short of heresy. They resented the insinuation that the progressives' appropriation of the classical tradition expanded the frontiers of popular music or enabled kids to listen to music with more 'quality'. This attitude seemed like a betrayal and smelled of elitism.

Even the style's heavy reliance on instrumental music was looked on with great suspicion. Robert Christgau spoke condescendingly of my band-mate Robert Fripp's "rare if impractical gift for instrumental composition in a rock context".[5] In general, the neo-Marxist critics – Bangs, Marsh, Christgau, and the rest – were deeply suspicious in three main areas: the lack of a political stance within the music; its over-reliance on high culture; and its commercial success. In the critical court of law, the progressive rockers were guilty on all three counts.[6]

Chipping away at the foundations, the critics would eventually cause enough damage to bring the ever-inflating edifice crashing to the ground. Their view was not seriously challenged until Allan F. Moore's book *Rock: The Primary Text* of 1992, and it would seem we are only just now arriving at a place where we can view the cultural history of the 70s from a clearer, more objective standpoint.[7]

As with psychedelia and the Summer Of Love, I remained

disinterested through most of this. More by accident than design, progressive rock was the musical milieu in which I had to work, impress, survive. The usual immediate short-term considerations pressed hard as they were always to press: how do I stay relevant and stay in business, and who should I be doing these things with? Lofty considerations as to the music's value in the longer term were for the armchair pundit and for another day.

❏

Given the prevailing critical hostility, then, I was surprised to hear myself saying yes down the phone to my old accomplice Jon Anderson when he proposed a further foray into this by now most wildly unfashionable genre of music. By 1988, progressive rock was probably the least fashionable music imaginable, so it's as well my career decisions have seldom been guided by fashion.

Jon was proposing that I help out on what I took to be a solo record of his. It had been a while since we had even spoken, let alone played together. Turned out the recording was to be on the Caribbean island of Montserrat – a deal clincher. I agreed, and presented myself at Heathrow at the appointed date and time. To my surprise, with Jon at the airport were Rick Wakeman, Steve Howe, and Brian Lane. I thought I noticed the thin end of a wedge.

In the studio, Jon was on strong form. On sabbatical from the mother-group Yes and freed from the old democratic music-making methods, he conducted proceedings without fear of let or hindrance. The music was already partially recorded, so we were required to do no more than sprinkle our fairy dust over half-completed tracks and personalise them a little. Tony Levin, my old partner from King Crimson, was on bass. The Caribbean atmosphere was idyllic and working conditions sufficiently agreeable to allow me to postpone asking difficult questions, like: is this a group? that goes on tour?

It was indeed shaping up to be a group, and if I didn't want to go on tour, I had to get off the bus sharp-ish. Somewhere around

'Birthright' and 'Brother Of Mine', two key tracks from the record, it seemed that a window opened briefly into a genuinely interesting new musical area for these seasoned pros. If we had the strength and determination, it might be possible to give fresh legs and a committed future built on sound musical choices to the old beast that was Yes. What the heck: you can never know with these things. I decided to give it a go. For the next few months, we had the wind in our sails, and there was a fertile and confident feeling about the thing. If we could only hold onto it, there was a future for us away from the mother-ship Yes. We had only to cut the umbilical cord.

Legal manoeuvrings that centred on ownership of the name Yes occupied the suits around us for weeks. Remember, there was a whole group of people in California with names like Squire, White, Rabin, and Kaye who had plenty of claim to the band name. Eventually we 'Europeans' settled on the nifty little moniker Anderson Bruford Wakeman Howe, or ABWH; I put my young Earthworks on hold, and we lurched out on tour in July 1989 in Memphis, Tennessee, playing An Evening Of Yes Music Plus.

Irrespective of names, there were many who thought this was the real Yes, and most of them lived, of course, in Philadelphia, that traditional stronghold of all things to do with the group. Our return to the Spectrum arena on August 3 1989 produced the loudest sound I've ever heard: deafening, sustained applause, which was far louder than the group. Back then, you could still offer a mixed set of 50-50 new material and old familiar music and still leave the stadium alive. Unlike now, when to play anything at these big expensive shows other than a strict rotation of everything the customer knows may risk injury. When we had finished 'And You And I' the continuing blast from the huge audience sounded like a jet engine warming up. I was genuinely moved by this gargantuan display of affection, the more so because I'd long since forgotten how persuasive 20,000 throats could be.

Back off the road after a successful tour, and with a useful three-quarters-of-a-million record sales behind us, we decamped to France to have a second go round – meaning to undertake a second album and its ensuing touring and promotion. This one was not going to be so easy. Jon had been fermenting the block of music we had recorded in Montserrat for many months, years even, and this time we'd be working up fresh ideas together.

My happiest day at Studio Miraval in Provence was my first. Before I'd unpacked my suitcase, a sassy little trio of Tony on Stick, myself on regular drumset, and Steve pumping out big silvery chords from a Steinberger 12-string, laid down some possible sketches to kick things off. Jon, Rick, and Brian, bearers of bad news, turned up the following day, and it all quickly began to go pear-shaped.

Executives at Arista Records had decided that we weren't to be allowed to go round again on our own. Oh no. We were going to do a record that would include a contribution from all the other guys in California and it would be by a group called Yes. All those names in the USA would somehow be cemented on to this Frankenstein and, additionally, have a few tracks of their own. This concoction, it was hoped, would be sufficient to justify use of the name, and the dollars would follow as night follows day. Such tortuous thinking could only come from the treachery of manager Brian Lane, whose personal remuneration, naturally, would be intimately connected to the size of the record-company advance. We'd been sold out.

There is an old adage that he who pays the piper calls the tune, and when the piper is costing hundreds of thousands of dollars, you'd better watch out. Arista executive Roy Lott, who had dreamed up this nightmarish scenario with Lane, was the man holding the purse-strings, and he soon started calling the shots. The whole smorgasbord was to be presided over by producer Jonathan Elias, who would make regular reports on whether this bunch of miscreants was making the kind of record not that the musicians wanted, but that Arista thought it could sell. Rough demos of progress were Fedex'd to headquarters in New York City, and soon messages were coming back from the suits along the lines of "more tambourine on the bridge" or "I'm not hearing a hit". Allowing the record company to create the music is about as wise as having the musicians look after the money, and at around this point, any experienced musician knows that all is lost. Would the last person out turn off the light.

The project was eventually finished with an army of computer programmers and session musicians – there weren't enough musicians already? – because the money said it had to be finished. The whole monstrosity was called *Union*, and not only was it the most dismal waste of cash I've ever had the doubtful pleasure of being involved with, it was also a textbook case of how not to make an album. Rick Wakeman, in immortal style, re-christened the thing *Onion* because it made him cry.

For me it was a pivotal album, because it was the first time I realised that my performance need only be near the mark, because it would be 'corrected' in the computer. Until then, and leaving editing aside, we musicians were accustomed to thinking that the performance accepted by the producer was the one the listener would hear on the final record. On *Onion*, the rules had changed. At the end of a take, the musicians typically want to hear some favourable comment from behind the glass where the scientists sit, along the lines of: "Great! That's it! Come in and listen!" On this occasion, nothing was forthcoming. I remember saying: "Well, is that it, or do you want another?" Elias's voice came back: "That'll do."

"That'll do?" I queried, exasperated. "That'll do *for what*?" Even as I asked the question, I knew the answer. I had entered a brave new world of something called post-production, which means the whole thing will probably be fixed, altered, perfumed, and neutered, and certainly without the knowledge, permission, or acceptance of the musician. The drummer now supplies some drumming for later digital 'enhancement', offered as raw material for later shaping and 'improvement'.

The subsequent performances on the Union tour of 1991 were possible only because no new music had to be originated. I doubt all eight of us would have been able to get in a rehearsal room together – the lawyers alone would have filled most of the available space. The doubling of all instruments, except bass and lead vocals, left a lot of people marking a lot of time, until all hands finally joined together at the top of the birthday-cake stage, the entire cast of *Dallas* or *Dynasty* reunited. It was a synthetic and sentimental kind of party, performed largely for Roy Lott's benefit, and the tour is divided, in my mind, into those dates before and after The Massacre At Madison Square Garden. That was a fiasco of career-denting proportions and it came as a powerful wake-up call. In another world I would have considered my position, as politicians primly put it. I had been sleep-walking into the ever-more-preposterous and bloated world of stadium rock. It was time to get back to playing some drums rather than pretending to do so.

The collapse of the most expensive drum kit ever staged was symptomatic of the compromised nature of the enterprise that I was supposed to be serving, and I spent a rueful few nights licking my wounds and wondering how much longer until I could dismount from the revolving birthday-cake stage. I trust Arista was happy, because I doubt they got their money back. The window that had so briefly opened a year or so earlier with ABWH had cruelly slammed shut under the sheer weight of back-catalogue baggage, costs-versus-ticket-sale projections, and unrealistic expectations from audience and suits. It clipped our wings and confined those who wished to continue to the same old birdcage.

❏

Robert Fripp had stopped King Crimson, rather smartly I thought, in 1974, and we were able to leave the scene relatively unsoiled by the excesses that were fast entrapping the unwary. Fripp said at the time: "The band ceased to exist in September 1974, which was when all English bands in that genre should have ceased to exist. But since the rock'n'roll dinosaur likes anything which has gone before, most of them are still churning away, repeating what they did years ago without going off in any new direction."[8]

The history of progressive rock since about 1976 can be divided into two distinct periods. From 1976 to 1982, a watered-down, simpler version limped on as American stadium rock and British symphonic pop, but no new ground was being broken and the older bands started to lose commercial viability. Record companies were not above arm-twisting as the older bands, beached like mortally-wounded whales, leviathans twice harpooned by the twin lances of punk and disco, flapped around trying to maintain something now called 'market share'. If you want a really frightening record, I strongly recommend ELP's *Love Beach*, an excruciating example of a prog rock band trying to turn in a mainstream pop album while hoping no one would notice.

The Yes, Genesis, King Crimson, and Pink Floyd groups of 1972 became the lighter, more consistent stadium rockers such as the Journey, Styx, or Kansas of 1978. Since the 80s, we have seen the rise of both a neo-progressive movement, with young bands, many of them European, attempting to bring a more contemporary sensibility to the 'classic' idiom, and a post-progressive style following the implications of King Crimson's *Discipline* album of 1981, with its introduction of elements drawn from minimalism and ethnic musics, elements new to rock.

By the time John Wetton's Asia had sold millions of copies of its bland radio-friendly pop in the 80s, the post-hippie extension of the counter-culture that was progressive rock, based on the idealistic impulses of the 60s, had finally run its course. The dream, or illusion, of individual and global enlightenment was over. Progressive rock, like the period that gave rise to it, was essentially optimistic. Indeed, the whole underlying goal – to draw together rock, classical, and folk music into a surreal metastyle – was inherently an optimistic ideal.

At its best, the genre engaged the listeners in a quest for spiritual authenticity. We took ourselves too seriously, of course, and its po-faced earnestness could lapse into a moronic naiveté, but it never gave way to bitterness, cynicism, or self-pity. Perhaps that lasting innocence, a refreshing antidote to modern times, is where the attraction lies for the remarkably large group of listeners it has managed, over many turbulent years, to retain.

7 DO YOU LIKE DOING INTERVIEWS?

I am lying on the floor of Room 135 of the Ramada Inn, East Orange, New Jersey, ice cubes in a rolled towel around my lower back. I've pulled it badly, rummaging about in the garden two days before I left. (Further evidence of poor credentials as a rocker: I don't even have the decency to self-harm with chemicals, just gardening implements.) The Virgin flight over to the USA had been excruciating. My head is on a pillow, face turned sideways, phone balanced delicately, just so.

"Yep, it's a fantastic show ... the Japanese tour was a huge success ... new album doing really well. How long have we been together? Since about yesterday afternoon, but we weren't very together then ... ha ha ha ... can't wait to see you guys in Peoria, it'll be great to be back in town ... remember the last time? Of course I remember the last time! ... how could I forget Peoria? ... well, we've got Jeff Berlin on bass and myself on drums ... the Unknown John Clark on guitar ... why's he called the Unknown? ... because none of you seem to have heard of him ... ha ha ha. Yep, can't wait ... you too ... bye."

I hang up on my 9:30, *The Peoria Journal Star*. The 10:00, 10:30, and 11:00 will all be along shortly. They will all ask similar questions, and I will give similar answers, with just enough of a pause between question and answer as to indicate some sort of consideration of this interesting matter before me – wholly bogus, of course. The preview for the upcoming show will remain at the most basic of levels: who is in the band, are they now or have they ever been famous, have they ever played with anyone famous? Well, all right then, have they ever had lunch with anyone famous? Well, he's not exactly famous. OK then, and how was that? And finally, for the local angle, what do you think of Peoria, or what do you remember about it if you've been before?

This pathetic and earnest desire for the good but sentimental citizens of Peoria to have their city remembered, and perhaps even praised, by itinerant foreign musicians and B-list dignitaries of doubtful quality, speaks volumes about heartland-America's desire to be wanted, and liked, and remembered. It is matched only by my equally pathetic and earnest desire to want the same thing for my music, as I am all too well aware.

I doze off for a second. The phone rings, my head starts up too quickly, and a sharp spasm of pain shoots through my lower back. Damnation and hellfire. This is the 11:00. Four more to go after this, and I could maybe hope for a room-service burger at about 2:00pm. I field the questions with a howlingly synthetic enthusiasm and wafer-thin good humour, drenched in an irony that even this klutz must pick up on – but no, there is no one home at the other end of the line. He, like me, is on automatic pilot.

This ghastly ritual is called a phoner, dozens of which will have to be endured, starting about a week before the first date and finishing about a week before the last date of a tour, in a gargantuan effort to get the band's name mentioned in American newsprint as many times as possible during the trip. In pre-cell-phone times, all this had to be done from a hotel phone, so you had to get up early, or start immediately you checked in at the other end, while all those hours in between in the van went wasted. You've seen this – it's the same thing in the movies when they hand the phone to the politician to 'work'. God only knows what running for president's like, I ask no one in particular, as I lever myself up off the floor to go in search of more ice.

The big mistake is having the temerity to run your own band. Before you know it, music goes out of the window faster than you can say Ticketron, and you're just into intravenous sales and marketing. You need a hundred or so interviews in assorted national and foreign journals just to bring your artwork, your musical endeavour, your baby, to the attention of the public, and this is before anyone has even mentioned radio. (TV is unlikely to be a problem with music like this.) Just to let the public know of its existence, let alone any possibility of it being heard prior to a decision to actively seek it out and buy it, will require hour upon hour of patient, relentless self-promotion. If your music has the sniff about it that it could actually make the label some money, then they could be more or less helpful in getting the word out, but I have long since forsaken the idea of making any kind of music that will trigger meaningful promotional dollars. So the punishment is: you're on your own, buddy. And it's going to hurt, repeating the same thing to a hundred different writers of one sort or another.

The good news is that with the arrival of the net, you can target this stuff with increasing accuracy – press releases can be sent out with solicitations for interviews, databases can be compiled and continually updated on laptops in airports – but somehow it isn't quite what I signed up for. Whatever; if the workload doesn't kill you, it will certainly deaden your appetite for music creation.

I can only rationalise all this as the public's thinly-veiled message being filtered back to me through the ether. "Enough already," they seem to shriek. "We've got enough music and we can't take any more. The iPod's full. Only the fittest of you shall now survive."

I imagine a little sperm with my new CD under its arm, swimming up the birth-canal alongside thousands, no, millions of other little sperm with CDs under their arms, racing toward the warm womb of public acceptance, where only one will be favoured.

So this is the punishment for having the sheer chutzpah to bring fresh music to market for consideration and, hopefully, eventual purchase. Ordeal By Interview, with Threat Of Lockjaw. None of this has anything to do with music, of course, and everything to do with the need to be loved.

The Preview, the Interview, the Review: the Holy Trinity of press and public relations. Let's assume you are in Big Demand, then. It's possible that world-famous papers, say *The New York Times*, will honour you with all three. There could be a preview piece advising of the existence of the upcoming item for sale, be it CD, concert appearance, or both. A month or so later, the in-depth interview with the star while he's in town, perhaps with additional backstage or 'lifestyle' commentary. And finally the review of CD, concert appearance, or both. Throw in a celebrity affair or political shenanigans, and you'd move from the arts page to the front page quicker than greased lightning, and the object of all this public attention could be kept in the public eye almost indefinitely.

That is the model. Further down the food chain, where I live, there are far fewer dollars to grease the wheels, but the model is nevertheless applicable. What applies in New York City is theoretically possible in thousands of inches of newsprint around small-town America. Launching into my 12:30 phoner, I wonder how many column inches, feet, yards, I'd managed to occupy with this depressing, vacuous litany.

For about the first seven or eight years of my professional career, no one thought to request an interview from the drummer. As far as the press was concerned, it was always the singer's band. Through the platinum sales of my early years, my views had remained unsought. The embryonic music industry, still in its early-70s innocence, had only a few weekly rags that covered events, and they were mostly provided for by a handful of commentators writing reviews from the bar. Occasionally I had fielded the odd technical question in the British music rag of the day, *Melody Maker*, but not much more than that. But as the snowball began to roll, and the audience began to flock to the record store and ticket outlet, its apparently insatiable desire for more information had to be alternately slaked and fuelled by an increasing number of weekly and monthly magazines, all of which needed filling with the latest titbits. The further your material moved away from the mainstream, the greater the test on your stamina as you vied for space with the big fish.

Most of this stuff was provided by well-meaning hacks, who in their ideal world would have been musicians too, and most of it was highly subjective without the slightest attempt at journalistic dispassion. But at the top of the heap – particularly the jazz heap – were some genuinely interesting and knowledgeable writers who cared deeply for the music. Neil Tesser from the *Chicago Reader*, Bob Blumenthal at *The Boston Globe*, Don Heckman at the *Los Angeles Times*, John Fordham in the UK, Hervé Picart in France have given much in support of music and musicians, even if at times they have to be cruel to be kind.

Referring to King Crimson's melange of minimalism, village music, and electronica bundled together as the 1980 album *Discipline*, Robert Palmer at *The New York Times* offered such an interesting context in which to understand the music, that band-members reading it looked at each other as if to say: "So *that's* what we're doing!" It may come as a surprise to outsiders that the musicians frequently don't quite know what it is they're doing and that, at the highest level, it may be a critic who puts their efforts into some sort of perspective, as much for the edification of musician as listener.

One of the best interviews I ever did was for Pam Lambert at *The Wall Street Journal*. I turned up at a midtown Manhattan coffee shop at the appointed time, prepared to ignore the questions and deliver the same sales patter as usual – about 30 minutes for the round trip. But at the 30-minute mark, we'd barely got past the small talk, and I didn't bother to disguise my next glance at my watch. I asked the woman how long she thought this was going to take? Two to three hours. I said something along the lines of you must be kidding. No, she wasn't. She had a week to write this, and a researcher and staff of three to assist. She would be pulling all the music I referred to, mine and others, from the Library Of Congress, and it would be a thorough, in-depth piece on the life of this modern working drummer.

I took some persuading but came up with the goods, and some weeks later I saw the result. It was indeed the most accurate, astute, and well-researched piece on my work that I've ever read. Quite short, its precision and concision were breathtaking. Everything that needed to be included was in there, and everything that did not was excluded. I've been a fan of *The Wall Street Journal* ever since.

Considerably lower down the food chain are the British tabloids, those purveyors of 'stories' for mass consumption. Ladies with beards mutter into their chins as Elvis is again found on Mars, Jim Morrison is again seen in Paris, and the great British Public is again urged to "bomb the towel-heads".

The Sun of January 16 1989 managed a breathless interpretation of the riches that would greet the members of Anderson Wakeman Bruford Howe as we reformed under that name in that year. We were to play to "11 million people in 13 countries over 16 months, and rake in an estimated …" by whom? " … £50 million," this last stunner in bold type. I read that a major airline was "lending" us a "luxury 747 plane, complete with Jacuzzi". There is always a Jacuzzi in these things, with its promise of late-night romps with footballers' wives. Until recently, there always used to be shag-carpet somewhere, as well. Very 70s. We were spending "£30,000 to have the jumbo customised by top psychedelic artist Roger Dean", and the operation was so huge that we were apparently "negotiating with hotel chains worldwide to take over entire hotels to house their 160 personel [sic] including three chefs".

Not a word of this nonsense was true, of course, and I loved all of it, but it is apt to cause confusion when the Wimbledon dentist tries again to grasp the slippery notion of being a musician. "Yes, but what do you *really* do?"

❑

We can trace the more serious role of the critic in all this back to the beginning of the 19th century, when music became autonomous, made for its own sake, irrespective of audience response. The critic became necessary as the expert, to explain it to the public and teach the punter how to listen. Until the beginning of the 20th century, he was on the artist's side, championing the new and the difficult. But as music developed a mass audience, his role as mediator became equally significant the other way around: he had to explain the mass audience to the producers. In fact, criticism split into those on the side of the producers and those on the side of the audience. Generally, now, he's a traffic cop for consumer guidance, sometimes directing the audience to the producers, sometimes directing the producers to the audience, but more likely orchestrating a collusion between selected musicians and an equally select part of the public into a taste group.

These critics often start as fans and tend to be on a mission to preserve a perceived quality of sound, or style of playing, in short to define the ideal musical experience for listeners to measure themselves against. Critical musical judgements are almost always entangled with social explanations as to why the music is good or bad. In much of our day-to-day haggling about music, we confuse aesthetic judgements about beauty and ugliness with ethical judgements about right and wrong. In conversational criticism we certainly deploy assumptions about art, folk, and pop, which refer to the ways in which musicians and producers and consumers and critics speak and write, but we tend to muddle them up. Music is a powerful force for taking you outside of yourself, but also for taking you deep inside yourself. We know it does this, and the sociologist, commentator, or critic attempts to explain how, sometimes with considerable difficulty.

By way of further confusion, popular musics may, and do, change their perceived meaning and may cross apparently firm cultural boundaries. When jazz first appeared in Britain, no one knew what to do with it. There was a complete absence of any critical standard. What were we listening to here? Folk culture? Art? Craft? Minstrel song?

In the 20s, the critics were classical-music critics – no jazz criticism existed at this point – and to them it was critically obvious that white jazz was better than black jazz because of its refinement. That, however, was quickly followed by the opposite judgement, that black jazz was better than white jazz because of its lack of refinement. Roger Pryor Dodge in *The Dancing Times* in 1929 insisted that jazz be understood as "a musical form produced by the primitive innate musical instinct of the negro", and the task of the jazz critic was, in the words of B.H. Haggin in 1930, to "oppose arty refinement".[1]

So the discourse developed and changed. Latter-day high priests such as Wynton Marsalis have changed it further and brought it to the walls of the fortress, where it can be protected, conserved, and taught to the young under strict control, but also wrapped in cotton wool and prevented from further change, or what he would presumably call tampering with or dumbing down. The sociological point to underline is that the conservatory composer, the session player, the band musician on a cruise ship, or the rapper in the Bronx are all musicians trying to handle the issues of the commodification of their music – is it any good or not? They all face similar issues in trying to decide the position of the artist in the marketplace, the relationship of class and community, the tensions between tradition and technology, the distinction between public and private – all these being more or less pressing concerns.

If you've survived either the praise or the blame of the critic in print – and the practising instrumentalist will need to survive both – there is always the shadow world of television. I'm in Hampton, Virginia, sometime in the 90s, filming with Jim Baugh on his Fox TV *Outdoors* show. Jim is a keen fan of jazz and progressive rock music from way back and produces a 30-minute angling show with about 10 minutes of content and 20 minutes of ads. Patiently ignoring the fact that what I know about fishing and the great outdoors can be written on the back of a postage stamp, he makes the shoot as painless as possible. The idea is that we'll go out into Chesapeake Bay and, while we're waiting for the fish to bite, he'll grill me on my work, aspirations, and future plans. Jim evidently doesn't consider King Crimson, five-pound flounders, my group Earthworks, and the Chesapeake Bay rockfish remotely incongruous, and therefore doesn't see why his audience should. It's an admirable attitude, as unusual as it is refreshing. This brush with local cable television is a pleasure.

I wish the same could be said, however, for more recent entanglements with mass media. Most of the creative musician's career will be, as it were, on the bottom, along with the flounders, below the sonar, and he tends to reach the larger public only indirectly, surfacing sufficiently to influence other musicians first. King Crimson's meagre record sales were always eclipsed by the group's influence upon other musicians, and that's where its strengths lay. Generally we were happy with that, but once in a while mass media, dangling the possibility of silver and gold, sidled over the horizon and whispered seductively in your ear.

WABC's mid-morning chat show hosts Regis Philbin and Kelly Ripa (or late-night Conan O'Brien, Jay Leno, or David Letterman) may be prepared to put you under the closing credits, provided a) the cookery segment doesn't run too long, b) you play the hit from a quarter of a century ago, and c) you cut out the tricky bit in the middle. Perfect demographic, reaches 15 million homes, waddya say?

Even as you put up a half-hearted struggle, you know this will only end in, at best, tears and, at worst, outright humiliation. Whatever life there was left in your modest hit from 25 years ago is systematically bled out of it by appalling sound and worse lighting. Tragic versions of 'Roundabout' by Yes and 'Dinosaur' by King Crimson have thus been beamed to the masses, and had all further record sales stopped overnight I would have quite understood why.

I can confirm that television is at best a half-truth. In the old days, TV people would deny this; now they don't even bother. Those big cool studios with flashing lights are half the size they appear and are made of cardboard. The snappy clever-dick repartee between game-show participants is only that snappy because of the editing. It's all in the editing. TV is cheap and getting cheaper; nasty, and getting nastier; it preys on your fears and aims relentlessly at the lowest common denominator.

❏

Some young production assistant winds you through endless corridors to your dressing room. The chat-show host has the smile of a barracuda. You know this is going to go badly wrong. You're looking for the place where the accident is going to happen, but it's hidden somewhere in all those muffins, flowers, and coffee in hospitality.

The first run-through of the tune produces only smiles. "Perfect, phew, man, you were *killin'* – but one small thing. It's a little long. Waddyasay we take out that funny bit where the singer stops singing?" Sixteen bars – the sixteen bars with the real teeth that throw the sappiness of the rest of it into sharp relief – are dutifully binned.

Another run-through. Another "Phew, man, you were *smokin'*. I love it, man. Hey, if it were up to me …" always a key get-out, that " … we'd run the whole album. Thing is, we have sponsors, and we're still coming in at a bit too long – like another sixteen bars too long." This eviscerated heap of nonsense that used to be the piece of music, the very piece the TV people signed up to broadcast, is now about to lose an entire verse of lyrics, rendering the rest of it virtually meaningless.

By the time you play it at midnight, you know the band shouldn't be doing this, but somehow it's all unstoppable, even as you think back to Jimi Hendrix's immortal stopping of 'Hey Joe' on the *Happening For Lulu* show live on UK national television in April 1969. He would have been going through the same thing – the more things change, the more they stay the same. When you hear it back after the show, the sorry truth is you've just treated 15 million potential US customers to an enfeebled and emasculated piece of dross that dribbles from the speakers with such half-heartedness it can't even be bothered to curl up and die.

Further south, things can be more fun. It's not every day that you get a national TV interview in Mexico City, but today is one such. Nobody at Channel 22 warns me that it is 'customary' for visiting musical guests to sit in with the house band, who happen to be a blazing little piano trio with a very skilled 24-year-old on his high-pitched bebop Gretsch set.

Sensing a trap, I decline, of course. This may have been acceptable if the house band had obviously been 'beneath' me, but it is clearly in no such place, and this is an invitation that, as a matter of honour, cannot be declined. This I understand as, cameras rolling, I stride manfully to the drumset. The pianist gives me a smirk and rolls up his sleeves. I lash out aimlessly, and with considerably less cymbal control than the kit's owner, and rather enjoy it. The previous night's gig at Lunario was hugely gratifying, and I'm on confident form. I had done what I had come to Mexico City to do: I had played everything I knew to a standing ovation and a degree of respect from the band, and it was one of those all too rare 'carrot' days that make this reluctant donkey want to do it again. Heck, I can handle this little twerp on the piano. In the event, we agree it's Mexico 2, England 1.

"Well, I guess I've got everything I need... ." The voice from Peoria is trailing off. Of course you have, you moron: it's on the back of the album sleeve, it's in even simpler language in the press-kit that my label has expensively mailed out to you with the album, and I've now told you the same thing in words of one syllable down the phone. You've got a great photo that should get us at least twice the space of any competitors, so get to work and let me call room service.

❏

Some can't live with it, some can't live without it, but room service never lets me down. It is unfailingly late, cold, overpriced, and the wrong thing. On a broader level, musicians are always involved with food: its absence, its paucity, its acquisition, its temperature, its age, its cost, its next appearance. Like soldiers, we spend hours doing nothing, or doing nothing in airports. In the vast concourses of the gleaming new shopping malls from which planes occasionally fly, the only seats to be found are in the eateries. Food has to be vigorously avoided one minute and equally vigorously sought out the next.

You are either too late for breakfast – everywhere except Japan – or too early – Japan, where terminal jetlag condemns you to sit forlornly outside the breakfast room with your neatly ironed copy of *The Japan Times*, waiting for the doors to open. In older, unreconstructed European countries, lunch has finished and dinner not yet started when you want to eat, at the admittedly unreasonable hour of 4:00pm, prior to departure for the soundcheck at 5.

In New York City, food is always available. Checking into the Drake Hotel as a youngster on my first visit to the Big Apple, I was told I could have a hamburger at any time of the day *or night*. It might cost the astronomical sum of $10, what with the tips and all, but the concierge could 'send out' for anything I liked. This was convenience of a proportion never before seen by a quiet young man from Kent.

On the plane, the limp salads and plastic cutlery of the 60s were almost forgiven with the arrival of steel cutlery. With the 70s hijacking threats, the prototypical terrorist alerts, the stainless steel reverted to plastic so that you couldn't stab your neighbour. There are few better barometers of national paranoia than the ebb and flow of acceptable cutlery on the national airline. Things must be improving: recent Virgin Atlantic Premium Economy flights have reinstated steel cutlery. Promotion to business class brought the untold luxury of a napkin and a choice of entrée. Oh heaven, I salivate.

The contemplation, acquisition, and consumption of food is both a pleasure and an occupational hazard. On the road, its appearance and availability come to dominate and regulate your daily schedule. In civilised Europe, the promoter will likely entertain you to a proper meal with tablecloth before or after the concert. In Protestant northern Europe the food is less good but the restaurants open earlier. In Catholic southern Europe, the food can be exquisite, but it won't be available until well after the show, so the bass player is probably falling asleep with his head in an exemplary minestrone soup around 2 in the morning.

In heathen North America, the food indicates the status your promoter perceives you to have. At the bottom, and jazz, it will be curly sandwiches and cold coffee. Grungy rock is pizza. A medium-level rocker's arrival as headliner is indicated by the appearance of the ubiquitous deli-tray, uniform throughout the continent – the one with the ghastly thousand-island dip. At stadium-rock level, there will be a remarkable choice of hot food at backstage catering, complete with a vegetarian option, to be shared alongside sweaty riggers, gaffers, drum techs, and runners. Beyond that I have not been, but presumably you are by then in Mick Jagger's inner sanctum.

Both Yes and King Crimson have had, on the good tours, their own catering. After the show, you may dine out with silver-service attention under the stars in Pisa, Perugia, or Portland, or eat from a menu of freshly-bought food at any time you choose, with candles, tablecloth, and all the trimmings. Doesn't seem like much, but to the weary road-warrior, this can be heaven. It may also just cause fewer upset stomachs. I have avoided the Indian subcontinent after percussionist Pete Lockett's harrowing and indelicate stories.

A promoter of world music that I know, long experienced in bringing African musicians in to the West, has become so dismayed by their falling like nine-pins to the twin lances of air-conditioning and processed food that he encourages them to bring and cook their own food in the dressing room around the show. The backstage of De Doelen in Rotterdam looks like a Senegalese marketplace when 17 drummers and dancers from Dakar insulate themselves from the poisons of the West by lighting their own portable stoves and cooking up some rice and fish.

My cast-iron stomach has come to be one of my most treasured possessions, and I never leave home without it. Part of the interest in food lays in the quaint idea of trying to keep body and soul together and in good health, the better to complete the endurance test that is the modern tour. Musicians try hard to avoid getting sick – it's too expensive to miss the gig. Insurance is only applicable to the chronically overpaid.

We don't get sick, but I have been around an awful lot of buckets on stage. We can be dying up there before the audience will notice anything is wrong. Three-quarters of Earthworks had the shellfish dinner the night before an important and much advertised show in Pontevedra, Spain. I declined and had the meat. That night, all but the lucky drummer retched as if retching for England. A particularly malodorous concert eventually took place the following evening, with B12 shots in the dressing room at half-time and three offstage fire buckets receiving a steady stream of visitors, as the music lurched forward in brief moments of intestinal respite.

An abiding image of a Houston, Texas, gig with Anderson Bruford Wakeman Howe involves a stetsoned beauty smiling, waving, and gyrating away to the far side of a bent Tony Levin, vomiting profusely into a bucket by the drum riser. He'd unwittingly contracted hepatitis and was to leave the remainder of the tour completely. Not that the beauty was aware of any of this.

Organist Tony Kaye of Yes is pictured on the front of *The Yes Album* with leg in a full plaster cast, the result of the inevitable car smash that we'd been due for a while. For many gigs around that time, he hobbled on stage with crutches. Playing with flu is so common it fails to attract a mention. We had to beat an undignified retreat after no more than 15 minutes of the show in front of 12,000 Romans when Jon lost his voice at the PalaEUR with Anderson Bruford Wakeman Howe in November '89. But, generally, anything short of life-threatening, and the show, somehow, always goes on.

Personally, my heart sinks and my stomach cringes when I'm told it is to be a location recording. The studio owner and chef collude in trying to keep you in some farmhouse for months by plying you with endless 'free' food and drink. I nearly died of over-eating in a perpetual grande bouffe in Provence, France, making the *Union* album with Yes in the early summer of 1990. Tables groaning with vast quantities of fresh croissants and pains au chocolat and gallons of café au lait would be set out under the apple trees for a leisurely breakfast. As the sun grew warmer toward noon, musicians would reluctantly retreat to the studio to hack away at the coalface of this preposterous, directionless enterprise.

With the studio door left open to capture what little breeze there was, our efforts were soon accompanied, regrettably, by the merry clinking of cutlery and glassware – the sound of lunch being laid up. Since it was important to get a good place, all workers soon downed tools, all noodling stopped, as we trooped out to the early afternoon snack of patés, olives, charcuterie, salads of all description, and long sticks of bread, followed by cheeses and chocolate mousse with a change of wine.

A light sleep after all this would of course be necessary, by which time the sun was low and it was time to return to the studio for the serious work of assessing exactly how directionless the enterprise was. Until again interrupted, that is, by the call to the main meal of the day, three courses with more wine and stories late into the evening. After several weeks of this, one meal sliding imperceptibly into the next, and the amount of food consumed moving in inverse proportion to the interest of the participants of this *grand projet*, I begged for mercy and managed to escape to the UK for a frugal and parsimonious weekend at home. It was a miracle we didn't all die of obesity. I still have the additional pounds around my waste as a daily reminder of that most difficult of experiences.

Food is a constant reminder of your value and status in the marketplace. Dividing up the bill at a Chinese on the Ball's Pond Road in East London after a wailing jazz gig, and squabbling over who had the extra rice, is not the same thing as being entertained in royal style by the celebrated Japanese promoter Mr Udo, for whom you've just made a small fortune.

The steak sandwich and scotch-and-coke at the Speakeasy in 1968, the champagne and canapés at a record company launch, the omelettes and salads on a health kick in the USA in 1973, the borscht and vodka, the sushi and seaweed, the curly sandwiches and the cups of tea – all these culinary delights produce a taste redolent of particular times and places and a smell of the music made. To this day, a curry anywhere in Britain makes me think it must be midnight on the outskirts of Stoke-on-Trent. All British musicians of my generation learned to consume substantial amounts of Chinese and Indian food, the only sustenance available after 11:00pm in a British town of any size until about 1990. The 80s were Japan and vast quantities of tempura, shabu-shabu, Kobe beef, and sake; the 90s were a well-catered-for King Crimson in Europe. The 2000s are dinner from a restricted menu in a dark corner of the jazz club before they let the punters in. That's what we really eat.

❏

On occasion, I need to remind myself of the reasons I do this. Hungry or stuffed, musicians perform for many reasons, and any reason is good enough. Personally, I see music as a path to change. It works much like a mirror: music will show you your reflection, but if you don't much like what you see, you can change through music. You can become a different person through your striving, possibly a better person. Those of a religious nature would claim that right artistic endeavour could bring you closer, no matter how infinitely small the distance, to God. However bad you are today, honest application will render you a better musician than you were yesterday. Musical endeavour offers a sense of progress.

It is also, for me, intensely social. I am unlikely to prefer working with my computer on music on my own above the upcoming social rehearsal. A rehearsal is a place where you and I look each other in the eye, count to four, and try to play four sweet-sounding notes in time and together so that they might produce a total that is greater than the sum of the parts. That's the nucleus, the DNA of the procedure. For me, whole compositions are just a rather superior superstructure built upon that elemental idea. We need to co-operate if we are to produce decent music when we play together. This small-group human co-operation, as manifested in the great string quartets and the almost telepathic qualities of a first-division jazz group thinking on its feet, is a template for how society could and should operate under perfect conditions.

If the British Prime Minister's Cabinet could co-operate on the same level as the great Miles Davis quintets, we'd be experiencing a different form of government altogether. As the theorist Theo van Leeuwen has put it: "Music can be seen as an abstract representation of social organisation, as the geometry of social structure."[2] Add to this the possibility that you might – a slim chance, but you just might – produce a music never before heard on the planet, a music greater than the sum of its parts, a music greater than any one of its individual players, and you have several reasons as to why my current work is acoustic, dependent for its success on improvisation, necessarily an extreme form of human co-operation by like-minded people, and played in real time. From this I derive a personal sense of worth. I sincerely hope that the resulting music would speak volumes to onlookers and buyers of concert tickets, but if it didn't, I would continue to make it anyway.

Music remains a mystery, in the best sense of the word, stubbornly refusing to be accurately caught in language despite the millions of words spent trying to do just that. Music begins where language leaves off. Great music invariably has something beyond the personal about it, because it depends upon an inner ordering process, which is largely unconscious and thus not deliberately willed by the composer. This ordering process is something to be wooed, encouraged, waited for, or prayed for. You can prepare yourself for music, but you cannot force its appearance.

You might want to prepare yourself for music to enter your house, by working on your technical abilities, by stilling your mind, by tidying up a bit, so music may pick your house to visit. Sometimes it doesn't visit, and I'm sure we've all been to or, worse, played at musical events where music stubbornly refuses to appear despite the striking of many notes. The shit ain't happenin', as some would say. Desperation sets in. We play faster, louder, turn up, and thereby ensure music won't come visiting for a long while.

People often talk of music passing through them, or using them as a vessel. Igor Stravinsky said that the germinal idea for *The Rite Of*

Spring came to him in a dream: "Very little immediate tradition lies behind *Le Sacré du Printemps*. I had only my ear to help me. I heard and wrote what I heard. I am the vessel through which *Le Sacré* passed."[3]

Much is made of the close similarities between mathematics and music. Both exemplify the fact that making coherent patterns out of abstract ideas is a deeply significant human achievement that enthralls and satisfies those who are able to understand such patterns, whether or not they are related to life as it is ordinarily lived. Aesthetic appreciation of this sort is not just cold and cerebral, it is full of human feelings – we delight in perceiving coherence where there was none before, we take pleasure in perfect form, we like to make order out of chaos. The patterns of both mathematics and music engage our feelings, but only music affects our emotions. Unlike feelings, the more extreme emotions involve the full body. First attitudes, then feelings, and then emotions.

The greatest creative achievements of humans are a product of the human brain, but this does not, as Stravinsky shows, mean they are entirely voluntary constructions. The brain operates in mysterious ways that are not necessarily under voluntary control. We must sometimes leave it alone, stand aside, get out of the way of the music. Some people find one of the great religions provides them with a belief system that makes sense of the world and their place in it; others look to music for the provision of something similar.

Anthony Storr puts it well in his book *Music And The Mind*: "Although music is not a belief system, I think that its importance and its appeal also depend upon its being a way of ordering human experience. Great music both arouses our emotions and also provides a framework within which our passions 'enjoy themselves', as Nietzsche put it. Music exalts life, enhances life, and gives it meaning. Great music outlives the individual who created it. It is both personal and beyond the personal. For those who love it, it remains as a fixed point of reference in an unpredictable world. Music is a source of reconciliation, exhilaration, and hope which never fails."[4]

8 WHAT'S IT LIKE WORKING WITH ROBERT FRIPP?

Robert Fripp had always been a handful: interesting and exasperating in equal measure. Winston Churchill's description of Russia as "a riddle wrapped in a mystery inside an enigma" could equally be applied to the seated, bespectacled guitarist of King Crimson. As soon as I had laid eyes on the band in 1968, I'd wanted to be part of it. Like an enthusiastic puppy, I'd ask Robert, "Now? When? Soon?" and he'd say "Not yet, not yet."

That response probably had as much to do with inter-band politics – Yes and Crimson knew of each other and played dates together, particularly in the USA – as anything to do with me, but I felt like a young tomato, ripening on the vine and not yet ready to be plucked. Eventually, and with a shock-horror headline in the national *Melody Maker* paper, I made the move from Yes to the Mighty Crim to general incredulity and astonishment from those in the music industry who cared about such things.

King Crimson had rocketed to early success but then fallen into a briar-patch of personnel changes. Yes, on the other hand, was slow out of the gate but by late 1972 was as hot as hot could be.

Why would this exciting young drummer want to leave the band he'd laboured in for four years just as it was hitting it big? From my view, it was all entirely logical.

For a start, I certainly wasn't about to go through *Close To The Edge* again. It had taken three months of all-nighters, and if I knew one thing at the end, it was that I wouldn't be able to improve on that effort with that group of people, so I could see no point in hanging around.

Secondly, I'd only played with these four musicians for the majority of my short professional career, some four-and-a-half years at that point, and I was becoming desperate to hear myself in some other context. I never subscribed to the notion that after a few hit records rock musicians were supposed to atrophy, become a laughing stock, and then just stop. Thirdly, I could no longer wait for the torpid Chris Squire. The grossest form of insult any musician can bestow upon a colleague is to keep him waiting. Endlessly and repeatedly.

Finally, King Crimson beckoned. To this I could add that there was a certain reckless bravado to the move that appealed to my romantic young senses. When Brian Lane had showed me the chart position in *Cash Box* magazine in the limo in New York, my strongest feeling was "Well, what do I do now?" The job, it seemed, was done. The bank was robbed; a clean getaway had been made. Time to divide up the spoils back in the farmhouse in Devon and forget we ever knew each other.

Almost immediately, Robert Fripp and I took up positions that we seemed to defend for most of our working relationship. I was the ingénue, the man with too many ideas, too much enthusiasm, and a genuinely thick skin. It required several rounds from an elephant gun to get me down, and even then I was only winded. Perhaps Robert was unused to having such artistic resilience in the band.

He was the superior intellect with a silver tongue, in possession of some arcane or possibly occult knowledge to which the rest of us weren't privileged. The Man With A Plan – but since he wasn't exactly letting on what the plan might be, a certain amount of inspired guesswork was called for. I might have known it was going to be an interesting ride when the first of the two gifts he gave me in some 35 years was a book entitled *Initiation Into Hermetics*. I wasn't given a set-list when I joined the band, more a reading list. Ouspensky, J.G.

Bennett, Gurdjieff, and Castaneda were all hot. Wicca, personality changes, low-magic techniques, pyromancy – all this from the magus in the court of the Crimson King. This was going to be more than three chords and a pint of Guinness.

I agree with Robert's analysis that I wasn't ready when I joined the band, but after a year with the older and wiser percussionist Jamie Muir, I became ready. Had I not joined, I would have been less likely to develop any potential that subsequently surfaced, and for this I have King Crimson to thank. Robert always insisted the band was "a way of doing things" and that he was no more than "the glue that held it together" – certainly nothing as coarse as the bandleader. But as the only remaining original member, and the only man without whom the group could not exist, he was the de facto leader. He decided when the group stopped and when it started again. It was his blueprint that was adopted for each successive edition of the group. It was he who decided to bin an entire repertoire of well-known and loved material in favour of a complete stylistic makeover in 1980.

This was a spectacularly daring manoeuvre that tested the audience's stamina and nerve as much as it tested ours. The album in question was called *Discipline*, for which we had developed a notably different style, itself requiring radical new technology and a couple of Americans to help realise it. The only fly in the ointment was a shortage of material. When the band showed up in one German venue on tour to support this new oeuvre, the audience was in a bad mood. In an achingly slow procedure, they had been put through a metal detector and relieved of cameras and recording devices, a gesture that Robert insisted upon and one guaranteed to engender hostility within the most welcoming of crowds.

As the music ran its course, and it became clear that the audience wasn't going to hear a single note of anything recognisable, the applause at the end of each piece diminished to all but inaudibility. Bravely we battled on to the conclusion of the prepared material, which, at the 65-minute mark, was a dangerously short presentation, given the circumstances. In a particularly Germanic way, the audience, having shown little life in the preceding hour, began to demand an unrefusable encore. It is a feature of German crowds that no matter how little they appear to have enjoyed the music they *will* demand an encore, which you *will* play.

But in King Crimson they had met their match, and, not being very good at being insisted at, we began to leave the stage. As I descended from the drums and followed my fellow musicians off the stage, there was a huge squelching thud as a sizeable packet of meat, later identified as uncooked liver, landed squarely at my feet. I paused for a moment and then walked around the bloody missile, pondering on the nature of the punter who brings a parcel of raw liver to the gig with him, presumably to hurl at the drummer if things don't go to his liking.

It was Robert who finished the band 'forever' in 1974, reconvened it in 1980, finished it in 1984, and reconvened it in 1993. I felt I could contribute no more after a series of abortive rehearsals in Nashville, Tennessee, in 1996, and it was the right time to move on. "What's it like working with Robert?" is a question I should be thrilled to never hear again. A short answer is that it's like working with a man who is one part Joseph Stalin, one part Mahatma Gandhi, and one part the Marquis de Sade, a description that I suspect would make him roar with laughter.

Oh yes, this difficult man possesses a wicked sense of humour. Many a hotel lobby has been treated to Robert at the piano making a brave attempt, with overbearing earnestness, to sing '(I Wanna Be) Bobby's Girl' or 'When I Fall in Love' – hopelessly romantic songs from a man who patently doesn't do romance. On several occasions, the whole band has ground to a halt, incapacitated by mirth, happily mostly in rehearsal.

His impression of one poor bloody applicant for the post of singer following the departure of original chanteur Greg Lake is enough, even as I write, to bring tears to my eyes. It centres on the feeble attempts of said applicant to deliver the poisonous lyric of '21st Century Schizoid Man' with a venom equal to or greater than the original. There are three vocal lines accompanied by slashing guitar, and the fourth, the punch line, is delivered solo vocal, without accompaniment. Robert's impression delivers the first three with insufficient muscle, but nevertheless a modicum of hope, only to be dashed as the fourth collapses into a moment of extreme winsomeness, as if delivered by a gay waiter.

He is disarming about his technical difficulties, maintaining that he has learned music as others learn French, implying a grind, a sweat, repetition. Only after many years has he found a place that he can inhabit, in which his guitar stylings will work. He enjoys solo work – this music thing is all so much easier without the added difficulty of a relationship with human beings. When you play with him, he appears to be in uncomfortable attendance, rather than inside the group or inside the music. He maintains a safe distance on the edge of things, as evinced by one tour with Peter Gabriel during which he delivered his contribution from the wings, offstage, safely removed from proceedings. His admiration for other guitarists centres on their ability to be completely inside the music: Robin Trower, with whom we worked occasionally in the 70s, or Adrian Belew, or Jimi Hendrix.

As Fripp will tell you, the listener tends to pay most attention to an instrumentalist on two occasions: when he begins, and when he ends. On the micro level, this is the beginning and ending of a phrase; at the macro, it might be the beginning and ending of a long set of music. Less attention is paid to events in between. Exits and entrances, stopping and starting, taking the saxophone out of your mouth, as Miles Davis is alleged to have suggested to the musically-verbose John Coltrane – these are of the essence. But they require rhythmic skill, the ability to jump in and out of the music at just the right moment, with the sure-footedness of a mountain gazelle, an area in which Robert was not strong.

It seemed to me that his notion of the clanging gamelan as a basis for an 80s King Crimson was brilliant on many levels, not least that he could safely start clanging at the beginning and finish clanging at the end, with minimal requirement for rhythmic adventure in between.

And the drums could do the coming and going. Several of the tracks from those days – 'Discipline', 'Frame By Frame', 'Neal And Jack And Me' – are characterised by his guitar providing an unbroken run of 16th notes from beginning to end. He was happy having assigned unto himself the function of providing the continuum. Like a drummer's right hand on a cymbal, he could get it going and forget about it.

He invited me for a drink in the bar on one occasion. A simple sentence, that, but this was an event as unexpected as it was unheard of, never to be repeated. We had a loose evening in a hotel on the night our bassist Tony Levin's garage burned down, with the sad loss of many fine instruments and personal possessions. In some seven or eight years of roadwork with Robert, I had never been to his room, and neither he to mine. It was more out of respect for each other's space than any kind of antipathy that one would steer to a separate table at meals, even if we were the only two inhabitants of the restaurant.

It was a little strange, however, when he would then take out a notebook, write something, pause, look at me across the vast space of an empty mid-afternoon dining room, scribble some more, look in my direction again, scribble some more. This material, I concluded, would either be submitted as evidence in court for some terrible misdemeanour involving a drum kit that I had no idea I had committed or was about to commit, or, more probably, would contribute to some voluminous memoir that is no doubt under construction as I write and will prove my own gentle assessment of our relationship to be tragically misguided and woefully lacking. Most of my contribution to King Crimson has been so assessed in the past by Our Great Leader – so there'll be no change there, then.

Despite our best efforts, this chequered relationship produced moments that neither of us were able to prevent or destroy. For a couple of years at the beginning of the 80s, we were the right band in the right place at the right time – not to get hits, but to do useful, fascinating, and right work.

Western composers, becoming bored and restless with the familiar devices that play on memory and anticipation in Western composition, had stumbled across fresh attitudes to rhythm, time, and the function of music that were very close to the cultures of, for example, the Chopi of Mozambique, or the Javanese and the Balinese. King Crimson was well placed to transmute some of these ideas from the New York City art world to the rock arena.

The talk in the group back then was much of village music. Nobody seemed to have quite formulated the concept of world music at that point. In attendance also were strategies from what became known as minimalism, and ambient music, an area in which Robert had just made a seminal album, *No Pussyfooting*, with a young Brian Eno, late of Roxy Music.

These all seemed like unusual and exciting ideas, and we had a whole new generation of tools to bring down off the shelf to help reformulate them into a rock context: guitar synthesizers, electronic drums, the Chapman Stick, and the emerging Musical Instrument Digital Interface or MIDI, which allowed the new keyboards and guitars to 'talk' to each other – all were enlisted.

For a while the group renamed itself Discipline, and that eventually became the title track of the album of the same name. The discipline referred to was essentially that required from the performers of the piece to avoid attracting attention to themselves, to affect the posture of the village musician who may have a modest part, requiring no virtuoso technique, but which is an essential element of a slowly and subtly changing fabric of interwoven parts. To the casual listener whose attention to the music may be superficial, nothing appears to be happening. A deeper listen will reveal that there is, to the contrary, a great deal of very small activity as different cycles of guitar notes weave in and out of phase with each other over long periods of time.

There is a deliberate playing with timelessness here that actually promotes an extraordinary attention *to* time. There are wheels within wheels, pulses within pulses, as one cycle of notes concludes only to start again immediately. As John Miller Chernoff has noted: "African music is both slow and fast."[1] This piece, 'Discipline', is probably the closest a working rock group of the day came to a synthesis of minimalist and non-European attitudes to time.

Being a rock group, of course, it occasionally became undisciplined, over-excited, and literally untogether. Then, playing the tune was like pushing sacks of coal uphill with muddy boots on. A good performance, however, was like making circles in the air with a feather duster, a somewhat childlike activity that required no effort and produced an enormous sense of wellbeing. Imbued with a kind of undeniable rightness, such occasions are what people like me struggle to create for much of our professional lives. That's what we *really* do. All the hours of practice and struggle are validated in such moments of pure pleasure.

The gig with King Crimson was without doubt viewed by drummers as one of the three best rock gigs available in the last couple of decades of the 20th century (the other two being, arguably, with Peter Gabriel and Frank Zappa). Any drummer would kill for it. We had built up a reputation for innovation through the 80s with the trilogy of *Discipline*, *Beat*, and *Three Of A Perfect Pair* that seemed to outsiders to be second to none.

No one, inside or out, seemed to care too much about record sales. Warner Bros tried their best with videos of our songs 'Heartbeat' and 'Sleepless' in the mid 80s, but it was never going to work. Whenever radio people saw a record with the name King Crimson on it, they dismissed it out of hand as unsuitable. Seeing themselves as guardians of the public, ever protectors of the people, they saw it as their sworn duty to ensure that listeners never got to hear the dangerously imaginative racket that might spill from their speakers.

Denied record success beyond the faithful few, what we did have was infinitely better. We had influence. This was the band that every musician from London to Los Angeles, from Moscow to Monterey, from Paris France to Paris Texas would drop everything to see. If you wanted to know what you were going to be playing tomorrow, you went to a

King Crimson show. If you wanted to hear what kind of sounds you were going to be using, you went to a King Crimson show. If you wanted to hear musicians playing stuff that you weren't allowed to play, you went to a King Crimson show.

We were paid to try the stuff out. We could play in unheard-of time signatures and two keys at once, and still stay in decent hotels. It was hip for jazz guys to be there, it was hip for metal heads. The drumming could be anything, so long as it didn't sound like the other guy, or Robert hadn't heard it before, or, better still, both. If the band had a motto at that time, it would have been: Go further. Whatever you thought rock music was, we were going to take it further. And with the Mighty Crim, it had ever been thus.

It's 1969, and I'm with the guys in Yes. We roll in to the Speakeasy for steak sandwiches and scotch-and-cokes, as is our habit. Whatever is happening on the bandstand receives the usual musicians' cursory glance up and down, before we straggle through to the quieter room to eat.

But on this night something is wrong. Nobody is moving. Everybody is staring at the stage, transfixed. Waitresses, inured to almost anything short of nuclear attack, stop serving. A strobe is running, and some guy is singing about the 21st century. Then comes this rapid unison passage over a blues form, with unison snare drum and guitar – and loud. Then a repeat, only this time so quiet you can hear the hairs stand up on the back of your neck. I know immediately we are in the presence of a very serious and very disciplined organisation. Even the cadenza at the end is organised to peak at a shriek before it hits a brick wall of absolute silence.

It takes more than a few moments after that before people remember where they are and start to move and reassemble their lives. There is little applause. And that's pretty much how it will always be. Most people you meet went to one King Crimson show, and whether they liked it or not, they'll tell you they have never forgotten it. And there was never much applause.

Several Crimsonesque notions and modus operandi entered my

bloodstream that night and have been with me ever since. The notion, for example, that, whatever you did before you joined the group, you were required to leave it behind and find something else to do when you were in it, so that you might bring about change. Change was everything. Changing the way you sounded would change the way your colleagues sounded, and the way the ensemble sounded, and, on a good day, the way rock music sounded. Whatever you were previously known for, you probably wouldn't be doing much of it in King Crimson, and you certainly wouldn't be the same man when you left. It was a black hole that sometimes swallowed musicians if they didn't look out. Violinist David Cross may still be in there.

After the shock of the band's initial impact at the Speakeasy, I saw it again on many occasions. I always liked the first minute after they walked on stage, before the ensemble played a note, because no individual played a note. In those days, one was accustomed to the sound of a shambolic lot of hairy behemoths plugging in to amplifiers amid a howl of feedback, thuds and clicks from the guitarists, rattles and booms from the drummer, and muffled one-two-one-two's from the singer as he found – remarkable this – that the microphone was still working. All this heralded the massive display of incompetence you were about to witness. The physical stillness and silence before a King Crimson performance heralded the massive display of competence you were about to witness.

The silence was the loudest silence you ever heard. And the longest. In the dark stillness, you wondered if they were all asleep, or dead, before all hell broke loose. Obviously these people knew something I didn't, and whatever it was they knew, I wanted to know it too.

❏

Outside my room, the fully erect eight-foot grizzly bear's claws are fully extended, head twisted, teeth bared, ready to attack. He is huge and he is stuffed, so I am in no immediate threat. Despite the obvious drawback of his immobility, he seems to me to make a sufficiently intimidating sentry. I don't bother to lock the door.

It's February 1983, and I haven't had any meat thrown at me in a while. The grizzly and I are in the converted bunkhouse at the Caribou Ranch and Recording Studio in Nederland, Colorado. It is a rough and ready sort of place, miles from anywhere and more than a mile above sea level, beautiful in the thin air and blinding in the bright morning snow.

I have made the breathless crunching trudge across from the bunkhouse to the studio in good time for our 12:00 call. My employer, I understand, likes to start late. It is to be a trio session, and the other man involved is my good friend, bassist Tony Levin. Our work as the Crims rhythm section has clearly not gone unnoticed by Al Di Meola, the celebrated guitarist whose record we are about to make and a man not given to wasting time with rhythmatists from the second division. This is one of the few periods in my career when I'm in some sort of fashionable demand, and I propose to make the most of it by accepting well-paid work from guitar stars such as Al.

Tony turns up, we josh and jive, get the drums up and running, and wait. More coffee and more waiting. No sign of the main event. We wait some more. Hours pass. The February sun, sensing trouble, dips below the horizon with indecent haste. Tony, not a man who likes to be kept waiting by any kind of a musician, good, bad, or indifferent, is weighing the odds about the kind of fallout he would receive if he just abandoned ship on this no-show.

Eventually the door blows open, and in a blast of chill air and a flurry of flakes our leader and guitar supremo makes an impressive entry. More joshing and jiving with me and the engineer, a lot of changing of strings, and Al seems to be ready for something. It might be music, but don't hold your breath. I'm behind my drums, Tony is stone-faced on a chair in the corner, bass not yet out of its case, and it's four-and-three-quarter hours after our appointed start time. Al begins to run the tune down. Tony and I listen. I practise a few bits, try a couple of options, ask him to repeat a section. Still not a word from the bass department. Al suggests that Tony might like to get his instrument out of the case, because this bit is going to be really tricky, as he lets rip a blazing run of notes that, evidently, he's going to want the bass to double.

The engineer is ready, I'm ready, Al is ready, and Tony's bass is still not out of the case. I can tell he's brought the Chapman Stick on the date. The Stick is an unusual kind of stringed instrument, half in the treble register and half in the bass, played by tapping with the fingers of both hands as opposed to plucking with the fingers of the right hand only. It's an unfeasibly tricky beast, and Tony is the leading authority on it in a pack of about ten. Even if he practised what Al is proposing for a week, I doubt he'll remember it, let alone get it right. But we are in the land of machismo here, and I sense Tony is about to establish who's who on this session.

Al is rightfully acknowledged as one of America's leading guitarists on either the electric or acoustic version of the instrument, but right now Tony couldn't give a damn. We are ready to roll, and Al is becoming increasingly insistent that Tony is never going to get this unless he gives it some attention. This is ignored, and Tony asks Al to run it down one more time. He gets out the Stick, plugs in to the amp, and, without striking one note to make sure the instrument even works – it'll work – he just says: "Roll tape." He remembers the four-minute piece exactly, and produces a note-perfect bass part: no slips, no fluff, no guff. Then he doubles it.

It is a remarkable feat of musicianship and establishes a different sense of authority in the studio. We touch up some drums, add a few additional guitar parts, and break for dinner. But Tony hasn't quite finished yet. After the break, there is time for another piece, which goes down quite quickly, but the engineer and Al are now having a larky time, and a few beers have also gone down. The track is all but done, but a clumsy error on the engineering side erases a bar or two of Tony's work.

It's getting late. Tony already has the bass in the case and is making for the door. "Tony," pleads the engineer, feeling foolish and, in the pre-digital age, dangerously exposed for having erased a key portion of Tony's playing. "Give me one last run at it: it'll take five minutes." Tony pauses, one hand on the door handle. He considers, relents, says, "Five minutes," and gets the Stick out. The track runs; the missing section is recorded again and deemed acceptable. Tony packs his instrument, click, click, and heads to the door.

"Oh no!" the engineer whines, as he tries to make the join. "We're two notes short! Hey, Tony – *just two notes*." If he doesn't get these, it'll mean plenty of extra work finding the same two notes at the same dynamic, assuming they exist somewhere else in the track, and then copying them, sliding them in – and it may not sound right anyway. But Tony's gone, leaving a whole lot of extra work on Al's budget. Time is money, even if, or especially if, you're Al Di Meola.

❑

I'd heard a lot about Tony Levin, even before I met him for the first time in a rehearsal room in Manhattan. Robert and I knew we wanted him for the 80s King Crimson, even though we went through the formality of auditioning a long line of wannabes snaking around the block. After about three customers, Robert announced that he had an appointment elsewhere and left the rest of the auditions to me. After all, it's all about drums and bass, right? I struggled on manfully for another couple of hours, at which point Robert and Tony turned up. Tony played the first chorus of 'Red'; we dismissed the last of the straggling hopefuls and went off to toast the new King Crimson.

Tony has played with everyone and still has that childlike sense of discovery about him that we all try to preserve but seldom succeed. Many things exert a greater appeal to him than playing the bass: still photography, handy-cams, cycling, laptops, emailing, and coffee – these have all been spectacularly obsessive diversions from the tedium of the road. Not many bass players strap wooden drumsticks to their fingers to see what the added attack would sound like and then market the product of their invention as Funk Fingers.

Our conversations are usually about luggage or phone bills, seldom about music. He has the understated way of the older jazz musician, a style of music that didn't score highly in his view. Trained at the Eastman School Of Music in Rochester, New York, he had played *The Rite Of Spring* in the bass section under the elderly maestro Stravinsky before deciding classical music was too snobbish, precipitating a move to jazz. As a member of The Buddy Rich Orchestra and Gary Burton's quartet in the 70s, he was not without success in that arena, but abandoned that style of music, too, for rock'n'roll and the company of the likes of Paul Simon and John Lennon. I presume he enjoyed King Crimson because it was the sort of place you could strap drumsticks to your fingers and no one would pass comment.

The first time we played together, he didn't play very much. Thinking I was not providing enough stimulation, I redoubled my efforts and played more, faster, and louder. This had the opposite effect to my intention, and he reduced his contribution to scarcely more than a trickle. Again, I revved up on all cylinders, and by this time he had ground to a halt altogether. It took a minute or two before I absorbed the essential lesson for beginners: the more I played, the less he was going to play. If I wanted to hear him play at all, I had to start with nothing. It's all about space and holes, stupid, and he let me find that out for myself.

Once asked by an interviewer about the difference in style between Bill Bruford and Steve Gadd, he deadpanned: "One of them shows up on time." The world of the drummer – its competitiveness, its petty vanities, its showmanship – was of little interest to Tony. Either it swung in steady tempo or it didn't.

Unlike my relationship with Tony, Adrian Belew and I never worked together outside the confines of King Crimson and so never quite got to know each other without the shade of the Fripp hovering above. Adrian and I both came by our music more easily than Robert, and we both struggled in King Crimson with the way strong musical beginnings could so easily be suffocated at birth. If you wanted your idea to enter the Crimson lexicon, it had to have a lot of legs and at least two other guys taking it beyond its initial state. Others had to make something of it, and ultimately Robert had to feel bound in as well.

When Adrian arrived in the re-vibrated 80s incarnation of the band, it was nominally as singer–songwriter–guitarist, but he was also to act as a drawbridge to be lowered from the gates so the unsuspecting customer might be lured into the inner Crim. The original onstage 'act' – except it wasn't an act – was the seated, frowning, owl-like bespectacled headmaster, the beak, bemused by the prancing of this gifted new young upstart in a pink suit. Would he let him get away with it or give him a good thrashing?

For the upstart's part, his fluid post-David Byrne body language existed in stark contrast to the impassive, slightly suspicious owl, and he was going to get away with a lot. Occasional forays back to his amp for some feedback, the trumpeting of elephants, or the extraction of a shriek from his harmoniser would be accompanied by a sly smile in Robert's direction. "What do you think of *this*, sir?"

In the early days, the possibility that these antics might raise a smile in return from Our Fearless Leader – that was the ticket-buy. That was The Onstage Relationship – Aretha Franklin to King Curtis, Bruce Springsteen to Clarence Clemmons, Roger Daltrey to Pete Townshend – that defined it as a group, not a solo performance.

Sometimes we'd all be rewarded with a smile from the beak, but as things started to fall apart, and by then scarcely visible in the minimal ambient light, Robert adopted the habit of staring unflinchingly at a spot on the floor slightly off to his right and about six feet in front of him, this for the majority of the two-hour set. The owl raised its eyes only for the most essential of cues, blinked only when necessity dictated. The floor never moved, and the big sign that might as well have been hung around his neck saying "I wish I wasn't here" became increasingly frustrating to play behind.

The sixth manager in my career had assigned himself the delicate task of holding the 80s King Crimson together for as long as possible, a job that must have been rather like feeling grains of sand slip through your fingers. Paddy Spinks had initially been given the task of day-to-day management by his employers at EG and immediately proved skilled in the arts of arbitration and divorce counselling, or what used to be known as listening.

Much of Paddy's time was devoted to massaging Adrian's surprisingly low self-esteem. As the frontman in the group, responsible also for its lyrics, Adrian was permanently irritated by the press attention afforded to Robert, who appeared to be doing his best to avoid it. Adrian's insistence that his solo career be given equal credence, and that Crimson's work schedule should allow suitable time for its development, was clearly a cry for attention. If I had been the bad boy on our first record, *Discipline*, then by the time we got to the second, *Beat*, attention had shifted to an uncomfortable Belew, far away from home and under pressure to produce words and melodies to order and deadline. To a difficult-to-please Fripp, the increasingly overt challenges to his authority were becoming unsustainable, and the atmosphere was poison.

Eventually, Adrian told Robert to leave the studio, which was equivalent to the first officer telling the captain to leave the bridge. Robert went straight back to Dorset and was silent for three days. The two men most interested in keeping the dysfunctional crew onboard – the manager and the drummer – went into hyper-drive. A barrage of letters, phone-calls, visits, and apologies followed Fripp to the West Country. The captain was duly coaxed back to the bridge, and we heaved a sigh of relief.

Paddy's skills were to keep us all onside for a third and final album, *Three Of A Perfect Pair*, but that was about as long a tenure as Fripp could manage, and reasons were found to scuttle the ship in July 1984 after the final dates in Montreal, Canada. Paddy went on to a distinguished career as Vice President of International at Capitol Records, bringing them much success outside the USA, and now runs his own music-industry consulting firm, Global Spins, in Los Angeles.

With hindsight, many would agree that 1980–84 was a golden age for King Crimson and that the creative tension produced valuable work. Adrian was the owner of what Crimson biographer Sid Smith has called an "almost beatific"[2] voice with a clarity unusual in rock. No matter how lousy the front-of-house PA or my onstage monitors, Adrian's vocals were always clear as a bell, intelligible, rhythmic, sassy. There must have been something in the frequencies of his voice that was extremely microphone-friendly, and I think of this every time I have to struggle to hear singers caterwauling down a mic.

Adrian was also a respectable drummer, a skill we used to great effect as he declaimed the deranged lyric to 'Indiscipline' in sinister fashion over a slow ostinato from a second drum kit, allowing me to feed in improvised percussion and electronics in response to the words. 'Waiting Man' saw the two of us standing at a set of six hexagonal pads, arranged tabletop-flat in a honeycomb shape and played from either side. We had two interlocking motifs, which ran for a while until cue. On a balmy night at some European show – perhaps in the Roman Amphitheatre in Fréjus, France – the moths and fireflies, attracted by the lights, would weave their perilous way in between and around the choreography of the four sticks of the two drummers as the airy but persistent marimba-like rhythm soaked into the subconscious. After a few minutes of this, Robert and Tony would join in, and the music became unstoppable. Much more, and you feared that either band or audience might levitate. These were the great moments, undeniable and indestructible, and I know we all felt them to be so.

Adrian's relationship to the group tended to be dominated by his unfulfilled expectations. As the frontman, principal songwriter, and lyricist, positioned nightly at centre-stage, he was clearly engaged, agreeable, and willing to please. The majority of the attention, however, persistently skidded past him to his left, where sat a neat-looking man with round spectacles staring at the floor, disengaged, disagreeable, and unwilling to please.

On a good night the seated man appeared unhappy about

something, and on a bad night unhappy about everything. Adrian might reasonably have said this state of affairs wasn't fair, which sensibly he didn't, although it was evident in his offstage demeanour. His solution to this was to divert much of his energies, and the band's, and Paddy's, into his solo career, an area in which presumably there was no one else receiving greater attention than he. It needs a character flaw of no greater dimension than this to prevent a good musician from becoming a great one, and Adrian seemed unable or unwilling to put down this particular burden.

Ade and I would not have naturally found each other had it not been for Robert, and having found each other, we toiled mightily to bring treasures to the court of the Crimson King. I felt confident enough to have most of mine spat on – plenty more where they came from – and was in receipt of more than adequate reward for the few that were accepted. Adrian, it seemed, lacked confidence even when most of his treasures were gratefully accepted, and he perceived his efforts to be less well received than they should have been. It is for me an article of faith to expect nothing whatsoever from audience or colleagues in return for any treasures – that way at least I am unlikely to be disappointed.

Some of this may have determined the short life of our collective working relationship, but we did plenty in the time allotted. Ultimately, the magic of the 80s Crim could be spun out for just four years and three albums, but all I knew or cared about back home in Ewhurst through the long August of 1984 was that I was once again out on the street. Little did I know that in only ten short years, Adrian and I would both be back on the bed of nails again. In my case, for the last time.

9 WHAT DO YOU MEAN, YOUR 'SPIRITUAL HOME WITH A BED OF NAILS'?

I spend a lot of time in coffee shops. On the road, they are the only place outside your hotel room that you can get any peace and quiet, and at home, they are the only place you can get any peace and quiet. On the road, they offer consolation and escape from the suffocating proximity of your colleagues.

In my younger days, I used to run (I never knew how to jog) for 30 minutes as soon as I'd checked in to the hotel, and that provided much the same anonymity and aloneness in unfamiliar surroundings. As I grew older, I craved these two indispensable preconditions before I was able to do anything more than just keep up with life. Lofty considerations of possible futures took place in the warm womb-like coffee-and-cake atmosphere of the coffee shop or, as my gut ached and lungs burst with aloneness, 20 minutes into a 30-minute run on the wrong side of the railroad tracks.

In a perfect world, the coffee shop will have no music, be located in an interesting old part of a European city, perhaps the student quarter near the university, and be bustling with the thoughts and ideas of young people. I scour the local rag for a preview of the upcoming performance, or a review of the performance just delivered, hoping for a few kind words. Most of the local papers can't afford the services of a knowledgeable critic, so either jazz is farmed out to the rock writer or both rock and jazz go to anybody in the office who has a few CDs, probably the gardening correspondent. This poor creature's modest efforts and myriad mistakes are the source of much mirth on the plane or in the van the next day. The more irrelevant, idiotic, and just plain wrong the review, the higher the marks awarded. And they get pretty high.

Nobody, however, has yet been able to surpass the astronomic heights of the hapless Dutch writer who managed the previously unheard-of feat, in a group of four musicians, of pairing every first name incorrectly with every surname, and every surname incorrectly with every instrument played. Were we The Beatles, to illustrate, we would have been identified as George Starr, bass; John McCartney, drums; Ringo Lennon, lead guitar; and Paul Harrison, rhythm guitar. It takes a stratospheric level of ignorance to pull that one off, and he was naturally awarded the highest possible recognition for his efforts, and his health was drunk lustily for several days thereafter.

If I can't find anything in the local paper, there is always the set-list to concoct and the endless postcards home. When they were young, my children were inundated with a barrage of cheap and nasty specimens, usually with a biro'd arrow pointing at my room in a concrete-block hotel with an implausibly blue sky. I fancied they liked getting them, but I'd actually never asked. Maybe they hated it. In earlier times, too, maps of exotic countries, particularly the United States, were pinned to the bulletin board in the kitchen, peppered with coloured pins, and on one occasion even with string joining the pins together. The string snaked north, south, east, and west as the tour progressed and the weeks passed, a countdown calendar to the day daddy came home. An hour or two in silence in a good coffee shop could be like a vacation. There you could write, think, get a grip, and avoid people you knew.

It was to the warm fug of one such place in my local town, Guildford, that I repaired one late December afternoon in 1993 to compose a letter that needed a little extra thought. There was a long list of Christmas-flavoured domestic chores quietly suffocating me at home, and I had something else on my mind.

I knew Robert Fripp was proposing to reinvent King Crimson and that there was another drummer in the frame. I badly wanted the gig. Django Bates, the wonderful E-flat horn and keyboard player, had given me notice of his need to move on from Earthworks a couple of months before, and the first edition of the band had played its last gig at Cabot Hall in London's Docklands that September.

Earthworks had to pause for any number of reasons, but principally, and with hindsight, because I was running it as a rock group. The only way I knew how to run anything was as a rock group. Managers, tour accounts, agents, someone else doing everything: the works. The costs associated with the complex Simmons electronic rig I was using were becoming unsustainable, and this was starting to look like a replay of my first band, Bruford, whose back had been broken by, among other things, freighting a Hammond organ around.

It seems you got two or three studio albums and a live album before either the musical blueprint for the group needed updating, or technology had moved on, or costs became prohibitive. Django sensed rightly that his departure would precipitate a healthy change; I was too exhausted to pretend not to see it. After Bruford sank with all hands, Crimson had been there as a lifeboat. So again this time. This was evidently becoming the band I could swim back to when life outside became too choppy. That worked fine in 1980, was about to work well again, I hoped, in 1993, but by 1997, after my last Crimson, I knew I had to renounce it completely if I were ever to make progress as a jazz musician. But this Christmas 1993, I needed the band.

Robert had made a number of pre-conditions to my rejoining. The first involved renouncing any further relationship with EG Management, who had hitherto been doing a poor job of representing Earthworks in the wholly unfamiliar arena of the European jazz scene. No problem there: just a lot of divorce papers. The second requirement was that I cede all creative control of the new King Crimson to him. The old argy-bargy above boathouses in Kingston or in the backrooms of music stores – that was to be a thing of the past. I was better with the first than the second of those conditions, but still I knew he would want to know not how much I wanted the job but how much I needed it.

In a three-cup marathon at the top of Guildford High Street, I composed a grovelling little number, one-third promise of good behaviour, one-third apology, and – important this with Robert, or indeed any musician – one-third flattery. It produced the required result. A few days later, I was, rather to my astonishment and certainly to my relief, back in the band.

Fripp has often suggested that his job was to throw balls in the air. Some would be caught by band members, some would slip out of their grasp, and some might be allowed to drop; all possibilities were fine with him. One of the balls he now threw in the air expanded the previous quartet format to sextet with the idea of a double-trio. This was initially exciting: the iconoclastic jazz altoist Ornette Coleman had worked with a double-quartet in the 60s, with the two bassists Charlie Haden and Scott LaFaro, the two drummers Billy Higgins and Ed Blackwell, and a frontline of himself with Don Cherry, Freddie Hubbard, or Eric Dolphy. I should have liked to have heard them just tuning up, because the record pointed the way to great possibilities. Taking a leaf from their book, I guess, it was proposed that Crimson would field two drummers, myself and Pat Mastelotto; two bassists of a sort, Trey Gunn and Tony Levin; and Robert and Adrian at the front. This looked better on paper than in reality, and it should perhaps have generated more roar than it actually did.

Our Leader tabled, according to form, a piece called 'Vrooom', with various extensions and codas as 'Vrooom Vrooom' and 'Vrooom Vrooom: Coda', along the lines of 'Larks' Tongues in Aspic' Parts One, Two, and Three. This was essentially medium-tempo guitar-led instrumental music dating back to his own 'Red' and back to an honourable tradition of guitar twanging from the likes of Bert Weedon and Duane Eddy. This was a dissonant Shadows on steroids with two drummers, more chromaticism, and so many effects processors that Tony was one day despatched to the stage after a soundcheck to find out exactly how many boxes, pedals, and buttons the band had available to manipulate its sound. He came backstage to dinner triumphantly bearing the number 84.

The sound of the sextet was a fabulously dense din, best heard, to my mind, on headphones so that some aural space can allow the detail to be revealed. We drummers spent hours in the back of the bus on tour working out detailed and complex interlocking parts for pieces such as 'Sex Sleep Eat Drink Dream', 'Thrak', or 'B'Boom', the drummers' response to 'Vrooom'. The album, called *Thrak*, also contained some lovely moments – 'Walking On Air', 'Inner Garden' I and II, 'One Time' – for which a sextet was certainly not necessary and in which the idea of a double-trio, with its implications of counterweight, doubling, two-for-one, simply evaporated.

The music was almost entirely pre-arranged. An improviser by nature, I thought we might find a more profitable avenue in the modest amount of improvised music we attempted, but despite moments of good luck on the heavily-edited live recording *Thrakattak*, moments when the idea of a double-trio really was audibly present, we lacked the collective sensibility of the long-experienced acoustic jazz improvisers, and our efforts in that direction also fell on somewhat stony ground.

Nevertheless, we toured the best handpicked rooms to critical approval. We stayed in the best hotels and were adequately remunerated, but this to a growing chorus of complaints from Our Fearless Leader. His discomfort with proceedings appeared to stem from the old bugbear of privacy, and its invasion, to which were added newcomers such as unsuitable venues and sound difficulties. He opted to sit centre rear, immobile, and with only ambient light from which he might be dimly perceived, staring gloomily at the floor.

His invisibility was beginning to cause mutterings from the audience. They had, after all, paid a lot of hard-earned cash not only to hear this bloke but also to see him. Here, we were sailing perilously close to the Trade Descriptions Act. If you buy a concert ticket to The Three Tenors, or The Rolling Stones, does the contract not imply that you will be able to hear *and* see them? Are the contracted performers required to be lit, and on stage, or could they, with impunity, deliver the music from the wings? I've struggled through a lot of mayhem on stage, but sitting next to this fellow in the dark was becoming a distraction. One customer wrote to Robert complaining that he could only be seen for a third of the show. Fripp wrote back, in a questionable piece of public relations, enclosing two-thirds of the ticket price and telling him to never come again.

Given that rhythm was not Robert's strong point, and an air about him indicated discomfort with almost anything a drummer played, it may surprise the reader to note that he hired two of them. Life with Our Leader was full of such minor inconsistencies. He maintained that both of us were too loud, and his audio problems were worsening rapidly, so Perspex sound-reflective screens appeared on stage overnight, like a nasty rash. Tony, himself with a hearing problem, was unfortunate in having my bass drum behind him on a riser at his chest height, so naturally a screen was called for to ameliorate that situation as well. This, of course, was a sound with which I was becoming quite familiar, the sound of a band falling apart, and from here it was only a matter of time until we would be in separate transport and with separate dressing rooms. I'd just been through all that on the Yes reunion tour of 1991.

Double-trio or not, we were playing fresh, high quality music of our choosing to an appreciative audience of supporters, so it was a sadness to me to have to spend several months separated from them and my colleagues by the plastic Screen of Shame, especially since I am not the loudest of drummers, and I pride myself in my dynamic control and the ability to play appropriately to the sound that I'm hearing. I was too tired to be bothered to tell anyone, but to make thing worse, the angle of my screen caused it to act as a reflective mirror, so for a couple of months I had to stare at my own image for two hours nightly. The discomfort is readily visible in the excruciating footage of the band from around this time made available for posterity on a DVD called *Deja Vrooom*.

By the time we arrived at Merriweather Post Pavilion, Columbia,

Maryland, for the penultimate date of what had been a long three-month tour through Europe, the US West Coast, down to Mexico, and all the way back up through the Midwest to the Northeast, my body was beginning to match my mood. At the soundcheck in Columbia, my left wrist began to give me a stabbing pain as I laid down the beat, and I feared I might permanently damage it. I played that evening as lightly as possible in the company of ice packs whenever possible, and the next day I flew down early to Philadelphia.

The promoter had found me a hand surgeon, an elderly man with long experience in his calm, cool fingers. He silently, gently, and very slowly felt all over the wrist and palm area, his face remaining impassive. After what seemed like hours, he pronounced his initial diagnosis that this was not serious, it was only a strain that would cease when the tour ended, and he would take some X-rays to confirm.

I performed my last concert with King Crimson at the Mann Center that evening: carefully, with the ubiquitous ice pack, and in a fog of painkillers. I didn't know, exactly, that it was the end, but had I done, I would have known from the top of my brain and felt from the bottom of my heart that I could give no more to the Mighty Crim.

❑

There is an in-between-ness to flying. There were a whole lot of problems, hoops, and hurdles that you've jumped through back at the place you've just left, certainly, and doubtless even more problems, hoops, and hurdles are waiting at the place you're going to, but for now, in the clear freezing blue at 36,000 feet, there is neither hoop nor hurdle. Just the contemplation of them. If I stay up here forever, no more problems. Well, there'd be the localised problems of the horrific cattle-like proximity to my fellow man, the incipient backache, and the terminal boredom, but nothing I couldn't cope with – well down on the Richter Scale of hoops and hurdles that usually await me at my destination. Up here is a dream-state, a vacuum, a suspension, so long as the fuel holds out. Then back down to earth with a bump.

How exciting, those early trips on the half-empty jumbos, before the mass travel market had kicked in with cheap travel for all. When George Glossop, Crimson's sound engineer, had ruined his back lifting heavy gear at the last concert in Tokyo in the 80s, there was no problem finding him four seats to stretch out on for the long flight home. Under the glow of a solitary reading light, a doctor on board peppered his back with acupuncture needles like grapeshot and slowly eased the excruciating pain. George landed in London in tolerable condition. Not possible now. Now every seat is occupied, and frequently by an overfed passenger carrying about 30 pounds of excess baggage around hips and thighs.

I've recently started to scrape enough air miles together for promotion to Business Class. After a reasonable dinner, I stroll about to stretch my legs and, particularly, to enjoy the view as I push aside the curtain that separates Business from the back of the bus. Three-hundred-odd Faces Of The Damned, lolling, pink, trays akimbo, shoes in the aisle, eyes glazed, fixed, staring at the back of the seat in front, an aerial Black Hole of Calcutta. You wouldn't be allowed to transport cattle in this way: they're too valuable. Hieronymus Bosch would have done a good job of getting this particularly medieval kind of hell down on canvas. I fancy that after the Big Explosion, beings from a more advanced civilisation will leaf through the charred papers and documents at American Airlines headquarters and find late-20th-century diagrams and schematics as to how you could cram more people into a 747, resembling those found three centuries earlier for the most efficient shipment of slaves from Africa to the colonies. The sight warms me with a feeling that life has indeed been kind, exempting me from this, and that I have indeed been well rewarded for my efforts.

But when I land at Heathrow to be met by Harry, my local taxi-man, it is with an overwhelming sadness. It is a beautiful autumnal morning in 1997, and the last couple of weeks have been spent fruitlessly in the rehearsal from hell – maybe the rehearsal for hell. Six Crimson musicians and assorted road crew have milled about aimlessly in a rehearsal studio in Nashville, Tennessee, utterly unable to find anything to play together, while incidentally consuming thousands of dollars in hotels, tickets, and charges of one sort and another.

Two or three guys would noodle on something, individuals contributed a passage here, a song there, a refrain here, but nothing worked. Our Fearless Leader, guitar in hand, stared at his favoured spot on the floor, slightly to his right and a few feet in front of him, for minutes on end. The Active Ones – myself, Belew, Levin, and Trey Gunn – ran up ideas, toyed with this, rejected that. The stare didn't waver. More music came and went; ideas from which the average rock group would make a whole album. Some were destined to be stillborn. Others would howl once with pleasure at their arrival into the world, only to be ignored by He Who Could Give Them Life.

Eventually, exasperation got the better of me, and I heard myself voice my unsolicited opinion on the proceedings with a clarity that surprised me. This provoked reaction. The stare wavered; its owner put down his instrument and wordlessly left the room. The following day he could be persuaded to return only with profuse apologies, but it was over. By now Robert and I couldn't even agree where to have dinner. And if you can't agree that, you sure as heck can't play together.

My days with Crimson were finally and irrevocably over. Most of the time I hadn't known whether to laugh or weep. On one hand I felt like I'd been let out of prison early; on the other I felt I might rather prefer to stay inside. It's scary out there – maybe I wouldn't be able to play with anyone else. After all, the band had been my spiritual home, albeit with a bed of nails, for a quarter of a century. Good thing I don't much care for comfort or convenience, because spiritual homes can be very uncomfortable and very inconvenient, as this one had proved to be. Maybe I didn't know at the time how rough it was to be – and it was rough – but all the pleasure comes in looking back.

Two or three Crimson CDs exist that, when I listen to the kid on drums, give me a warm feeling inside. The studio album *Red* certainly had something about it, but we were better live. *Absent Lovers*, a double-

CD live in Montreal, Canada, proves that beyond dispute. The last gasp of the 80s band, that music was recorded over the last two nights of an edgy North America–Japan–North America tour, distinguished only by its length of over two months and Robert's acute unhappiness. Montreal's Spectrum was a great club back then, and probably still is, with a wonderfully encouraging and attentive crowd. Seemed like any other date to me, but the recorded evidence shows a level of playing ability and musicianship that can still bring a smile to my lips. And this was before the days of cosmetic enhancement and digital manipulation in post-production. Damn, we were good.

The next day, Robert broke up the group, again, for the umpteenth time, dwelling at length, I suppose, on our lack of imagination, ability, direction, and a thousand other things we were doubtless missing. I suppose this only because I remember not listening to this litany of failures. Might as well quit while you're ahead, I thought.

I'd had the transatlantic flight to begin to consider my future, and already its direction was clear. The days of the Big Beat were over. The publicists, the record companies, the personal managers who told you what to do, the tour managers who told you where to go, the girl back at the office who knew where everyone was, the caterers, the security staff at the stadium, the nice bloke who set up the drums, the record-company hamper at Christmas, the good luck telegram and (eventually) the embossed tour accounts – gone, finito. The whole creaking shooting-match of co-operative rock, its attendant compromises, its bodged efforts at marketing, its opening nights and its last nights, were about to be consigned to my personal historical dustbin. And I felt great!

Boarding school or rock tour? Anticipation at the beginning, the packing of the clothes trunk or drums, the goodbyes, the confident start with sharp pencil or new sticks, the bit in the middle from which you can neither see the end nor remember the beginning, the climaxing toward the big exam, or big gig, in which you will be sorely tested and after which it will seem you can give no more. And then it's all over, the pack-up, the anticipation of the last day of the term or the tour, the ritual laying-out of the last set of clean clothes miraculously saved for just this occasion, the triumphant return home to loved ones, bloodied, exhausted, but not bowed, wrung out and bruised, but confident and secure in the knowledge that the best has been given, the licking of the wounds, the taking stock, the future plans, and the doing of it all over again.

This pattern had been the defining rhythm of my life for too many years. I would need to imagine life without it, because where I was going it would have a different rhythm.

❏

I had begun the 90s at Madison Square Garden with Yes, 20,000 people, and a faltering electronic drum set, and ended the decade at the jazz club Birdland with Earthworks, 200 people, and an absolutely reliable acoustic set. The two venues may only be separated by a few blocks across town, but the cultural gulf between the music played in each is considerable. Conventional wisdom has it that most musicians spend a whole career trying to move in the opposite direction. I had been spending most of my career trying to find my way back to jazz. And I was making real headway.

Rock drumming and jazz drumming differ in myriad ways, not least in matters of articulation. Coming from rock, I had given a lot of thought to how you could get away with things – the kind of things that interested me but may not interest the audience. For example, if you want anything delicate to be heard at the back of more than a thousand seats, you're going to have to make room for it in the music and articulate with care. If you want to say something clever, it will have to be said clearly with as few notes as possible. If you want anything at all to be comprehensible at the back of 10,000 seats, don't attempt to go any faster than the lugubrious Pink Floyd plod. Somewhere there is a music PhD to be had involving an analysis of the correlation between various compositions and the rooms in which those compositions are to be heard.

Stand-up comedians and jazz musicians, conversely, may speak at the tempo they want. In the small and natural habitat of the jazz club, everything is audible. The skill on the drumset here does not revolve around clarity of articulation. On the contrary, the jazz drummer is looking for an ambiguity of expression. Was it this, or was it that? Maybe it was, maybe it wasn't. Was that a wrong note on saxophone? Not really: the piano harmony made it right. Does jazz have wrong notes? Maybe: it depends on the context in which you hear the note; it depends on the other notes surrounding it. The seductive rhythmic play of two beats against three, so common in African music and increasingly so in Western music, is as old as the hills. The essence of jazz rhythm, this ambiguity can flourish within this quicker, more adept music in this smaller environment. A whole band may morph from the initial duple pulse to its triple-pulse variant at the nod of a head. Its rhythm section may stay in one, while the top-line melody or soloist moves to the other. A drummer's feet may be outlining one, while his hands outline the other, in an endlessly appealing play on pulse. But that stuff doesn't work at Madison Square Garden.

Jazz, as both a music and a way of life, is an altogether different beast from rock. It doesn't promise to make anyone money, so it gets little attention. There is only a handful of practitioners on the several instruments in each nation who make a decent living as working jazz musicians. A select few, with a quality of vision and endurance denied to us lesser mortals, can fill concert halls around the globe – Keith Jarrett, Wayne Shorter, Jacques Loussier, Herbie Hancock. Singers – Diana Krall, Dee Dee Bridgewater, Kurt Elling – naturally do considerably better than instrumentalists.

But broadly, the jazz musician scrapes by, keeping several plates spinning in the air at the same time, with the mortgage and kids' shoes never far from his calculations. He lives on his wits as a salesman of his own talent, a product available for hire to his colleagues who are also his employers. Tonight he's at the bar at Ronnie Scott's in London, letting it be known that he's available, but not too available. Tomorrow he'll be down the Six, the 606 Club in Chelsea, doing the same thing before his support slot in front of the main band. With a bit of luck and some smooth talking, he'll wind up in two or three bands that he might be able to dovetail together to produce the mortgage, the kids' shoes, *and* the musical environment in which he can live and move and have his being.

He might end up in my group Earthworks. Nine men did, mostly hired straight from the stage. It's not much, but you'll be shown every consideration by a leader who has the ultimate respect for his employees, not least because he usually hires people who are better than he is. Being a musician himself, he knows what they want, because it's what he wants. His employee wants reliable, interesting work outside the parochial UK scene and clean sheets in single hotel rooms. He wants a leader who does what he says when he says he's going to do it, and pays what he says he's going to pay when he says he's going to pay it. He wants some musical space in which to contribute, and he doesn't need to be told every time he slips up, socially or musically. Not a lot to ask really, but if you can find it, it's a gig worth holding on to, and there are surprisingly few of them.

In return, the employer is getting a remarkable creature. He will have been the best jazz musician by far in his region of Idaho, Devon, or Provence before he seeks national acclaim from a foothold in New York City, London, or Paris. He's adaptable and can absorb and retain prodigious amounts of complex music by ear or by sight. In common with other people in a buyer's market, he doesn't whine, moan, or bring his problems to the bandstand. He isn't late: to keep his colleagues waiting is the gravest form of insult. He's reliable because he wants and needs to be there; you can agree to meet him three weeks hence at a departure gate at Madrid Airport, and he'll be there without further reminder. In my experience he drinks less and does fewer drugs than any number of professions, from doctor to city-trader, because, firstly, the music is difficult enough as it is, and, secondly, if he is a British musician, he has to drive back after most gigs, and if he loses his licence he's dead in the water.

This person never gets sick, and is prepared and expected to give of his or her best a few hours after a sleepless economy-class flight halfway across the world. He must get used to playing unfamiliar music with people he only just met ten minutes earlier in the dressing room and having the results 'reviewed' by 'critics' in what may amount to little more than a character assassination without right of reply.

Generally he is at his employer's beck and call, until and unless he can find an income stream that will once again allow him the luxury of a degree of self-determination. Only then may he be able to reconstruct some sort of family life, assuming there is some sort of family life left by this stage worth reconstructing. Only then can he be there to participate in the hundred-and-one domestic issues that define such a thing. If he can do all that happily in the music industry, while still looking after the mortgage and the shoes, he is already the very definition of success, irrespective of what a fickle public may think.

He may not be much in control, but his modest amount of musical self-determination is much envied by his institutionalised classical colleagues.

There is a growth industry in counselling for musicians, with the aim of maximising performance potential, reducing anxiety, identifying strengths and weaknesses, knowing yourself as a musician, and so forth. Contrary to common belief, the jazz musician, with apparently so little, is the least frequently in need of the counsellor's skills. The pop and rock musicians are rather more in attendance, and our regimented and highly organised classical colleagues appear to require more or less constant succour. The degree of attendance, you'll note, has everything to do with musical self-determination and the ability to control your immediate musical surroundings.

As in all walks of life, we prosper as musicians only insofar as we know what we want and are honest with ourselves and others in the pursuit of it. Happiness may be a by-product of meaningful or 'right' work, but knowing the right work for you implies that you must know yourself first.

❏

Andrew Evans founded Arts Psychology Consultants in the UK, and as his book *Secrets Of Musical Confidence* indicates, he is interested in all aspects of the production of confident musicians. It is confidence, he maintains, that is the cornerstone of professional success. He suggests that foremost to the idea of confidence are two main things, consistency and reality. His work helps the musician to identify the 'unstable' or inconsistent areas in his inner and outer life and replace them as far as possible with the known 'stable' or reliable qualities and talents that can be nurtured to give him confidence. A reliable source of personal effectiveness makes him feel equal to, or stronger than, obstacles that lie in his path.[1]

We need the feedback of doing well because, as they say, nothing succeeds like success. Down the pub we all talk of 'making it', as if there were no other route to happiness. The industry promotes itself as a permanent jackpot or lottery: winner takes all; losers never even get a hearing. But there is an important, less glamorous middle way – neither perfectionism nor low self-worth – that can ensure that you do well and are well regarded by your fellow musicians. It's the way I've chosen, and it is walked by more intelligent, wise, and healthy musicians than *The Daily Mail* would have you believe.

Such a path may not be the stuff of newspaper headlines, to be sure, but some of the finest musicians have never made headlines. Some of the best music I've ever heard has been made by people playing to three men and a dog. An early Weather Report performance in a tiny club in San Diego, California, comes to mind. Bassist Miroslav Vitous spent most of the evening trying to get distortion on his upright bass with a reluctant little gizmo on the floor, but his distraction didn't register with the indifferent crowd of locals.

Equally, an early UK date for The Jimi Hendrix Experience at the Bromel Club in the Bromley Court Hotel, Kent, performed to myself, a smattering of celebrities herded in by manager Chas Chandler, and a couple of cloth-capped regulars at the bar, seemed, from where I was sitting, to fall on stony ground. The set ended with a howl of feedback as Hendrix's guitar was left moaning on top of an amplifier, and I distinctly remember a cloth-cap, who'd had his back to the miniature stage all night, slowly turning around and staring in disbelief. Why is this black guy with a feather in his hat trying to spoil his pint?

By the time these innovators have figured out what they're doing and taken it to Madison Square Garden, the music's usually gone pear-shaped anyway. Most people never make headlines, and if you want to be around for a while, best to avoid making them for as long as possible.

❏

I'm inclined to agree with Frank Zappa, who told *Telos* magazine that "the single most important development in modern music is making a business out of it".[2] But the rules of this particular bullpen are at best a bit sketchy. The music business is, and always has been, highly volatile, a continual struggle for control as to whether the content of the mass media is to be decided by established authorities, be they the BBC, Sony Records, or Bugs Bunny, or by popular demand through the market. The role, importance, and market value of the individual musician fluctuates alarmingly within that, depending on how valuable his services may be at any given time.

It is a game certainly, but a dangerous game, disorganised and unregulated, governed neither by traditional ways of doing things nor by the culture of what may be called a status group, whose members share a common outlook, lifestyle, and sense of fair play. You have to be able to trust people, but where there is no sense of shared attachment to a moral order or a status culture, social and economic relations are going to be problematic and stressful.

Interviewed back in 1971, Allen Klein, the American former business manager of both The Beatles and The Rolling Stones, outlined his view of this 'game'. He said: "The music business is about 99 per cent no-talent losers who can't stand a winner in their midst. I'm a winner, and if they want to sour-grape my success by calling me names, let them. I don't give a shit."

He was asked if he would lie. "Oh, sure." Would you steal? "Probably. Look, you have to survive; you do whatever it takes, because if you don't stay alive in this business you can't help anybody. ... It's really like chess: knowing all the moves. It's a game, for chrissakes, and winning is everything. It's a shame it has to get nasty sometimes."[3]

Klein's approach was far from unique, and it reminds me of an early personal introduction to the questionable level of integrity in the industry. At Advision Studios in London, in the early Yes days, work had again slowed to the pace of a snail. Killing time in reception outside the studio proper, I was waiting for the others to extract themselves from any one of several self-made quagmires. Also waiting was an ordinary-looking American middle-aged fellow with a seersucker jacket and something funny about his hair.

We fell into conversation, during which he told me he was in the industry too, in fact in artist management. He was looking to book time at Advision for a female singer under his care and protection. Thing is, he went on to explain, she's really good but has had a very difficult time of it so far. I felt my jaw slowly dropping as he proceeded to recount a list of Dickensian horrors as long as my arm.

Evidently this poor thing had been the victim of early child abuse in some Southern state – Alabama, I think – and run away from home at 15. She had adopted a new identity in another state and by 18 years of age had mothered an epileptic child with an army deserter, only to suffer internal injuries and a broken left arm in a hit-and-run accident shortly after the birth. Unable to pay for either her or her daughter's mounting requirement for medical attention, and with the child's father no longer in attendance, she eventually fell to singing and 'hostessing' in nightclubs to make ends meet. At one of these joints she had been spotted by a Nashville talent scout, who had immediately paid for high-end demos to display her natural musical talents to a major record company. The label had decided to send her to the UK for a meeting with Beatles producer George Martin, with a view to George producing her first album at Advision for global distribution.

And here they were. What did I think? What I thought was that this was the most terrible story, and I warmed to the girl, who was not present, and hoped her stamina and fortitude would pay dividends in her future career as a singer.

Her manager handed me the press release on which this tragic tale was faithfully reproduced. Yes, he was insisting, but what did I think about her story? I told you what I think. But what about the bit with the hit-and-run? Is that a bit too much? The scales fell slowly from my innocent eyes as it dawned on me that not a word of this fabrication was true, and, worse, he assumed that I and everybody else just made this stuff up. We all do, don't we? He was pleased with his invention and was eager for approval. What did I think? More about the internal injuries?

Of course. Silly me. I thought an artist's biography was supposed to have a passing resemblance to the truth. But no, we're in the Industry of Human Happiness here. We're in fantasyland. Welcome to the whacky world of press biographies. I went back into the studio to continue work on *Close To The Edge*, a fantasy if ever there was one, and never again believed what I read in an artist's 'official' biography.

The working musician is a long way from operating in a vacuum. He or she is from somewhere – real, imagined, or invented. He is the product of his times; his views and tastes will have been shaped by the cultural milieu in which he grew up, by the taste-group of which he is a part, and by everything that ever came out of his iPod. He will be operating in a world in which large forces are at play, some of which may be more of a help than a hindrance.

Maybe the wind will be in his sails, as it was for the swing-era musicians leading up to World War II, when, despite the Depression, bands were hiring more than firing. Maybe the wind will be against him in one of the industry's periods of reassertion of control, as in the 1949–55 era of manufactured pop stars and shortages of shellac, rubber, and gasoline – all essential to the recording or touring musician – when employment was, for the instrumentalist, hard to come by.

Often the desire is to do something 'completely new' or perhaps 'shocking', both of which are difficult to achieve, even if desirable. A completely new music would be meaningless, in the sense that society would have had no time to form the taste groups and develop the listening conventions that would attach meaning to it. And shocking people requires that these conventions be contravened just enough to pose difficult questions about them in the first place, but not so much that discussion is meaningless. That was nicely played by The Sex Pistols in 1976, Village People a little later with the gay, disaffected, multi-racial subtext that they had running, and N.W.A from the Compton ghetto in Los Angeles in the 80s.

Not the least of a musician's skills, then, is to develop a strategy for survival based on an understanding that there is only so much he can do to move things his way. At some times it's quite a lot; other times, very little. But the periods change quite rapidly. I started in a very welcoming music industry that trebled in size every year, and one in which the playing and opinions of even the drummer were valued. After a downturn in the late 70s and early 80s, my move to jazz was happily coincidental with one of those periodic occasions when the UK media had decided that jazz was to be The Thing, jazz was to be fashionable, and you could even see a jazz big-band, Loose Tubes, regularly on British television. I was able to co-opt skilled and enthusiastic younger players for Earthworks direct from Loose Tubes.

Now, in the era of fame schools and reality TV, there won't be much around for the performing musician, who probably, chameleon-like and ever resourceful, has hunkered down with his home-recording system to do library music – music by the yard for TV – while he waits for things to get better. The moral of the story is that the path to a fruitful career will inevitably involve perpetual change in a continual redefinition of yourself and your goals. So much of being successful in music is no different to being successful in any other field. It hangs on knowing what is and what is not possible and, like the goldfish, on swimming around the rocks rather than continually banging into them.

It is also an industry for which the constant stream of technical innovations – phonogram, wireless, recording, vinyl, cassette, long-player, multi-track recording, CD – has been both the lifeblood and a constant source of disruption and disturbance that threaten the established ways of exploiting musical materials to yield a profit. If the music *industry* was all about banging out bits of black vinyl on an assembly line and delivering to a vast number of retail outlets, then its modern replacement, the music *business*, is about the never-ending war waged by record companies, composers, and publishers to establish and then protect copyrights on their material and collect royalties for its use.

When record sales started to slump in the mid 70s, it was home-taping that was to blame, like downloading today. The industry has for much of the last 30 years been preoccupied, as Russell Sanjeck put it in *American Popular Music And Its Business*, with "public larceny and its cure".[4] Pirate radio, home-taping, bootlegging, cassette piracy, and illegal downloading have all flourished in their day and continue to fuel, for example, much of the Chinese music industry. In the same way that I would make more money by immediately stopping all further production of fresh music and devoting my entire working life to collecting the correct, contracted publishing and recording royalties owing to me but not yet paid, so doubtless would EMI make more money by ceasing fresh production and going after unpaid royalties from China. Neither is likely to happen, but the point was made well to me by EG Management's director and accountant Sam Alder: it's all about collection.

It's hard to escape the implication that there is already enough music in Western society, and Western society tends to point out to the musician through the market – sometimes quite brutally, because the stupid musician doesn't get it – that it doesn't really want any more new music, that it's stuffed with the music it's got. Especially if it's going to keep it all and prohibit a natural decay. This is the environment into which the young pretender is ejected at the end of his college course in commercial music, and survival will require new modes of thinking about what it means to be in this exasperating, frustrating, and exciting music business. We don't want anyone getting hurt, now.

10 IS IT DIFFERENT, BEING IN JAZZ?

Everything sooner or later needs a name. Cats, children, this book, my hundreds of individual compositions and recordings, my house, my groups; every name is the wrong name until I find, or the item or creature acquires, the right name, at which point I am unshakeable. Until appropriately named, we only half exist. When correctly named, we begin to acquire personality and a future.

Despite an uneasy feeling that we already have too much music, I have continued to create it, and it all needs naming. I prefer to title the instrumental music I produce in an oblique, rather coded kind of language, as if to say: "This is what it means to me, but it might mean something else to you, and that's fine."

The phrases will have an internal meaning, considerable rhythm, and may only allude in a crossword puzzle kind of way – 'Some Shiver, While He Cavorts'; 'No Truce With The Furies'; 'Sarah's Still Life'. Alliteration, double entendre, dusty words – bring 'em on. I over-use images of dance and song, because that's what I think I'm causing my sticks to do up there on the stage. It's those that you should watch, not me. 'Making A Song And Dance'; 'Every Step A Dance, Every Word A Song'; 'The Wooden Man Sings, And The Stone Woman Dances'.

In 1986, my first jazz group, The Bill Bruford Quartet, was self-evidently in urgent need of the correct moniker, and not only because

Virgin Records was breathing down my neck for it. In a panicky phone call between keyboard and horn player Django Bates from a payphone in Wales and tenor saxophonist Iain Ballamy and me in my kitchen at home, we settled finally on the only one of several names upon which we could all agree.

The word Earthworks has a multi-level meaning. It may refer to a man's work here on Earth, or perhaps the fortifications and ramparts of early bronze and iron-age man, also known here in these ancient British Isles as earthworks. In order to build a building, you have first to excavate, to find solid footings upon which to construct, and maybe to construct a jazz group that will last a couple of decades. There are also implications of musical works from across the globe and styles from across oceans. All of this was to be sewn into the fabric of the band. Musicians entering would hopefully use the band as a vehicle for personal change and growth, and, Crimson-like, be different players with different outlooks when they left.

Part of the reason I was edging rapidly toward jazz was because there had to be better ways of creating music other than by staring at your feet in a room full of expensively unprepared musicians – one of my least favourite pastimes. Jazz players not only don't like to rehearse but also are unable to afford anything more salubrious than an afternoon or two in somebody's front room. If it's Django's front room in a large tumbledown and unheated house in Beckenham, Kent, where we ran through the early Earthworks material, it'll have ice on the inside of the windows as well as the outside.

Generally, the musicians come together to rehearse music already specifically designed for the project in hand. The basic harmony and melodies pre-exist in written form by the time the kettle goes on, so the band is only adding suggestions and making sure fingers go in the right places. With superior musical training, good ears and memories, and the ability to sight-read, it's all over in a few hours. If the collective doesn't like the piece, you bin it and do somebody else's. No tears, no recriminations, no blame.

Jazz moves faster than rock in many ways, not least the amount of musical material that good players get through. An accomplished saxophonist like Tim Garland might, for example, be in a couple of groups of his own, perhaps a trio and a big-band, and also is available for another couple of groups under other leaders. He'll also be working on a couple of other projects on an ad hoc basis, while composing on his laptop a large piece for the BBC Concert Orchestra. He's good, he's in demand, and he has perhaps six plates spinning at the same time. The wide variety of music he's playing, much of it memorised, feeds his own enthusiasms and creative juices, and keeps him match-fit.

But Tim's not usually working on them simultaneously in rehearsal. We'll meet him in greater depth shortly, but Tim's colleague and current Earthworks pianist Gwilym Simcock also possesses a prodigious ability to multitask. Like others, musicians now work on the move, booking dates, arranging travel, preparing music, and paying taxes, all while waiting in line to board the airport bus. At a rehearsal, however, phones are usually off and your full concentration on the task in hand is both required and expected.

Simcock handles the material of music with such ease (and with perfect pitch) that at one such recent rehearsal for a broadcast of Garland's new concerto 'Homage To Father Bach', doubtless intricate enough for we lesser mortals, Gwil raised the bar on multitasking. With his laptop out on top of the piano, he was seen to be simultaneously scoring parts for his own concerto, 'Progressions For Piano And Orchestra', the nationally televised premiere of which was just over the horizon, in the gaps between comments from conductor Garland on the immediate work in hand. Father Bach would have loved it.

By the time Yes had managed to decide what day of the week it was, Earthworks would have considered, deployed, or rejected enough music for a couple of CDs and a BBC broadcast. The modest sums of money allotted to jazz mean that the musicians need to be quick, resilient, self-confident, and know their strengths and weaknesses. It's a warts-and-all music that lives in the moment. There is not much make-up at the beginning of the date and even less cosmetic surgery at the end. Jazz doesn't brush her hair or hang around for long. Even if she wanted to, there isn't time or money to do it again.

❏

The first Earthworks, born 1986, was an electro-acoustic outfit based around the idea that the electronic drumset – recently enabled to play all manner of chordal, sampled, and pitched or unpitched rhythmic material – had come of age and was a serious instrument that could be used seriously in jazz. The plan was that I would play much of the chordal material, and that I would find some young open-minded players from the exciting and growing UK jazz scene and have them play single lines on top.

Saxophonist Iain Ballamy was a local Guildford musician who, by the time he was 17, had already been pictured in the London *Times* playing at Ronnie Scott's famous jazz club. He was picking up the knowledge fast by playing alongside great tenor players like George Coleman and Dewey Redman. Iain introduced me to the equally precocious Django Bates, who played all manner of keyboards and the small E-flat 'peck' or tenor horn. Django was a fugitive from the Royal College Of Music, from which he had absconded after only two weeks because he'd seen a notice affixed to a piano that read: "Not to be used for the playing of jazz music."

Django's compositions were far more interesting than mine and went about smashing as many sacred cows as possible in a gentle, self-effacing, English kind of way. He is now a much-feted composer and a professor at the distinguished Rhythmic Music Conservatory in Copenhagen, Denmark. I liked both Django and Iain individually, but better still they were very close as people, a musical double-act, a real partnership. It seems that neither had heard of Yes, King Crimson, or Genesis, and it was refreshing to be able to abandon that legacy and strike out fearlessly into a braver, newer, less rehearsed world, in which survival would require some fast thinking on my feet. Bates and Ballamy were essentially the backbone of the first edition of Earthworks, together with the dark and extremely intense bassist Mick Hutton, a man about whom and of whom you immediately understood it was best not to ask too much. The same Mick was shortly to rearrange the cutlery in Bergen University Students Union kitchen.

We were in business to break some rules and ask some questions, and the first question was: "What should, or could, a drummer be doing in an ensemble like this? Is there a right or wrong?" All I had to do was configure some bizarre confections of percussion from this unique kit and give the others space to write something on top. At least we could be sure they wouldn't sound like they usually sounded.

We made three records quite quickly for Virgin. The first, *Earthworks*, sold spectacularly well to my rock crowd, who clearly had failed to notice there was no electric guitar involved and declined to show up again for the follow-up, *Dig?*. It would take another five years for the band's sales to bottom out and start to rise again in the warm attention of a new audience less familiar with my past.

Meanwhile, trying to configure the electronic pads to produce chords and melodies eventually became a self-inflicted punishment that was threatening to drive me crazy. Wisely, no other drummers seemed keen to leap into that particular quicksand. Any musician worth his salt always wants to push new instruments past their design capabilities, and the manufacturer, in this case Dave Simmons, always wants a high-level endorser to get behind the instrument, often before it is really ready for the market. A recipe for disaster.

In return for free kit, Simmons would annually require my help at the enormous musical-instrument trade shows. Frankfurt, Los Angeles, and occasionally Tokyo play host annually to distributors, store-owners, and the general public in its thousands, all interested in musical gear of every conceivable description. I was enlisted to play the new offering from Simmons hourly, on the hour, in a cramped and packed show-booth. Elaborate claims were made in the marketing literature for these electronic drums, even though they would frequently stall on me, or perform erratically, and I could see unconnected wires trailing out of the back of the machinery. The inventor had not quite bundled them all back in during the last few minutes before the doors opened.

I spent months in my studio at home with hexadecimal MIDI code, trying to get reluctant instruments from several manufacturers to co-operate, and it was a heavy ride. But the results could be spectacular: 'Industry', 'Waiting Man', and 'No Warning' from King Crimson; 'Stromboli Kicks', 'Bridge Of Inhibition', and 'All Heaven Broke Loose' from Earthworks. In the 14 or 15 years I was actively on board, I suppose I gave rise to no more than a couple of dozen compositions that were absolutely a function of electronic percussion, and whose charm arose uniquely from that instrument. At about one a year, that's not a great output, given the time it took. But I don't regret a minute of it. I was driven then, as I am now, by both the necessity and the desire to find unlikely things to do on a drum kit.

I was changing, and I could sense the audience was changing with me. Some of the braver progressive rockers followed me over to the jazz side and took a keen interest in their discovery of this new less-obvious music, but more generally the rock guys were beginning to stay away. The jazz crowd would not really begin to attach themselves to the group until the all-acoustic second edition, with *A Part, And Yet Apart* in 1995. I was always too rock for the jazzers and too jazz for the rockers, so I was prepared for, and didn't mind, any of this. I was proud of my baby Earthworks and thought the music displayed skill, depth, and muscle. I was on a roll.

❏

It's about ten o'clock on a blustery late-October morning, 2001. A two-hour struggle through early-morning traffic, and I pull my car into the tiny parking lot of the converted church in North London. I unload drums. Earthworks is about to make its seventh CD, and it will be called, appropriately, *The Sound Of Surprise*. The first surprise is that the reasonably clean recording studio is deserted, despite my request for the engineer to get things started so all would be ready for the other guys arriving at about 1:00pm.

Between now and then there is plenty of technical dinking-about to do – reconfiguring the recording board to accommodate individual monitor sends, choosing the right place for everyone to be with regard to sight lines and acoustics, setting-up, tuning, miking and test-recording the drums and piano, checking the digital recording system.

Around 10:30 the assistant engineer turns up, 30 minutes later the engineer appears, and by 1:00 most problems are sorted and we're roughly on target. This is 30 years after *Fragile*, and unlimited company-paid studio time is a thing of the past. Here the clock is running, and I'm paying.

Musicians begin to wander in, are given coffee before they ask for it, and in varying degrees make clumsy conversation and gossip to fill what would otherwise have been an edgy silence. Everyone pretends there is nothing to it, this recording thing. But it is on record that you will be remembered. When your grandson sits at your knee in 25 years time and asks, "What did you do, grandpa?" and you reply, "I was a musician," and he says, "What kind of musician?", you'll reach up for a little slice of audio, put it in the machine, and you'd better be happy with what you hear when you play it to the little fellow, because *that is it*. Everything else is just your or someone else's foggy memory of what you or they think it used to be like. But the mics don't lie, at least not in jazz they don't. What you are, what you can do at that moment, what you did with those guys 25 years earlier: that was it. Today you'll make the stuff you leave behind, and you may never get a better opportunity to create something worth leaving behind than you will today.

The band is pretty well rehearsed, and we should not, by now, be worrying about where the fingers go. There is a very high level of musicianship here: hundreds of hours of study and practice and performance should ensure that the fingers go in the right place, but that alone will be no guarantee of any music worth listening to. I have just had us all out on tour for 15 dates learning this material, examining it, playing with it, tackling it from a number of different angles. We've discarded the one-way streets that all musicians visit from time to time and that lead nowhere, tried all manner of variables in phrasing, fingering, colour, tempo. We've selected, chosen, discarded. Today, all we have to do to create a work that has a life of its own, that is greater than the sum of its components, is to put it all together at the same time.

The human components are, as yet, far from settled. It's nearly 3:30 and we haven't recorded a note yet. Like jockeys at the Grand National, we warily circle the starting gate, each one reluctant to commit himself to being ... well, ready to play. Most time at this stage is rightly devoted to, and thirstily consumed by, the 'prima donna': the lead voice, the singer, or, in this band's case, the saxophone player. He, like all the players, needs to hear just the right blend of himself and the piano for intonation purposes, but he's hearing too much drums. Changing that mysteriously alters the bass-player's headphone balance. Having been settled ten minutes ago, he has now become unsettled again. I look at the clock, and hurriedly opt to work with pretty much whatever racket is spewing from my headphones.

We need to record three masters a day to get this thing in on budget. After many years experience, I've got a pretty shrewd idea of how many copies this will sell. I know the revenue it will create and the cost of making it. So I also know that at about this level of cost, I can take three days to record and three days to edit and mix the results, pay everyone a bit more than the going rate, and leave myself enough of a profit to make me want to do it again. I'm obsessed by the idea that the recording of this music, of my music, this artefact, must be profitable. No vanity publishing for me. No sir. I'm sure as heck only going to go through this kind of grief if people are going to buy the result with their hard-won money. Profit proves that the music is connecting, that it really means something to thousands of people out there, that you're not just playing to your own mother-in-law.

At last we're settled, and we run the first one down. It falls apart half way through. We complete a second take and go into the control booth for a listen. Here comes the hard stuff. As producer, I must listen sympathetically to everyone's contribution and take on board a thousand small and not so small suggestions of both a technical and musical nature that are flying around the room in the adrenalin rush of actually having completed the first piece of music.

The bass drum sounds woolly, the saxophone too harsh and nasal, the piano is sort of OK, the bass sounds like a rubber band, and could we have some more biscuits? Worse, the bass player thinks his sound is working and warns both engineer and producer away from the precise remedy that will tighten up the bottom end. I agree, knowing the bass sound can be improved another day. The engineer wants to know should he be bussing the reverb to separate channels or will a mono version be acceptable? And we haven't even begun to discuss the playing yet.

I need to make the technical adjustments speedily before we all go off the boil, so I recommend coffee out in the lounge and then pull them in one by one to make minor but all-important sound adjustments. Eventually, we're in a position to discuss the arrangement. All agree that it should diminuendo into the section at letter B, and it will need to gain muscle, but not tempo, as we return to the main melody for the last time. The sax will now go around three times as opposed to the agreed four, and there will be a break for the piano entry, which now has replaced the return to the head. If we cut the last four bars of D, that would make a better transition to E. Concentrate, Bill, concentrate.

Meanwhile, an ancillary discussion between the bassist and saxophonist has been getting heated on the phrasing of the main groove. The sax player feels it's too complex for him to work with effectively, but the bass regards his part as an indispensable component. Everyone, always, regards his part as an indispensable component. I referee this to a barely acceptable compromise. And so it goes on. Head reeling, I lead the group out to the studio again for take 3.

Its 4:30, and the music sounds lumpy. The pressure begins to mount as everyone realises that it'll be a late night. Take 3 falls apart again. Take 4 completes, but we forgot at least two of the five proposed improvements, and the drums misread the exit from the bridge. At this point, I think of and refer to myself only as "the drums". It seems less personal that way. Take 5 is our first clean one, and has been completed correctly, but I know there is better to come, so long as all parties remain focussed. We've been playing hard for two hours or so now and take ten minutes to wander about.

Another factor is coming into play here, and I'll have to tread carefully. Different players have differing stamina and are inclined to peak at different times. An electric bass player can go for a lot longer than an acoustic player on an aggressive piece. Fingers and wrists get tired on the upright instrument. Few horn players can blow all night with this level of concentration – lips and mouth go. The pianist may solo effortlessly and give his best on the first two or three takes, but, like most improvisers, the quality of thought wanes with the repetition, and that's what's happening here.

The pianist is saying he's done his bit – the last two takes did indeed have blinding solos from him – but the saxophone player is just settling into it. I get a firm feeling that the sax player would do this all night if he were allowed to. There is no more dangerous individual in a recording studio than the performer who doesn't know when he has done his best, which drags others through progressively worse takes because he's sure it's just around the corner, man. To avoid this breaking into open hostilities, I prevent them from going into the control room to listen to the probably unacceptable take 5 and encourage all by claiming unconvincingly that we'll have it in the next two. We settle down for the next shot at it.

I abort take 6 because I stumble irreparably in my own playing, something I haven't thought about for at least the last hour. But at last, take 7 seems good: all parts in the right place, intonation good, strong feel. But just as I put the sticks down on the drum kit with a triumphant flourish, I look up to see the sax player drawing a finger across his throat and the pianist throwing up his arms in exasperation.

The engineer says: "Do you want to keep it Bill? Because we haven't got space for another." Now I have to gamble. Do I take a 30-minute break to re-stripe the tape with sync-code, which will allow us to keep the successful take 7, albeit with all kinds of grief from the saxophone player, but the delay may cause a possibly fatal lapse of concentration? Or do I lose take 7 in the hope that we are within inches of a golden take 8, for which there will just be room on the tape, so long as the pianist's open section doesn't run too long? How long is too long? Double or quits. I gamble.

We record and complete a take 8 that has most parties happy most of the time. The pianist and I are probably past our best, but the saxophonist is triumphant and the bassist, who tends to hear only his own contribution, and thus will not become the band's record producer any time soon, doesn't care any more. Its 8:30, and we have the best version we can do, of that song, on this day, in the can. For better or for worse, that's what I will have to play my grandchildren.

Dinner is always a takeaway that I never want and takes forever to come. My digestive system, in its present highly acidic state, is saying: "I shouldn't if I were you." I eat without tasting it. Eventually I manage to cajole everyone downstairs for the easier, slower piece I've been saving for the post-prandial evening blow. It won't get any easier, but as the hours slip by I can let the pianist and bass player go as the saxophonist and I try as many alternative takes as the project can afford.

In the event, the cards fell broadly my way. The digital system worked well and fears about its capacity and reliability proved unfounded. The 15 gigs before the recording were a godsend, the cheap hotel was tolerable, and I even played mostly OK, although I cannot stand to listen to it just now, of course. Such a painfully accurate representation of my abilities needs some distance, needs sufficient time to forget where the bodies are buried.

My family seem joined in the idea that I should make this "easier", maybe "get some help", or take longer in the studio, in the mistaken belief that such measures would make things more comfortable. My instinct refutes this. It always is, will be, and must be uncomfortable. It's about the ability to deliver the goods in difficult and perhaps unpleasant surroundings. Being a performer doesn't mean being able to do it once perfectly in perfect conditions; rather, it means being able to do it imperfectly in imperfect conditions night after night. That's when you polish the diamond; that's the imperceptible removal of grime and accretion over hundreds of nights and thousands of concerts that will let your light shine forth more brightly. Polish what you have, polish and refine. Find it and refine it.

Thinking about it and talking about it and thinking about talking about it are no substitute for just doing it. And after 32 character-building years, you are just as good as you are: your light shines forth just as brightly as it does on those four days in Livingston Studios. Nowhere to run, nowhere to hide, and no one to help. A fifth day won't help or hinder; either way you are going to stare your mortality in the face and hope you can live with yourself a little easier than last time. For me, that's what making an album is.

Why do I like the CDs so much? The actual, physical CDs? Because *they got made*, dammit, and made to the best of my ability. Despite it all, despite the self-recrimination, the guilt, the resentment, the phone calls, the sleepless nights, and the endless opportunities to quit, the hoops and hurdles were all jumped and *the music got made*. The CDs stand as a permanent, undeniable testament to the fact that I got the job done. I triumphed, when I could have just packed up and gone home.

❏

Almost all musicians seem to perform under less than optimum circumstances, and it's probably best that way. Any tour manager will tell you, if you are unwise enough to ask, that any given musician is either starving hungry or completely stuffed from cramming down the remains of a chicken jalfrezi that, ordered at 7:10, has failed to materialise until 7:44, precisely 16 minutes before the 8:00 show. He either arrived at the gig too early and is complaining of boredom or has screeched into the car park with seconds to spare, utterly unable to compose his thoughts before the downbeat. Air-conditioning off, and the sweat gets in his eyes; on, and the music will blow off the stand, or he'll get a cold. Offer coffee, he wants tea; offer cash, he wants a cheque. It's reasonable to assume, therefore, that these people prefer it, and perform better, when things aren't right.

Ralph Towner is a brilliant guitarist and leader of the group Oregon, and a man with whom I made an album in 1996, about which we'll hear more shortly. He had signed to a distinguished German record label, which preferred their artists to record with a particular engineer in a particular studio in Oslo, Norway. Ralph, based in Seattle, Washington, explains that he would arrive after about an 18-hour journey, try, and fail, to sleep, and face the microphone at 11:00am the next day jetlagged out of his mind. He'll tell you that his entire body of recorded work has been extracted from him between stifled yawns and that he has never made a record yet on which he wasn't half asleep.

On the few occasions that circumstances are optimum, the results are often and strangely below par. Musicians complain because they want to have something else to think about, anything to stop that front part of the brain cutting in at the moment of performance and saying: "I wouldn't do that, if I were you. Most unwise." In the same way as the body can only feel one kind of pain at a time, the conscious mind seems to require distraction before it will leave its owner alone to get on with it.

At one time or another, most of us have arrived at a gorgeous concert hall with a spectacularly sumptuous hotel room within walking distance. You have the whole afternoon to relax, prior to a leisurely and professional soundcheck in which everything works, everyone can hear everyone, the coffee is fresh, and you can't think of anything to complain about. Then to dinner, in agreeable company, before the short walk back to the dressing room in a gentle and balmy

Mediterranean breeze. The sea shimmers in the distance, the crowd seems on fire with anticipation, and a pleasant phone-call home establishes that all is well back at Central Command. The gig is rubbish.

Conversely, the equipment arrives late in some dirty, smelly dump; the backstage sustenance you wouldn't offer a dog, and there's no coffee anyway, hot or cold. The soundcheck is a lot of shrieking in several languages to a background of a wall of electronic feedback, your head is killing you, Iberia lost your suitcase, and they are letting in the punters in seven minutes, so dinner is out of the question. What do you get? A blinding gig.

❑

Like football teams, rock or jazz groups can look awfully good on paper, but success or failure lies as much in the co-operative and interpersonal skills of the players as anything overtly musical. If there is any kind of a nominal leader, his job will sound easy: make the calls, put on the kettle, define the perimeters of the ballpark in which you're going to play, maybe produce a couple of pieces of music to indicate that, and then get out of the way. If the band has been offered an interesting blueprint, they'll only need half a prompting and they'll be off and running with it like hounds after a rabbit. Clearly defined blueprints for the *Discipline* King Crimson of 1980 and the first Earthworks of 1986 produced early results of high quality.

But it can get a little trickier than that when it comes to the personal relationships. People have varying abilities to cope with the musical lifestyle, and a couple of months on the road will throw light on collective or individual weaknesses with the force of a laser-beam. Personal and musical idiosyncrasies that may be acceptable for a few gigs can be intolerable after three months, and you don't want to threaten the very existence of your group, in which any number of people may have a considerable investment. Six weeks into a long American tour and nearing Texas in an insufferable heat wave, one band member decided, for reasons that never became entirely clear, that he needed a handgun. Couldn't buy one in New York state – the gun laws were too tough – but in Texas he'd be just fine. I can't remember the outcome of that one, but it all got extremely oppressive. If you want the tour to complete, it may be wise not to ask too many questions.

Sometimes there's grief even before the band hits the road. One musician decided to hold me to ransom – to jeopardise an entire American tour – over obscure details of a deal with EG Music Publishing. I can see him now, as the last call to board the plane to JFK is being made, arguing the fine points down the payphone with the group's equally stubborn manager, Sam Alder. I guess he got what he wanted, because we got on the plane, but only just.

On yet another happy day, guitarist Allan Holdsworth called me to pull out of a French tour with about four days notice. "Allan," I fumed, "you can't do this. Not at least without leaving me with a workable replacement." Allan, one of the most spectacularly individual guitar voices on the planet, would be unlikely to produce someone who could begin to come close to what he did.

"Funny you should mention that," he said, "because there is this bloke in Slough that I've been teaching a bit, and he could probably do it." There was indeed a bloke in Slough. Incredibly, he was willing, able, and available to learn this impossible music, come on this tour, and pretend he was Allan Holdsworth.

I'm not sure the deceit was perfect, but we got away with it. The 'unknown' John Clark stayed with us through to the end of that band in 1980 and wisely retired to the far calmer pastures of Sir Cliff Richard's group, where he has been ever since. To this day, there are those with not very good ears who think he doesn't exist and that John Clark was a pseudonym for an unhappy Holdsworth.

A decade later in Earthworks, I would have to separate a fight between two band members. It had been brewing for months. Iain, our saxophone player, had a beautiful young girlfriend called Jess, who, tragically, had contracted cancer. Separated from her on the road, he naturally attracted most of the available attention and sympathy. The

bass player in the band, an ex-London Underground train driver called Mick Hutton, with a dark personality that seems to attend members of that profession, took a dislike to the disproportionate amount of attention lavished on his colleague, and his niggling and needling at Iain reached a peak on stage at Bergen University in Norway.

We got to the dressing room at the end of the set, and they flew at each other. This dressing room happened to be the student canteen kitchens, a large facility with rows of stainless steel pots and pans hanging neatly above the work surfaces, next to an elaborate array of kitchen knives. We separated them as Mick had Iain's head pushed back into an industrial sink, knives dangling much too close at hand. The next 24 hours were spent shuttling between hotel rooms pleading for them to recant on the sworn intention to never play together again – I had a tour to do. It was like the Arab–Israeli peace negotiations, but somehow I got the only acceptable result, and we were on stage again the following night in Stavanger.

The situation with Jess came to a head the following month at a hot and dusty July Riverfest in St. Paul, Minneapolis. Her surgeon had been on the phone all week giving Iain updates on her progress, or lack of it, and eventually he said that if Iain wanted to see her again while there was still life in her body, he had to come now. I cancelled the West Coast leg of the tour, got him on a plane, and faced the evening's music as one-third of a gravely disabled trio.

I was all for cancelling the show that night, but our redoubtable keyboardist and horn player Django felt he could cope with playing not only his usual second harmony parts but also the lead lines themselves. These he had of course heard on many occasions but never played. In a remarkable feat of musicianship, he spent the gig running to and fro from his keyboards to the front stage mic, a position usually occupied by his absent partner, to deliver the necessary lead melodies and solos. The work of two was done by one, sight unseen, with astonishing musical skill. Iain returned to England and was married and widowed within a week. "But what do you *really* do?"

❏

Flexibility, adaptability, and good communication skills are, of course, basics for success in any walk of life, but in a successful jazz musician you will find these qualities at an exceptional level. Like Django, a good jazz player can make music out of anything, often with people he's only just met, and in the most unfamiliar of circumstances. Music at the highest level is not formulaic or standardised in any way. A little rehearsal may be necessary to get started, but after a while the musicians will inhabit the musical terrain in a unique way. With luck, your group will be producing a sound that others could not make, or would not make, or would not have thought of making – and then you're getting somewhere. But this highly personalised music becomes so because it is specific to that group of people, thus making a short-notice replacement of any one of them extremely difficult.

As a bandleader, the email you don't want is the one announcing illness or an unavoidable clash of dates. Still, in the fog of war, stuff happens, and it is still just about possible to find a true professional who will take the written music and an audio tape of the band, spend whatever time he can on his own with it – it's too late now to arrange a rehearsal – and tackle the whole thing unseen.

Earthworks' two-hour set was a long blow. There was written music, up to a point, but jazz happens off the page, and many a fine player has been lost, adrift in a barely legible sea of repeats, codas, and chord changes, while depping (deputising, or substituting) in some band or other. I found Julian Arguelles, a master of the saxophones, to do exactly this for me when the band's regular saxophone player, Tim Garland, was unavailable for some reason or other. Julian was about to depart for a tour of Mexico when I called him. My date in question was in Oxford the day he got back. Julian agreed to do it and was duly equipped with audio and charts. He was unable, however, to do any work on the material until the flight home from Mexico, which he doubtless spent with earphones strapped to his head, poring over the music. One long rehearsal at the venue the following night, and he was on the stand with people he only vaguely knew, in a band he'd only just heard of, as centre-stage principal voice, playing faultlessly. Exceptional work from an exceptional musician, and all of this for a lousy £300.

If I threw a party for my 20 greatest musical friends, past and present, the room would divide down the middle with ten on one side and ten on the other. The ten on my right would be millionaires with salaries so unaccountably large that more time would be spent in charitable dispersal of the stuff than its actual acquisition. The ten on my left would be among the finest jazz musicians in the world, with an average salary approximately equal to that of a supermarket checkout girl. And I would be standing in the middle.

The disparity is taken for granted in this business, but it nags and gnaws away at the less fortunate, sapping self-belief, corroding relationships that might otherwise be more supportive. It may cause bitterness, and it is the fount of the musician's advanced and perennial black humour.

The miracle is that most jazz musicians have the stamina to keep going in the face of such disparity. They may have deserted, insulted, or reneged on you, but then go out of their way to deliver a blinding performance that comes from so deep down that it makes your eyes water, and all is forgiven. They will do the impossible for free, because they love the music. As awkward as some may be, as neurotic as some may become, these brilliant musicians are capable of co-operating with me and others to produce the sort of music I was put on this planet to play. You may not want to take them home to your mum, but the best can play like angels.

11 IS IT DIFFICULT, WITH A FAMILY?

Harry Levett cultivates the malodorous, dishevelled look. His dark blue 'chauffeur' jumper – you know, the one with the shoulder pads – is always covered with a light smattering of dandruff. He is slightly deaf, so it is best to speak up if you feel the necessity to break the oppressive silence, and it is always stuffy in the Peugeot diesel taxis he favours. This trivial list of minor irritations is, however, easily outweighed by Harry's overwhelming advantage: he knows all the possible back roads to Heathrow Airport from darkest Surrey. He's been driving there in all conditions since before the M25 was but a twinkle in the eye of some highway planner. He's watched that road descend from acceptable flow to unpredictable jam to inevitable and wretched car park, and its presence or absence in his life matters to him not a jot. Heathrow was and remains always one hour away, come overturned truck, multiple pile-up, ice, snow, hell, or high water. You can set your watch by it, and I do.

I give Carolyn a hug and a kiss, whisper an unconvincing "I'll be home before you know it", and am relieved to be on my way. As I watch the family recede in the mirror, the car picks up speed and the tour has started. By the end of the lane, I've survived the first couple of minutes of a nine-week stretch. The mere thought of the 63 days ahead produces a lump in the pit of my stomach. I fool myself that now, separated from domestic attachments, I'll be free to concentrate on one thing only – the job in hand. It is a complex feeling that every soldier, sailor, sportsman, salesman, indeed anyone who travels for a living will recognise: at once a red-blooded enthusiasm to get to the work that he has been anticipating, and for which he has been preparing for months, while shaken with a consuming love for the ones left behind and stirred with an equal dash of guilt at having left them behind.

At least others have some excuse for this desertion – to protect the country, perhaps, or oil the wheels as a captain of industry – but me, I am going off to *play music*, for God's sake; barely an excuse, and certainly no kind of reason that could possibly justify abandoning wife and young family for nine weeks. And increasingly it is to play music I really love and don't even earn much money from, so I can hardly shelter behind the old 'putting bread on the table' riff. Ah, the guilt, the guilt. It was with me from the first time a crestfallen girlfriend had unwisely shrieked "It's either me or the drums!" and will remain with me until I hang up the sticks. It is a guilty pleasure, this musical fantasy, masquerading as some sort of a job. I've managed to incorporate it, to equip it with health benefits, salary cheques, and VAT returns, just like the real thing, but I fool nobody, least of all myself.

The idea that I might be left to get on with it, to face my touring and performing demons in the best manner I can devise, with full concentration and all the strength I can muster – that too is an illusion. Domestic life pulls and tugs with all its strength in the direction of normalcy, of routine, of dutiful paternity. Fathers are people who go out in the day, come home at night, fix bicycle tyres on Saturdays, and are there for parents evenings and sports days. Professional life pulls with equal strength in the opposite direction, toward uniqueness, exaggerated behaviour, extreme endeavour, standing out from the crowd.

Musicians may be self-centred, monastic, or profligate, and capable of charming thousands, but usually only with the aid of a small arsenal of psychiatric or psychotropic weaponry to keep any one of a long list of demons at bay. Many a useful player has foundered on the rocks between the public and the private, has confused the two channels, and become disorientated in the fog. All those music schools are noticeably short on the provision of any navigational aid. I know these are dangerous waters. I know these ideas will ricochet around my head for much of this tour, the same as they always have on previous tours, slugging it out in an inconclusive boxing match, at the end of which these two old adversaries, the public and the private, both bloodied but neither bowed, will slink back to their corners to fight another day.

Even on the other side of the world, you're never far from domestic issues. Modern telecommunications see to that. Computer, phone, and fax deliver with startling efficiency, fresh off the press, a long litany of school horrors, accidents, near-accidents, real or imagined effronteries, domestic crises, hospital visits, animal deaths, sibling unpleasantries, and gardening upsets. I don't blame the messenger, or particularly want her to stop, or particularly care whether the news is 'good' or 'bad'. It comes with the turf: it just is. Even now, at the end of a good innings, the first thing my eyes search for on entering any hotel room is the red flashing message-waiting light on the phone (or, in the old Holiday Inns, on the wall). Only when I am sure there is no message can I relax.

Time was when communication across continents allowed for cooling-off periods, for moments of reflection both before pen was put to paper and during the putting of pen to paper. No such luxury now exists. Voluminous quantities of domestic grief pour unedited from fax, from email, and directly from the mouth of the telephone receiver. Iain Ballamy, Earthworks' first tenor player and specialist in musicians' black humour, describes a call to his wife and mother of his young family as a call to the war department, and rather than commencing with the tentative but marginally hopeful "Is everything all right?" prefers to get straight to it with the utterly hopeless "Is anything all right?".

"Daddy's going on his holidays again" is Carolyn's default explanation to the children as daddy and Harry slip away down the drive. Daddy has about 45 holidays a year. She also encourages the confusion, evident enough in the lives and heads of most musicians, between the words 'work' and 'play'. Most children understand work as something less agreeable than play, but musicians evidently play their instruments at work, and go to work to play. Daddy, explains mummy, is always going away to play on his 'holidays', so whichever way you skin it, he is bound to be having more fun than the child's poor suffering mother, who never seems to go anywhere further than Sainsbury's.

Mostly, this is all understood as the light-hearted banter of domestic life – the gentle and playful surface that disguises the darker undercurrent. But occasionally, my ability to absorb the guilt will be compromised by a particularly bad day with the demons. The circuit will overload, and sparks will fly. Every musician can tell you about the five-minute phone call home, anticipated and begun in good humour, that mysteriously turns into a £58 69-minute analysis of Where It All Went Wrong, complete with tears and long sullen silences, broken only, if you were in France or parts of Eastern Europe before about 1975, by the frequent interruptions of that dragon at the switchboard, the hotel operator.

"I'm not actually out here for my health, you know. I do do some work," you say.

"Oh yes? So how come that's a party I can hear in the background?"

"Oh, that. That's not a party. Its just 30 young people with female company emptying the combined mini-bars of 30 rooms at three in the morning in the tour manager's suite."

(Rock tour managers usually get a suite. They buy so many rooms in the hotel that the reservation people will often throw in a suite for free, which of course the tour manager assigns to himself. The musicians, his employers, relieved that they won't have to wade through empty beer cans and over-flowing ashtrays in their own rooms, usually overlook this privileged accommodation so long as the 'entertainment officer' makes the suite fully available to his superiors for rest and recreation as required.)

Click. Brrrr. "Operator, what the hell are you doing? You've just cut me off!"

"She doesn't want to talk to you any more. Maybe she doesn't love you any more ..."

"Don't be idiotic. And don't listen in to private conversations. This is the second time now, for God's sake. Get this number again – zero, zero, four, four ..."

There is an erroneous assumption that musicians like to stand around talking about music, whereas the two favoured topics of conversation at check-in or baggage claim are, in my experience, telecommunications and luggage. Some years back, there was the introduction of the phone card, or global calling card, or something similar. I had one that required the input of 23 digits into the phone. Not easy when it's late, early, or you're inebriated – that is, most of the time. Twenty-three digits later, the pitiful engaged tone tells me my teenage daughter is gassing at the other end.

I imagine the life of a 20th-century musician in the archive of a black museum of communication 30 years hence. The visitor will file listlessly past glass exhibition cases containing, in order: telegrams; postcards; love letters; the red light from a Holiday Inn wall; the clicking unit-counter under the front desk of a 1970 French pension; a tableau of a disagreeable Polish hotel phone operator depicted hard at work listening in; fax machines; in-room fax machines; bedside phones; bathroom phones; early laptops; email; in-room broadband advisories; a VOIP-enabled laptop; cell phone; and iPhone, right up to the present day. All these items would speak more about the life of a musician than any similar archive of his personal instruments or effects, because much of it was about staying in touch with home.

❑

The subject of family life and its attendant responsibilities in a book about a rock musician is about as welcome as a flat tyre on the tour bus. The modern musician tends not to bring his domestic or personal life into the dressing room, unless invited in a rare moment of interest in anything other than the band, the show, or the album. No rules here, really: some are more forthcoming than others, some more interested to hear about it than others. But generally, a front of relentless optimism prevails among the men who are 'spoken for', in a world where the admission of a problem or even a difficulty can ultimately cost you your job.

Most beginners in a music-industry relationship seem to fall at the first hurdle. The girlfriend has typically managed to survive the rebuffs of the first few weekends, but it will inevitably dawn on her that he will be working most weekends of their relationship if he is to make any headway at all in his chosen line of endeavour. The minuscule amount of glamour she thought she may have detected, the occasional glimpse of celebrity on the horizon, the possibility of a ride in a limo – these things in no way compensate.

Not unreasonably, the wiser partners throw in the towel before becoming seriously committed. Better then than after the arrival of a child or children. You know, all that sex, drugs, and rock'n'roll can't be interrupted by the inconvenient appearance of a few sprogs. The cliché, reinforced in a thousand hagiographies, is of the rock party-animal with a girl and an unwanted infant in every port. At one such port, mother and child turn up backstage 19 years later to present child to father for the first time. All parties kiss and make up; tearful smiles in celebrity magazines; the daughter of this liaison goes off to be an actress and the boy to join a band. Just like dad. *Party on, dude.*

Would that life were so simple. It's a recurring fault of mine that I take everything much too seriously, and far from last on my list of things to be taken seriously is my family. My experience in this arena is, as a consequence, infinitely more prosaic and mundane, and my one wife and one family have put as much into this man's modest achievements as could reasonably be expected. Infinite patience, stamina, and flexibility – because the plans are going to change, they always change – a familiarity with single-parenting, some skill with a screwdriver, adequate belief in the intrinsic worth of her husband's occupation – these are minimum requirements on her side. On his side, infinite patience, stamina and flexibility, absolute belief in the value of his work, and coming home when he says he'll come home – these seem to me to be minimum requirements for a relationship in the music business to exist for more than ten minutes.

The institution of marriage is an astonishingly flexible beast, and there seems to be no end to the tailor-made variations on the basic theme that my colleagues have come up with that appear to work adequately. Consenting adults without children and with some imagination can and do devise elaborate ways by which their union might survive long separations and huge phone bills, and yet strengthen at the same time. But it's going to need a whole lot more effort than just a phone call home.

I write from a personal male perspective, but the problems and experiences of road-life would seem to be genderless and interchangeable between the genders. In my day, rock music was predominantly peopled by partnered males on long tours wrestling with the absence of girlfriends or wives, or single men wrestling with the problems of too much choice. In a more recent age of Madonna, Kylie, and the increasing feminisation of the culture, the balance, certainly in pop music, has been tipped in favour of the female singer-songwriter, with a male partner just as likely in domestic support.

Sometimes the partner comes too. If she's the star, he may be in the band if musical, or perhaps involved in the administrative or technical side if not. If he's the star, she may be useful in any number of areas. In jazz, a common ploy is for her to become his manager, with a number of obvious attendant advantages. The manager–wife can be a fearsome tigress in defence of her husband's interests, as many a promoter or agent can testify. Back in the wealthier rock world, Rolling Stone Ronnie Wood's wife Jo frequently accompanied him on tour. In her case, she told *The Sunday Times*, the job involved getting Ronnie to interviews and "sorting out his clothes, and so on. [In 2006] I earned

$5,000 [£2,700] a week from the tour".[1] Clearly the rest of us are in the wrong game.

But in the absence of meaningful work on tour, just hanging around your partner is a non-starter. An itinerary that reads like a travel brochure – Paris, Rome, Milan, Zurich – can look mighty fancy when you're the American girlfriend of a lighting man on a King Crimson tour and you've never been out of state before. But a couple of weeks in, her stomach is playing up, she hasn't had any time alone with her fella since the tour started, and she hasn't actually seen anything of these places. The dawning realisation that she isn't going to be able to get Kleenex at four in the morning in Bilbao is the nail in the coffin, and she's headed for the next plane home, with or without our lighting man.

At least the principal combatants have the couple of hours a night of activity to look forward to. Non-combatants have neither control nor responsibility, their lives slipping away as observers on the fringe of the pantomime. If one girlfriend or wife comes, her mate will be sidelined by the rest of his colleagues in the decision-making process. Other females remaining at home may understandably feel less privileged, causing resentment. Best, maybe, if all partners come, at the risk of the whole thing descending into an elaborate mobile holiday-camp.

The complexities involved in maintaining a solid relationship inevitably increase tenfold with the arrival of dependent children. I'm increasingly of the opinion that there are but two types of adult on the planet: those with children and those without. The distinction between male and female is as nothing compared to the distinction between adults with and without children. Adrian Belew is a father; Robert Fripp is not. When my children were small, there was always a cookie-monster in Adrian's suitcase when he came to visit. When Robert came to visit, his idea of fun was to tell the same children at the same age that their necks were so pretty and appealing that he'd like to sink his teeth into them and lick their blood. Their mother was speechless for days.

Musicians of both genders with more or less complicated family considerations compete with those with minimal or no direct family concerns. This goes entirely unrecognised in professional magazines, where the music stars swan through life with never a mention of the wear and tear that such swanning might cause on the family unit. The non-combatant partner must learn to live with the spouse's habitual absence from family occasions and social events. He or she may miss the first time his child walks or talks, the school play, the soccer match. There will be a long list of missed parent–teacher evenings, entries to and exits from the doctor's surgery or headmaster's office, high school proms, first dates, driving tests, exam results, achievements and failures grand and petty.

In short, participation in all the milestones on the unfolding path of his children's lives may be jeopardised because of his insistence on playing his new songs in a dump seven hours drive away to the proverbial three men and a dog. What price, then, artistic vision? Up until children, it's remarkably easy to dream of changing the world with your music. Exactly how far are you going to persist with those dreams? Around the time you hear those baby cries, your horizons will shrink, maybe the world doesn't need changing after all, and a week's worth of work with the function band sounds suddenly convenient and very well paid. Ah, the guilt, the guilt. You can feel guilty for abandoning your family or guilty for abandoning your dreams. Take your pick.

Money can grease the wheels. Once I'd got over the trauma of my post-*Fragile* £16,000 tax demand, I managed, more through luck than judgment, to stabilise the flow of income, to smooth out the highs and lows, and to produce a salary on which we were always comfortable and never wealthy. As a keen beneficiary of the Copyright Act and its various amendments, my performances on record and my recorded compositions have generated quarterly royalties sufficient to produce an annual salary approximately equivalent to that of a section-leader in The Chicago Symphony. I've had the same salary for about 30 years and, unusually among musicians, have had little need to consider the financial implications of any course of action. There was always enough for me to do exactly what I wanted, musically. My good fortune can also be attributed to my manager Sam Alder, who dispensed wise personal financial advice to me, even while dodging a High Court writ from Robert Fripp for questionable business practices at EG Management.

So, before children, and despite the coolness of the welcome from Robert, Carolyn occasionally came on tour with the Crim, and later there was even the odd moment of glamour in New York or Los Angeles when we'd managed to get the babysitter in place. The occasional backstage natter with Sting, a dinner with Peter Gabriel, picking up most of Phil Collins's young daughter Jolie's omelette from the dining-room floor of a Swiss hotel, abandoned there in a fit of pique – these things may not sound like much, but briefly made her feel that she belonged, and a little goes a long way when you're the one keeping the home fires burning.

Long-distance relationships are complicated under any circumstances, but there is perhaps an added piquancy in the musician's case. In most professions there is probably some sort of regular pay attached, and the globe-trotting partner can, with some legitimacy, talk about putting bread on tables. The self-employed musician, however, may only be able to come up with some guff about "investing in his own future", or "this one's for free, but I should get paid for the next one", or "the tour made a bit of a loss".

Personal, financial, and emotional difficulties evaporate in the morning warmth – the sun shines relentlessly in the Industry of Human Happiness. Of course, our celebrities are hard at work doing an excellent job of breaking up, breaking down, drying up, drying out, rehabilitating, being outrageous, and being handsomely remunerated by the tabloids for their efforts. That's their job. But I'm talking about real people, the kind that bleed when you prick them.

❑

It took me a long time, as a young man, to register that some people don't want to have children. It never occurred to me. Being a father was a given in my world. Patterned as I was by a normal – and I'm not even going to put that into inverted commas – 50s childhood, paternity was as inevitable to me as night following day. Unfashionably, I have no complaints about my treatment as a child, and I assumed I would proceed down the path that my parents had walked with me, at least until I spotted some urgent need for a diversion.

Only difference was, the circumstances by 1968 were somewhat changed. Now there was something called free love. There was the contraceptive pill, the Summer Of Love, psychedelia, endless American tours. Even for a straitlaced, bookish student of the instrument like me, I was going to have to strap some blinkers to the side of my head, learn to say no, and find a life partner who could help guide me through it. She would need stamina, constancy, love, and patience in no particular order. No matter how much you tell her it's boring out here, an early-morning jet to Chicago for a two-hour concert with your mates, and a well-catered after-show party to follow, doesn't sound too shabby when all you have is the supermarket and nappies.

Carolyn and I were adolescent sweethearts. We met on her occasional trips to the UK from Boston. Her English cousin happened to be my best friend, and it was his family that had put up with my first public appearance on that Swiss holiday in Saint-Cergue. Carolyn had an American accent, American legs, and American teeth – three irresistible attributes that would make me a great deal of headway with my English mates. She loved music and pronounced England to be cool. The complete package far exceeded my modest requirements, and around 1966–67 we began to take our first hesitant steps in the not entirely compatible worlds of love and music. We learned about the music industry together and from scratch.

She was around to wave off the van, Big Red, and she was there when it returned at three in the morning. She was there when I brought back the test-pressing of my first album with Yes, and breathlessly we set up a record-player to hear it in a corner of the Fulham Road restaurant in which she worked. She was there in Courtfield Gardens

THE AUTOBIOGRAPHY / 11

when we huddled around the radio to catch our first broadcast on the John Peel show, and she was there when the band shared a house in Fulham. We had a trial separation for a while, during which she returned to her parents in San Diego, but it didn't last long, and she was there when Yes finally turned up in Los Angeles at the beginning of the group's long and distinguished career in North America.

For a couple of years at the beginning of Yes, we were housed in London at 50A Munster Road, Fulham. Jon Anderson and Jenny, Chris Squire and Sheila, Carolyn and I, and guitarist Peter Banks – we made a turbulent and classically dysfunctional family, with a permanently occupied bathroom and a permanently full kitchen sink. If you took the classic 80s British TV sitcom *The Young Ones* as a template, you wouldn't be too far wrong. Confined to barracks, we weren't actually allowed to go anywhere in case Jon's masterful haranguing of promoters produced a gig, which could be at 24 hours notice. Like a fire crew, we'd slide down a greasy pole – something the band continued to do for most of its subsequent career – pile in to Big Red, and charge up the motorway, all bells clanging. Some of the girls may or may not have been on board – no one would have commented.

When I arrived at the court of the Crimson King in the 70s, it was to find that partners on the road were actively discouraged. Girls, it was thought, would probably mollify and calm their boyfriends into being entirely reasonable, and this would have a detrimental effect on a close-knit masculine operation that relied on creative friction to produce the necessary spark. It was suspected that they would distract and offer balm, an entirely welcome contribution in most travelling organisations, but unhelpful when you need the wire-wound, over-caffeinated, testosterone-fuelled musicians to deliver the aural psychosis that everyone was expecting, six nights a week, five weeks straight.

There was an element of wisdom in this. The hopelessly muddled, mixed-gender, culturally confused, Anglo-French Gong, with whom I had enjoyed a brief sojourn, was a travelling misunderstanding, a mobile love affair in which no one was quite sure who was in love with whom. At breakfast the next morning, body-language would speak volumes. There was no time, as I recall, for the discussion of music – all discussion time was allotted to cross-national rows about, of course, real and perceived inter-band infidelities and, more pressingly, where to find a hotel that night that all could agree on. These arguments would have been blazing, except it's difficult to blaze in lousy English and worse French. I had the privilege of a couple of months with this lot, the end of which involved 12 people up in a 12-seater van with neither snow-tyres nor chains in Norway in December 1974. Carolyn was there for that one, too.

If the attitude to females and family on the road was wholly different between King Crimson and Gong, then Genesis was something else again. Here was the quintessentially family-minded band. By 1976, we were mostly childless young marrieds, and wives or girlfriends were encouraged on the road. Genesis treated touring as an extension of a trip to Harrods. All necessary requirements were laid on, the partners behaved themselves and didn't interfere unduly, and a jolly around North America was undertaken with the same kind of excitement that might have been engendered by an orderly picnic in Richmond Park.

Genesis were exceptionally considerate to employees, from the high-status sideman such as myself or, later on, drummer Chester Thompson and guitarist Darryl Steurmer, down to the lowly third drum roadie from the left. Even girlfriends of sidemen were welcomed into the bosom of this extended family, an unheard-of generosity. Easy, I hear you say, when you're a loaded and successful rock band like Genesis with private planes and plenty of manpower to help. But this warmly accommodating, family-friendly attitude had existed from the beginning in that particular band – it was just built into the fabric. This was ceaselessly pointed out to me by Carolyn in her many unfavourable comparisons of life as a camp-follower between King Crimson and Genesis: the one was bleak, spartan, and unwelcoming (my wife was never entirely sure if Fripp actually knew her name, and nor was I; he certainly never used it), the other generous and gently accommodating.

Without a similar culture of the permanent extended-family often found in rock, and with about a tenth of the money floating around, jazz finds it hard to match the warmth of the unusually gracious Genesis. Jazz gigs are usually Easyjet, a bumpy van, and a curly sandwich – not much worth following the camp for there. By the time I got to jazz, I had children who needed their mother at home, and anyway, absences were shorter – the typical tour is about three days.

Now under self-management, I and many of my colleagues spend more time working from home. We arrange gigs, rehearsals, airline tickets. We write music and email it to colleagues for comment or improvement. We record, promote, and sell CDs and register their contents with collection agencies. We monitor the activities of our competitors, evaluate our own headway, run websites, upload music to YouTube, and pay our taxes. In short, we attend to the thousand-and-one jobs requiring attention and save the 20 per cent management commission we would otherwise be paying someone else to do this for us. We do as much of this as we have stamina for, then some more – and we need to, just to stay visible in a highly competitive and perpetually changing global market.

Working from home brings a new dynamic to the central domestic relationship. When Harry Levett comes up the drive now, it's more likely a sigh of relief I hear as we pull away down the drive at the beginning of a rare tour. I can hear Carolyn thinking: "At last the old man is going somewhere – I can get the house to myself." Achieving the right sort of balance between the professional and the domestic has been a leitmotif purring through my entire musical existence. The energy and time spent dovetailing the two used to revolve around departures, absences, and returns, and has imperceptibly come to revolve instead around the 24/7 nature of the business, office hours, and adhering to them.

It used to be – in my mind, at least, if not in Carolyn's – that my work had precedence over domestic obligations. Somewhere in the last five, maybe ten years, it shifted. Now – in my mind, at least, if not in

Carolyn's – the domestic takes precedence over the professional. Work is now required to fit in around domestic issues, which are legion. Children, although grown, have not quite departed, and life seems to be more fully occupied with them than ever. Like others, we have been visited by serious illness in immediate family members. Where 20 years ago, a two-month tour would have been relatively easily absorbed into the domestic fabric of schools, birthdays, and the general chaos, now a two-week jazz tour seems to be all but beyond us.

My competitors – and we are all competing for gigs – never seem to go home. On an endless tour, the Americans in particular are fuelled with a work ethic beyond comprehension, their zeal paraded in the glossy music magazines as an example to us all. "Look, this is how it should really be done. Sweat, man, sweat!" In drum-magazine land, the domestic complexities of illness, bereavement, breakdown, even general wear and tear, are banned, swept under the carpet. Occasionally they peek out, inadvertently introduced by musician X who lets slip that his four-year-old daughter lives back East now, so "I don't see her as much as I'd like, but sometimes her mom brings her out on tour," or musician Y who "never did quite get to see my father before he passed away".

I don't much want to be associated with pop psychology, and I doubt that I'm much good at self-analysis, but I think it quite plausible that I was in a more or less permanent state of mild depression for a few years since the end of King Crimson around 1996. The departure from the band itself was neither here nor there, but one of the major symptoms that caused that departure – a seeming inability to run my life without endless domestic negotiation – was closer to the culprit.

There it was, right there: the classic male loss of control. There was the sudden and uncomfortable awareness that I wasn't particularly enjoying my music-making any more, and then that I wasn't particularly enjoying anything any more. It was certainly possible to live with it most of the time, but it was at its worst on high days and holidays. This seemed to be bracketed on my left by the gentle insistence that I might "do less" or "have a slower year", when I was anyway teetering on the brink of professional sclerosis, struggling to maintain 50 gigs a year, and on my right by the impossibility of living with the ever-changing nuances of complicated domestic arrangements. The whole combined on occasion to produce a deep resentment, and I know Carolyn felt something very similar from her side. We were both aware that it probably made us intermittently disagreeable.

Artists shouldn't be family men, they say: two incompatible skills, runs the argument. The essence of the artistic existence is relentless selfishness, self-examination, self-absorption. The successful parent, by contrast, sublimates self-centredness and looks out of himself to his family for sustenance. Maybe my exasperation with domestic requirements was at last a kind of proof – extrapolated by reverse engineering – that I contain a modicum of artistry. On the good days, I was simply embarrassed by my recurrent self-pity, the most loathsome of tendencies, which I urged others to avoid while I indulged myself. On the bad, I could find no words to describe the blackness, so thank God I had Carolyn to calm the fevered brow.

Mercifully, the bad days were few, and receded. As I reach the end of the race, and have learned to say no, life is regaining a semblance of being again under control. Carolyn and I have shared amazing experiences, extraordinary company, failures, successes, and heard a skinful of great music along the way. There has been no institution I can think of that would have held me together with a firmer, steadier hand than marriage, and no mechanism like the interplay of a family to recall me, reconstitute me, refresh me.

If music is to be no more than athletics, then this father of three cannot compete with the unencumbered athletes of the percussion world, all teeth and tattoos, bicep'd and oiled, thirsting for 300 dates a year on the road. If, however, it is about life rather than sport, then all of life's accoutrements will be included and reflected in the way one conducts one's musical life. The private will be reflected in the public character, and there will be a humanity in the music.

12 DO YOU SOMETIMES PLAY WITH OTHER PEOPLE?

The enterprising bandleader will have an encyclopedic knowledge of who's who on the European jazz-festival summer circuit, and he will spend a substantial part of his time ensuring that the buyers know that he's in the market, in one guise or another. In the UK, jazz festivals in London, Bath, Brecon, and Cheltenham are highly prized. Berlin, Marciac, Sous Les Pommiers in France, Vienna, Madrid, and countless other European festivals also have imaginative rosters of artists and, sometimes, spectacular settings. There is not much that can beat a large attentive crowd on a balmy evening, a beautiful stage and piano at the foot of the floodlit medieval castle, and an excellent dinner on conclusion, such as you might expect at, for example, Jazz en la Costa in Almunecar, Spain.

Canada has a string of well co-ordinated events across the country, ending up at the Montreal jazz festival. Only the USA appears to have difficulty welcoming European artists. The European circuit has for years welcomed American stars and lavished upon them the lion's share of the budget, while the local players prowl patiently waiting for crumbs, but the situation does not pertain in reverse. The vast majority of US festival slots are for US musicians, and so far Earthworks, for one, has been able to grace only Chicago's fine Ravinia Festival, despite weeks of club touring and plenty of visibility in that great country.

These summer events are well sponsored, organised, and paid, and thus are on everyone's shopping list. There is a furious jockeying for position among artists, agents, and buyers for most of the previous year, culminating in some sprightly horse-trading at the (recently deceased) International Association of Jazz Educators conference in North America and the (very much alive) International Live Music Conference in London in March, which acts as a clearing house for performers to be finalised on all the major festivals. If the artist wants an entrée to the better festivals, he will need to be offering something special or unique for that summer or, better still, for specifically targeted events that summer.

Regular touring groups tend to lose out over sometimes spurious and unlikely combinations of artists that will read well in the festival brochure and provide the necessary cutting-edge feel to proceedings so beloved of the fashion-conscious sponsors. If your group can count among its number John The Baptist on nose-flute, ex-President Clinton on tenor saxophone, a couple of tabla players, and a rock guy on guitar, preferably Andy Summers from The Police, you will do well on the festival circuit that summer.

Furthermore, if this ensemble were to write a unique piece especially for the occasion – perhaps 'The Lights Of Bratislava: Suite' to be premiered, naturally, in Bratislava, prior to further renditions in Fréjus ('The Lights Of Fréjus') or Barcelona ('The Lights Of Barcelona') – then you may expect rapid promotion up the schedules and to be accorded all the honours that small cities can bestow upon visiting composers who write music about and for them. Some of the material may at best be questionable, especially since this is an under-rehearsed premiere – President Clinton couldn't make it in time, and the tabla players had visa problems – but hey, it looks good on paper, and the whole town is talking.

The morning following the performance in Bratislava, bleary-eyed musicians and helpers of one sort and another begin to straggle into breakfast. This has long been my favourite time of the day on the road.

I'm usually the first down and, fearing the boredom of my room, the last to leave. Some are bleary-eyed because they have arrived early from the USA and will be performing tomorrow, while some are just bleary-eyed from the previous night's efforts on stage, or in the bar, or both.

Andy Summers, John The Baptist, and the one tabla player who finally made it are here. They played last night. A couple of tables to my right is a leather-jacketed old roué from Los Angeles, trim moustache, substantial middle-aged spread, telling his 30-something female companion the old Buddy Rich jokes we've all heard a thousand times before. "Only two kinds of music he hated, country *and* western" … "Hey, mister, I *am* the band … ha ha." The corner of the woman's mouth turns up slightly, indicating no more than a polite interest. He'll be playing tonight. God spare me from having to dine out on Robert Fripp stories when I'm 64.

On a quiet table by the window, with a great view of the river, is the brilliant New York tenor saxophonist and composer Bob Mintzer. He's on his own, and if I had half an iota of confidence I'd be sidling over, introducing myself. "Love your music man, hey, you're *killin'* … must get together sometime … how long are you in town for … maybe I could give you my number?" The luxury of my advancing years affords me exemption from this ordeal, but for young acolytes this is not optional.

Within the music community, networking, even at breakfast, is a sacred obligation. It is at jazz festivals that young aspirants meet potential future employers, that sidemen meet leaders, that leaders can earmark young Turks. Mintzer is a leader. He moves in a prestigious world populated with highly advanced sight-reading musicians, so my lack of skills in that area also permits me to avoid disturbing him as I slip past for another pastry. In the unlikely scenario of his calling me for a tour with small or large ensemble, or a record, would I even have the confidence to accept? What if I didn't make it? If I did do well, imagine the confidence-boost as I dropped that one into conversations with my British friends. The only way you'd find out, of course, is by just doing it.

There have been too many occasions where I've bitten off more than I can chew, when I've 'just done it', and my palms can get sticky just running through them in my mind. At the 1983 Percussive Arts Society International Convention in Knoxville, Tennessee, I showed up with the new-fangled electronic drums. Everyone was keen to hear these unwieldy beasts, to see if they lived up to the marketing hype. I could have just told them they didn't, without having to demonstrate that they were practically unplayable, as I launched fearlessly into a heavy-fisted version of Max Roach's superb 'The Drum Also Waltzes'.

On another occasion, rising Philadelphia bass player Jamaaladeen Tacuma invited me to play on his album when I was on tour in the USA. The only available slot was on the way to JFK after my last gig, so the job was done with one foot and half my head out of the country and almost home. The studio was so small my suitcases took up much of the space in the control room – there wasn't much in the way of a lobby. I didn't know what we were going to play, and there were few clues coming from the all-African-American remainder of the band. I was having trouble understanding the few comments that were going to and from the control room as I set up the house drumset and put my own set of cymbals on the stands. There was music playing on the speakers that I gathered was the thing we were going to play. Acting purely on instinct, and without further guidance, I launched into the first thing that came to mind, and wondered again about my fragile nervous system.

An altogether grander 1994 project centred on Neil Peart, the charming and successful drummer with Canadian rockers Rush, who had taken it upon himself to make a series of recordings of Buddy Rich's music. Buddy had passed away in 1987, but The Buddy Rich Orchestra was still very much a working organism, featuring several of the musicians who were in the band when their leader was alive, most notably tenor saxophonist Steve Marcus. The idea was for an A-list of the most celebrated drummers of the day to do a couple of tunes each from the standard Rich Orchestra repertoire. The resulting CDs were to be called *Burning For Buddy*, and time was duly booked at the Power Station recording studio in Manhattan.

For reasons best known to himself, Neil thought I'd be suitable for this project and got in touch to explain the plan. He suggested a couple of tunes, and I, with what must have seemed like arrogance but in fact was that old insecurity, said fine, but how about one of his and one of mine? Neil asked for a demo of my proposed tune, which was duly approved, and I went off to see English trumpeter and arranger Chris Batchelor to have the composition transcribed.

The night before the sessions passes in the by-now increasingly common fog of red wine, jetlag, and Temazepam, and I struggle to my feet, exhausted, at about seven the next morning to the mood-music of Manhattan traffic. When I arrive at the Power Station, it is like a dentist's waiting room, with half a dozen of the best drummers in the world sitting around leafing through magazines and, on a variable scale, dealing with their demons. Steve Gadd and Steve Ferrone are up next, Kenny Aronoff and Simon Phillips have completed, and I will be next up after Ferrone.

Each musician has been allotted two hours to move his drums in, set-up and soundcheck, rehearse each tune once, and then record them. To the layman this might seem like a comfortable schedule – to the crack studio musicians like Gadd and Ferrone it might appear a little tight. But it seems to me, with my leisurely art-rock background in which it took two hours to get the sandwich order straight, let alone move any instruments into a studio, that I have a better chance of getting a camel through the eye of a needle than I have of completing this on time.

Ferrone comes out of the dentist's office with a look of acute relief. The crew throw his drums more or less unceremoniously out of the room and mine into the place that his had previously occupied. The mics are repositioned, and thanks largely to a good studio, a great drumset, and an exceptional recording engineer, we spend no time at all making sure the drum sound is up to scratch. In front of me is a world-famous big-band stuffed with excellent jazz musicians. Behind me is a control-room with Peart producing. The place is jammed with players peering down at the proceedings, probably just interested to hear the only original composition on the album, but who are, I am convinced, secretly hoping the British guy will never get off the runway.

We start with my tune 'Lingo'. I hand out the music to the 16 players. The high trumpet does what I'm told the high trumpet always does: he speed-reads through his chart to see if there are enough high notes to justify his ride in on the subway. These are the high-wire artists of the jazz orchestra and they must be allowed to display their skills, or they may become petulant. There is a questioning frown on the bass player's face, but he doesn't say anything, so I pretend I haven't noticed. We run it down once, and I'm cleared for take off.

I count the tune in and we lurch down the runway, but 30 seconds in there is a malfunction in the trumpets and trombones, and we have to abort. The written music is intricate and involves some complex rhythmic interplay between the two sections. It's playable as is, but without serious practice it's not going to sound good. The question comes to me: do I want it as is, or do I want to cut? I want to cut, naturally – anything to make it sound good – but I'm uncertain exactly what, where, and how much to excise. Sharks are circling, sensing a wounded prey, and I'm at their mercy. There is a heavy silence while about 25 people wait for me to make a decision. I turn to the lead trumpet, who seems like a friendly face, someone who is not going to let this last forever, and ask for his recommendation. My acknowledgement that I need help is well-received, useful suggestions are made, and the offending phrases cut in trombones and saxes, leaving the trumpets to make the running at that point.

I return to the drums, we run the difficult passage, which now seems smooth and efficient, and the producer in the control room, with a very large clock on the wall, patiently suggests we go for a take. "This ain't no party, this ain't no disco, this ain't no foolin' around," as Talking Heads might have said. The whole thing is being video'd, and cameras and unbearably harsh lighting appear to be everywhere. We are by now at about the hour mark, and the first take of 'Lingo' is going well. The sound of the band in the headphones is exhilarating, and I begin to relax into the groove as I make a note that I must do more of this. We safely negotiate the tricky rapids at letter B and Steve Marcus launches into his solo. Then I catch sight of the bass player.

He's looking anxiously at me – what the hell is his problem? We keep rolling. The tune continues to sound good, but I'm losing focus, distracted by this guy. He stops playing his electric bass and raises his left wrist as if in pain. Shit – I've got it. I've written a part consisting of continual and repetitive eighth-notes in only one hand position on the bass. The repetition, so easy when you are demoing something on a computer, is effectively unplayable by a human. But this guy is a pro. His other hand is making a 'keep rolling' gesture: he too knows that it's a good take and doesn't want it to abort on his account. By now I can't remember anything I've played for about the last minute. My drumming is coming from a place that I've spent years preparing for – just this moment. I'm on a professional automatic pilot. The bass player waits a few bars for his wrist to uncramp, drops smoothly back into the music, and we both know that if this is the keeper, he can slip in and repair the pothole in a few minutes.

The take completes, and we go back in to listen. I'm unused to the huge organic sound and power of a big-band blasting and reminded of the advantages of an everybody-at-once-preferably-on-acoustic-instruments type of recording. My own performance is workmanlike but with a sassy twist in the tale. Deeply unwilling to go through that experience again, I vote strongly for keeping it, as, thank heavens, does Neil. The bass player repairs the pothole and we proceed to the second piece without further hitches. The job is done with five minutes to spare.

Back at the jazz festival breakfast, the room is beginning to thin and I am awash with coffee. It seems natural that, about twice a year, the healthy musician will want to put himself in a position in which, musically, he is completely out of his depth and where he knows for an utter certainty that he cannot do what is required of him under the pressure. This is good for the backbone – the musical equivalent of a cold shower in utter humiliation.

But this morning I feel I've had all the cold showers I can handle, and half of me thankfully relieves the other half of the artist's obligation to go searching, to test to destruction. My more accomplished colleague, saxophonist Tim Garland, would have exchanged numbers at Mintzer's breakfast table by now, and the two would already be sketching out plans for the Mintzer–Garland Symphony Number One. They probably know where and when its first public performance will be. Tim has the hunger, and the skill to go with it. His work rate is phenomenal, even for one who has effortless facility with the raw material of music composition: the composer's software program Sibelius, the orchestration skills, the black book upgraded to an iPhone with the numbers of dozens of musicians, the functionaries in the compositional process. Tim's zeal incapacitates me, and I am exhausted just being in its presence.

❏

You toy with this powerful thing called music at your peril. Music – not as entertainment only, but as literal power – is a force that affects all who hear it. Researchers are beginning to suggest that music, its use or abuse, plays a far more important role in determining the character and direction of civilisation than most people have until now been willing to believe. The powers of music are multi-faceted, sometimes uncannily potent, and by no means entirely understood. Some, like David Tame, believe we should consider carefully before we forsake the conscious, constructive use of these powers.[1] For most of human existence, until roughly now, music was understood to have, for example, immense healing properties for both mind and body and considerable influence over the purely intellectual and mental processes. Professor Grenville Hancox, Professor Of Music at Canterbury Christ Church University in the UK, recently told me he is trying to have singing prescribed on the National Health Service, and I sincerely hope he succeeds.

Whenever we are in the presence of music, its influence is playing upon us constantly – speeding or slowing, regularising or irregularising our heartbeats, relaxing or jarring the nerves, affecting blood pressure, digestion, and the rate of respiration. Even when you think you've tuned music out, these physiological effects are taking place. In the modern world we have reduced music to a commodity for purchase, to a non-essential and peripheral lifestyle option. It is often given away free on magazine covers, thus inadvertently encouraging the notion that it isn't worth anything. The philosophers of antiquity would have regarded such a viewpoint as not only irrational but also, ultimately, suicidal. From ancient China to Egypt, from India to the golden age of Greece, the belief was that music had the power to sublimely evolve or utterly degrade the individual psyche – and thereby make or break entire civilisations.

Here is the great violinist Yehudi Menuhin from the opening page of his book *Theme And Variations*: "Music creates order out of chaos; for rhythm imposes unanimity upon the divergent, melody imposes continuity upon the disjointed, and harmony imposes compatibility upon the incongruous. Thus as confusion surrenders to order and noise to music, and as we through music attain that greater universal order which rests upon fundamental relationships of geometrical and mathematical proportion, direction is supplied to mere repetitious time, power to the multiplication of elements, and purpose to random association."[2]

Tame informs us that "to the major civilisations of antiquity, intelligently-organised sound constituted the highest of all the arts". It was "the most important of the sciences, the most powerful path to religious enlightenment, and the very basis of a stable harmonious government".

Music was deemed to have a powerful effect upon the character of man. The great philosophers debated this in determining the morality of people. Aristotle, for one, wrote: "Emotions of any kind are produced by melody and rhythm; therefore by music a man becomes accustomed to feeling the right emotions; music has thus power to form character, and the various kinds of music, based on the various modes, may be distinguished by their effects on character – one, for example, working in the direction of melancholy, another of effeminacy; one encouraging abandonment, another self-control, another enthusiasm, and so on through the series."[3] Wars and politicians may come and go, but music abides indefinitely, never failing to affect the hearts and minds of those who hear it.

The irony of this, of course, is that it was taken for granted right up to and including the period of the great 19th century composers, almost until the 20th century. Since the dawn of time, or the dawn of music, it was self-evident that music possessed a mediating role between Heaven and Earth, that it was a communications channel from man to the gods, and the gods to man, and a key for releasing the energies of the supreme into our life here on earth. Powerful stuff, which we have done much in the last hundred years to lose, downplay, or deliberately forget.

We say music is important, but we circulate it for free, accord it no significance, fail to listen to it when we are in its presence, and ignore it, in a century in which, paradoxically, there has never been more of the stuff on tap. It has a good deal less status than water, which at least has the decency to be an essential for life. To be sure, there is the bottled kind, and the mountain-stream kind, and the posh fizzy kind with lemon bits, and good old tap, but you don't really notice it until it isn't there. Quiet round here, isn't it? We'll have to talk to each other.

Music is now everywhere. Has it no shame? Everywhere you go – shop, airport, restaurant, bank, church, job centre, funeral parlour – there it is, whirring away, hopelessly emasculated, obtrusive in its unobtrusiveness. Like a tart on a slow night, it has lowered its price so much that anyone can have it. It all smacks of desperation. The more there is of it, the less noticeable it becomes – unless you happen to work in that particular field of endeavour, in which case it remains quite noticeable enough. Maybe this sheer profligacy has dulled our senses. Our civilisation stands alone in history in according music so little value – and it remains an open question whether this is the result of modern man's greater wisdom and progress or his over-materialistic worldview and spectacular ignorance.

The sociologist Simon Frith understands correctly that music need no longer be framed by a special time, place, or occasion. No longer an event, it may exist only as background music; it is increasingly moving from foreground to background by dint of the sheer density, the sheer volume of material. "Most commentators take this as music's loss of power – the more it's heard the less it means," writes Frith in his book *Performing Rites*. "Background music has no sense of history or authority: it is anonymous, artificial, electronically enhanced, and so forth. It encourages 'regressive' hearing in Theodor Adorno's terms - 'alienated, narcotised listening'; listening that is in Joseph Horowitz's words 'mentally supine'."[4] Maybe background music also discourages the opposite, namely positive listening or actual engagement with the music.

Equally obviously, music is entirely disconnected from place. It is mobile, can cross national and political boundaries, follow us from room to room, on a bike or in a car. There is less and less a sense of music being appropriate to certain times and places, such as the restrictions on the uses of Indian classical ragas. Has it no sense of occasion? Elton John and Abba for your wedding and funeral, Elgar when you want some hope and glory, Chemical Brothers when you want to forget (or forget Diana Krall), Diana Krall at your dinner-party for the 'sophistication' of jazz without the jazz, Rock The Classics when you want neither rock nor classical music.

Every artist comes with an appended lifestyle, and I don't seem to want any that are on offer. I monitor the offerings of my colleagues, in a desultory kind of way, but that is little more than professional diligence. In the right hands, perhaps those of drummer Bill Stewart, composer Maria Schneider, or bassist and composer Dave Holland, the music can still be pushed and shoved into a brilliance that stirs embers deep in my soul. For better or worse, in sickness and in health, I am wedded to a particular style of music-making: small-group acoustic post-bop jazz. For certain, this is the frontline of development on my instrument in my culture, and that's were I want to be. Few others are doing anything half as interesting.

The people who flourish in that fierce musical environment are creating a paradigm of human social co-operation on the highest possible level. If prime ministers, statesmen, and captains of industry were able to interact at such a high level of understanding, the place would be a lot tidier than it currently is. The agility, the grace, the imagination, the fluency, and the sheer depth of understanding evident in that music holds a place in my heart from which I cannot depart even if I wished to. It has a hold on my imagination that makes it difficult to imagine any other future.

If you're a fiddle player who honestly believes that the Bartok string quartets are the apex of the development of the string quartet and, as you look around, all you could see is down, what are you to do? You're skewered, barbecued. When you can no longer imagine a better future, no matter what your particular musical viewpoint, then you have nothing to say, and anything you do say may be used in evidence against you. "Mr Bruford, you stand accused of contributing to the static. How do you plead?"

Music abounds. Everyone can now make a CD in his bedroom, and the problem is, everyone does. With no quality control, conscience, or suffering, the stuff oozes out from under the bedroom door, a blind slime looking for approval. Only a tiny little bit of it ever gets to the bottom of the stairs, let alone slithers off to market. The only person who ever knew of its existence, who watches its lamentable journey as it struggles out into an unheeding world, has forgotten all about it after the first dozen rejection slips. But the music had been given form and a kind of life, so where is it now? In that great CD rack in the sky, clogging up the place: that's where. The entire system is constipated, overfed, and unloved. My piano groans under the weight of unsolicited CDs from all corners of the globe. Russian progressive-rock groups, Italian King Crimson tribute bands, Chilean jazz quartets, aspiring young drummers from Finland alike – all gathering dust.

The implied deal from the sender of this 'gift' from a 'huge fan' is that I'm supposed to listen from beginning to end, make a detailed appraisal of its merits – which it is hoped will be legion – and return a glowing testimonial to the sender, while commending his or their undoubted talents to my entire address book. I never seem to quite get started on that chore. Every morning I stare at the pile as I wait for the computer to fire up. I swear I'll get started tomorrow, and the stack of CDs stares balefully back. Now that the whole world and his aunt produces the stuff, the sheer wanton wastage leaves you physically repelled. As when presented with a plate with too much food, the appetite suddenly deserts, and you don't want any of it. Music from all sources and all continents from a hundred years ago is endlessly repeatable. Its presence can no longer be defined against the everyday as being something unusual. It is the one minute's silence that is unusual.

Musical taste is now intimately tied into personal identity: we express ourselves through our deployment of other people's music. Musical experience has been individualised. Music is more like clothes than any other art form, not just in the significance of fashion, but also in the sense that the music we 'wear' is as much shaped by our own desires, our own purposes, our own bodies, as by the desires, purposes, and bodies of the people who first made it. We are stage managers, deciding for ourselves when, where, how, and with whom to listen to music, in what order, which sounds will go together, and, as the DJ might say, how sounds will sound.

❏

Some technological developments are so pervasive that their enormous effect is sometimes overlooked, and here I'm thinking of electrical amplification. Philip Brophy has pointed out that amplification "is integral to the cultural and social growth of rock. It changed not only the sound of the instruments but also the scale of the live event which contained them, thereby determining the nature of the audience experience."[5] The audience was amplified as well as the musicians.

Neither Hitler's Nuremberg Rallies in the 30s nor the Woodstock festival in the late 60s would have been the events they were without rapid developments in loudspeaker technology. The ear-splitting volume of modern rock gigs is received as a physical onslaught, a narcotic with ever-diminishing powers that has to be replenished in ever-increasing dosages to compensate. If it's not so good, it's going to sound a whole lot better if you turn it up. There's that word 'sound' again. The entire body begins to vibrate, heads begin to bang, preferably actually inside the bass cabinets of the PA, and oblivion follows shortly thereafter.

Brophy puts it well: "The lineage of Caribbean music is founded on bass: from ska (the Caribbean distortion of East Coast R'n'B) to reggae (the latter being the first major instance of subsonic bass intruding upon white-rock's favoured midrange aural spectrum) to black disco ... to the eventual bass explosion in 80s hip-hop. This explosion is regional: booming drum machines, pounding disco bass drums, cheesy subsonic synthesizer bass lines ... travelled from the East Coast ... throughout the nation (Chicago house and acid, Detroit techno, Miami bass) and over to the West Coast (LA hardcore rap and jack-beat swing). And on it will go."[6]

The body of the car is used to amplify the amplification, in an unforeseen use of automobile technology. We are advised to wear protective ear-defenders when we listen and play, and young rockers are daily becoming aware of the narcotic of volume.

But it doesn't all have to be loud. In the lull after my first edition of Earthworks and the blasting sound of The Buddy Rich Orchestra, I was vaguely mapping out an altogether more poetic scenario for my next album. All I had to do was to find some musicians and someone to pay for it.

13 DO YOU STILL SEE ANY OF THE OLD GUYS?

I t's August 1996, and I'm shaking hands with a few people in the lobby of a Kansas City hotel. King Crimson is in town to play the Sandstone Amphitheater, and the transport to the soundcheck is running late. A slightly built, undistinguished looking fellow proffers his album sleeve, and as I start my scribble I hear him say how much he would like to hire the band for a gig. Uh-oh, this one could be whacky.

I dutifully explain that this is going to be unlikely. We are currently on a tour with, mercifully, a beginning and an end. Deviation is impractical, as is crossing the ocean from our UK base for a one-off. However, he'd be more than welcome to call our agent and slot in a date next time around. Looking at him, I suggest that I have just saved him an expensive evening, to which he replies that cost would not have been a problem. My antennae rotate silently in their sockets. Always on the look-out for a little discretionary spending power, my tone softens, and I suggest we meet after the show for a drink.

Later, upstairs in the hotel bar, it becomes clear that Norm Waitt Jr., for this is he, is a keen music fan who would like to become involved in some way with some of the musicians who have given him so much pleasure over the years. It further transpires that Norm is the brother of Ted Waitt, founder of Gateway Computers. The company was born in a farmhouse in Sioux City, South Dakota, in 1985 with a $10,000 loan and a three-page business plan, entered the Fortune 500, and went public, trading on the NASDAQ and then the New York Stock Exchange. Turns out Ted has bought his brother out of his share of the company, and Norm has turned his attention to the arts as a possible repository for some of his excess cash.

I order another round of drinks and shift a bit in my chair. This could be a long and, if carefully played, fruitful night. This pleasant man appears wholly ignorant of the doubtful pleasures of the music business, and I sense that I am going to be thoroughly examined on several aspects of it before I can home in on the end I have in mind. We wade through manager–artist relationships, the funding of albums and expected returns, the demise of the major record company as a meaningful player in that field as far as I and my colleagues are concerned, the possible impact of this new-ish thing called the internet that I've heard about, the financing of King Crimson, and the past financing of my previous records. It probably also cost me a "What's it like working with Robert Fripp?" before I am able finally to ascertain what he wants and how much he is prepared to pay.

Essentially, he wants an entry-level amount of credibility by appearing as executive producer on a serious project on the 'art' side. And he is prepared to finance such an album. Well now, if there is one thing I'm good at, it's dreaming up album pitches and plots. Albums, like movies, need to be about something, with a definable sub-text. *Tutu* was Miles Davis's comeback album; *Face Value* was Phil Collins's divorce album; *Earthworks* was about letting young jazz guys loose with the tools and technology of rock and giving them more than 20 minutes to make a record. A month or two earlier, a young man called Russell Summers, about whom I knew nothing, had said, pretty much in passing, that he had a suggestion for me. One of the hazards of all this meeting and greeting is that the customer feels extremely free to tell you with whom you should *really* be making records. Most of the proposals are laughable enough to be ignored, but as Summers came up to have his

CD signed, he said in a dry, matter-of-fact manner: "You should make a record with Ralph Towner."

Now Ralph Towner is one of the great acoustic guitarists of our time. He has a golden catalogue of his own poetic albums on ECM Records and a musical association with most everybody you'd want to have a musical association with. Ralph always struck me as bit of an outsider, a classically-trained musician whose acoustic guitar playing centred on the silver shards of light he could extract from the unwieldy 12-string version of the instrument. If I'm too rock for jazz and too jazz for rock, then he is probably too jazz for classical and too classical for jazz. His most recent record with his main group, Oregon, was recorded live in the studio in Moscow with the Moscow Philharmonic – an ambitious project indeed. My two immediate thoughts were, first, that Ralph was completely unattainable and, second, that he was exactly the person I should be making a record with. I thanked Russell for his suggestion, and there the idea lay waiting for just this moment.

Now it's 1:00 in the morning, and I'm edging Norm toward abandoning any ideas about hiring King Crimson and investing instead in a chamber-jazz trio. I don't know who the third party is yet, but I'll think of someone. Norm knows of Ralph's work and seems remarkably willing to fund the creation of a project with the two of us. We swap details, numbers, and so forth, and I slide off happily to the elevator with, I believe, the funding for a new project in the can.

It had been six years since Earthworks' hundred-hour album *All Heaven Broke Loose* was recorded in Germany in the same hundred hours it took the coalition forces to boot Saddam Hussein out of Kuwait in the First Gulf War in 1991. There had been a worthy double-trio with Crimson in between, but now I was ready to air some new ideas with fresh players. I had to track down the third member of my chamber-jazz trio backstage at a club in, of all places, Kansas City again.

He was Eddie Gomez, a highly professional, highly regarded, and highly expensive acoustic bass player known for his soloing ability. I knew Ralph and Eddie had worked together before, and I ran the idea of the three of us working together past Ralph when he and I first met in London. Crimson had a good name among jazz musicians, if they had heard of the band at all, so I didn't have to introduce myself for too long. It took me the rest of 1996 after my meeting with Norm to book a studio, find an engineer, write some music, and get everybody in one place.

Ralph, Eddie, and I finally meet at the Make Believe Ballroom, a small rural studio in West Shokan, New York, in the bitterly cold February of 1997. Owner Tom Mark is our engineer. It's a tiny place, but that suits the intimate nature of the all-acoustic project I have in mind. Recent drummer-led records have all been about muscle and flash, targeted below the groin at that part of the drum community that enjoys those kinds of fireworks. But I'm after something altogether more poetic – softer, hazy, autumnal. Pete Erskine and Paul Motian are a couple of the very few drummers who could caress you rather than beat you up, and there is an intimacy in the quality of their recent work that I'd like to follow up on with Ralph. Two or three acoustic instruments can fill a huge sonic space on disc, as if the whole aural spectrum is available to them. I want everything played quietly and mixed loud, playing on that falsity of foreground that recording can give you. With titles like 'Somersaults' and 'Thistledown', I want the music to have a dreamy, 'secret garden' feel. The album will be called *If Summer Had Its Ghosts*.

I can afford to have Ralph and Eddie for four days only, and the sessions start promptly at 11:00 on the Monday. I play some scratchy demos and stretch out some sketchy charts on the table, and we hack our way through the undergrowth as speedily as possible. Right away I love the sound, and this intimacy agenda is going to work. The downside is going to be the compositions. I have produced too much fussy material, as is common with the amateur writer, gripped by a nervy and mistaken belief that the world will collapse if he doesn't have something to point to, to be able to say: "Play this." On the contrary, all that is required with people like this is the barest minimum that will get them going, and then you get out of the way. But it has to be the right barest minimum. In the absence of that surety, the drummer–leader on these sessions has fallen into trap number one – the material is too dense – and is about to fall headlong into trap number two – he's allowed no rehearsal time. These are capital offences from which many records never recover.

If you'd like to make a third mistake, why not write music that is effectively unplayable on your choice of featured instrument? I have neglected to take the time to familiarise myself with what is and what is not possible on the 12-string acoustic guitar. It does some things really well, but it doesn't play bebop. The bits of tunes that move in that direction break down amid a barrage of blasphemy from Ralph as the instrument goes out of tune repeatedly, usually three-quarters of the way through the take. But both my collaborators are sweethearts who give it their all, and things start to pick up after a couple of bleak days with a charming version of 'Thistledown', which, for once, was under-written.

We are on surer ground with a piece from Eddie called 'Amethyst' and a booting little rocker from Ralph called 'Now Is The Next Time'. At the end of our four days we are all shattered, and the music is all in bits, somewhere, but I know we have it. Practically delirious with relief, I say goodbye to two of the greatest musicians I've worked with and point my nasty little rental car back across the snowy and frozen Ashokan Reservoir toward the Kingston Ramada. At 3:00am in the parking lot, slipping in the icy snow and laden with music, tapes, instruments, cymbals, and session paraphernalia, I contrive to lock the car doors with the engine still running. This is no easy feat, even for a guy who's just completed a challenging week of sessions. Forty-five minutes later, the locksmith has sorted out the problem, and I'm in bed and in one piece. Just.

I tend to agree with Miles Davis when he said: "I don't lead musicians, man. They lead me. I listen to them to learn what they can do best."[1] But I also listen to other musicians to learn what *I* can do best. Learning on the job has something going for it, but I worry I'm getting a reputation for this.

As a postscript, our executive producer Norm Waitt was repaid his outlay of $60,000 in full from the record sales some two years later.

❑

It tends to be a continuing source of comfort to some musicians that the promoters and punters never 'get it', as if their never getting it in some bizarre way validates the music. I never joined in very wholeheartedly with that one. I am in favour of everyone getting everything, or at least something, out of the evening's entertainment. Moreover, what the punter 'got' was very much a matter for the punter, and he will alight on the strangest things. He has a nasty habit of applauding not the things the musicians like but the things that *he* likes.

One thing the he likes, invariably, is the possibility of disaster, and then recovery from disaster. At the micro level, it could be dropping a stick, followed by an elegant and unhurried recovery with a replacement appearing as if by magic, not a note missed. I have to watch that one. It's very easy to do, so I take my time. At the macro level, it can be the illness or non-appearance of a key figure in the proceedings, thus forcing the remaining performers to improvise around his absence – because, of course, the show must go on. What audiences also pick up on with disarming ease is humbug, fakery, and posturing of all kinds, and, conversely, honest effort, genuine skill, natural ability, commitment, and a general willingness to be present.

It never ceases to amuse me how differently the male and female tend to receive the musicians' collective efforts. The men are all "how?", the women all "why?". Men edge to the front of the stage and count the processing devices, check for keyboard manufacturers and drum-kit specifications, and look at the amplifiers' glowing lights; the women just want to know who likes or loathes whom in the band, and are the toilets clean. They seem, not unreasonably, to want evidence that some or all of the performers are appearing to have, or are actually having, a good time, or at least appear committed. But if the loos are dirty, or the band grumpy, or the ambience smoky, the group could be rewriting the future of music and it will go unnoticed. It is one of very few disappointments in my professional life that, even though I much prefer playing to women, they have generally and rather stubbornly stayed away. Maybe the toilets were dirty.

The customer can be demanding beyond reason, but that's mostly because we've trained him to be so. Thirty-five years ago, in an era of plentiful record sales, it was not felt by either party that musician or listener required a 'relationship', outside that existing within and provided by the music. You made the album, he or she bought it, and that was the beginning and end of the arrangement. I must have been about three years into my career before I started doing small interviews for journalist Chris Welch at the *Melody Maker*. It was probably another decade before anyone asked for my signature on the back of a fag packet. That started with our less reserved American friends, in clubs, and the preferred item at the time was the nasty napkin under the beer glass, this still being years before official group merchandise was available to sign. It wasn't long at all before people began to bring their vinyl records and then CDs to the event, hoping to waylay a band member on his way to the bathroom.

As record sales shrank alarmingly, it gradually dawned on us that if we were going to be 'allowed' to keep playing the music we wanted to play, we'd have to go on a charm offensive. Magazines were proliferating, and we could tell the ill wind of change was blowing when we had to start soliciting them for interviews, rather than the other way around. The speed of change quickened. Next we were selling merchandise at the concert, but many years after our colleagues in country music had opened that particular can of worms. The thing that gets the merchandise selling faster than hotcakes is if the 'star' or, better still, all band members are available after the show to sign the new purchase, grip the customer's hand, and put their arms around his shoulder while his friend snaps a picture. Before you knew it, there were trestle tables laid out, fresh Sharpie markers, and bottles of water, and you were up for another steady hour of gripping and grinning. The whole thing was starting to smell like running for president.

Then the arrival of the computer, emails, the online store, and the questions, the questions, the questions. Each customer has now to be courted like a girlfriend. The unwritten contract at time of writing is: I'll answer your question, on condition you join my mailing list so I can harangue you with 'newsletters' advertising my latest CD. The size of my mailing list is now infinitely more important than the size of any other appendage as a mark of my potency. Each man is now his own record company, so you are in the marketing game whether you like it or not, buddy. Mailing lists at dawn.

Back at the venue and signing away like a trouper, there is plenty of advice and instruction to be had from the customer. It's 2001 and I'm in Hollywood, playing a four-night run at Catalina Bar & Grill, a small jazz place on West Sunset Boulevard. Violinist and producer Eddie Jobson, an old colleague from the band UK, has very insistently invited me to lunch at his place along with my brilliant but elusive old colleague, guitarist Allan Holdsworth, who, it transpires, doesn't show. Lunch turns out to be a welcome diversion from the tawdry glamour of these few blocks of the Hollywood 'entertainment' district. In my younger days I would have been down frying in oil at the hotel pool shimmering below me, but now, in the late afternoon of my career, I only stare down dolefully at the young things basking, feeling hopelessly out of place. This is all about young things making it, and if that's not on your agenda there is only a powerful feeling of redundancy. Time, again, to move on.

Tonight is the last night I shall have to sign autographs for the earnest, pleasant, balding, upright middle-aged men who have flown in from Kansas City or El Paso because I once played on *Fragile*. Their comprehension of the newer Earthworks material is minimal, but it sure doesn't matter to them "as long as *you're* up there playing those drums,

Bill – been following you forever". This is attached to a handshake the size of the Rocky Mountains. "Do you still see any of the old guys?"

Too large a portion of my residual North American audience is old and sentimental, and no matter what I'm playing up there, they are only hearing *Close To The Edge* from 30 years ago. "Don't ever stop, Bill, don't ever change," comes the instruction, as I sign the wrinkly album sleeves somewhere near Jon Anderson's quick flick of the pen. If I avoid change, they are then also permitted to avoid change. Life was always better back then, and my job, as instructed, is to reaffirm that.

Critic Don Heckman's glowing reviews in the *Los Angeles Times* continue to fall on deaf ears. He surmises, correctly, that Earthworks has still not been taken to the bosom of the US jazz community, probably never will be, and I don't think it bothers me now. There is just too much baggage around my background to permit the necessary adjustment of thought.

The good news about working in the United States is that when the people have decided you're great, great you will always be. The bad news is you can only ever be great at the one thing the audience has decided you're great at. You are not permitted, as it were, to come around again for a second bite of the cherry. "You know you once thought that I was the Godfather Of Progressive Rock Drumming? Well, I've got news. Now I want to be A Great Jazz Drummer." That's evidently not going to wash in the land of milk and honey.

❑

In the land of the rising sun, however, it's a different dynamic. Japan was scarcely mentioned in my first decade as a musician. Early Yes, early King Crimson, Gong, UK, Bruford, Genesis – all came and went before we knew how to spell the word. All energies were concentrated on invading America, and it wasn't until the re-formation of King Crimson in 1980 that we began to look east. "But we're big in Japan" was rapidly becoming the unverifiable and exotic mantra from those who demonstrably weren't so big in North America.

With the Crimson *Discipline* tour of 1981, the floodgates opened onto this mysterious culture. My ensuing 25-year career in Japanese concert halls and clubs was to involve a dozen different ensembles, from the *Discipline* King Crimson through to duets with my Dutch pianist–partner Michiel Borstlap and the current edition of Earthworks, and allowed me to watch a substantial change in the nation's cultural attitude to Western rock and jazz.

When I first turned up with the Mighty Crim in the early 80s, the shows were early, at 6:30, and peopled by well-behaved and neatly-groomed youngsters who would have been kept firmly in their seats by the hall ushers had they shown the slightest inclination to jump up and move their hips – which, of course, they didn't. Applause was brief, leaving plenty of time in the long silence between songs to wonder whether they liked it or hated it. It would take another decade before American MTV would show them how to behave at a rock concert, so that by my last visit with Crimson in October 1995 they were a-whoopin' and a-hollerin' just like their Caucasian cousins. The tiny modular bathrooms, the bullet train, the sushi, the rice-culture conformity, and the sake became regular and enjoyable features of my touring schedule as the decade wore on.

But it was all a bit like working in a vacuum. The culture does not appear to allow for critical press reaction to visiting foreign artists, on the grounds that this might be considered disrespectful. A month of deference bordering on the reverential had you longing for a good drubbing in the Western press, in the same way as a month of sushi and shabu-shabu had you aching for a good old cheeseburger. Translation of magazine articles confirmed their content to be no more than listings: they recorded this, they played here, they went away. Ticket sales, naturally, were a strong indicator that the various groups were connecting, but I missed the robust exchange of views with writers, commentators, and colleagues that was the life-blood of the Western scene.

The natural arc of my career in Japan – discovery, peaking, and a long slow tail as work diminished – exactly mirrored the country's economic transitions as the boom economy of the 80s sobered into the deflationary 90s, and it came as a sharp reminder that what we musicians have to offer is largely inessential and purchased only after everything else of greater necessity. In all markets, the musician is among the first to feel the chilly blast of a downturn in economic fortunes and the last to feel the sunny warmth of an upturn. By the new millennium, the worsening jetlag, and the slimmer pickings were pointing to a rethink. I'd spent far too many hours clutching my book on *Understanding The Japanese* while waiting for breakfast to begin at 6:00am after hopeless attempts at sleep – convincingly portrayed by Bill Murray as he wrestled with his jetlag in the movie *Lost In Translation*.

But it was all worth it for a few dates with Bruford Levin Upper Extremities, or B.L.U.E., in April 1998. This was a loose-limbed, largely improvised quartet that Crimson bassist Tony Levin and I had recorded in Woodstock about a year earlier, immediately after my project with Towner and Gomez. It featured Chris Botti on trumpet and David Torn on all manner of guitars.

The offer from the Japanese promoter had at the top of the bill Fripp's ProjeKct 2, with old Crimson bandmates Trey Gunn and Adrian Belew, and B.L.U.E. opening the show. Coming only months after the stultifying rehearsals in Nashville, the backstage atmosphere at the Akasaka Blitz in central Tokyo was bound to be chilly. Our group was little more than an absurdly confident jam-band, rough and ready, and I don't remember much that anyone could call a rehearsal. We had never been on stage together before, but the intrepid professional kind of likes that. It means that at the least we are all going to be as interested in the proceedings as the customer.

It turned out that, in our embryonic trumpet star, we were fielding a secret weapon of considerable potency. Unfeasibly good-looking, and in possession of a beautiful warm round tone, Chris Botti modelled himself on Chet Baker, the much photographed cultural icon of the 50s

West Coast school of cool jazz. In that school, nothing was done in a hurry, and it was always done with the minimum of fuss and the maximum of restraint. This could naturally be very appealing to the ladies, and following several years picking up tips as a sideman with Sting, Chris was to go on to make a substantial international career as a smooth-jazz artist on Columbia Records.

But tonight he was the lark's tongue in aspic, the delicacy in the aural roughage. Slowly patrolling the front stage area, and bathed in a hazy spotlight, he would equally slowly deliver the fewest, longest, slowest notes he could get away with, the preparation for which was almost as interesting as the notes themselves. Behind him, I watched all this flirting with a great deal of amusement and interest, and resolved to inject a whole lot more control into my own performances. Get them to watch the sticks, not me. The trumpet's bell-like purity of tone cut clean through the clouds of Torn's stereo guitar loops, and with the ex-Crimson rhythm section on fine form smouldering beneath the proceedings, we were a tough act to follow. None of us had much idea what Robert's ProjeKct 2 would sound like, and in the event its performance was overlooked in the backstage celebrations.

With B.L.U.E., demand was still strong enough to ensure a visit to Osaka, Japan's second city, but by the time Earthworks showed up as a pure and simple jazz act in the new millennium, the country's economy and the not-rock nature of the music consigned us to performing in Tokyo alone. An April 2004 run of dates in the Shibuya district was notable for a wholly different kind of energy pouring from the newest and youngest Earthworker, pianist Gwilym Simcock.

Gwilym was an astonishing find from the British scene, a product of Chetham's, the elite classical-music school in Manchester. He had studied classical piano, French horn, and composition, and went on to graduate from the jazz course at the Royal Academy Of Music with first-class honours and the coveted Principal's Prize for outstanding achievement. If being feted by the chattering classes on both classical and jazz sides of the fence brought its own burden, Gwil didn't seem to notice, and his career went into hyperdrive. Such was his strength and energy as a musician, I was forced to dig deep into my bag to keep up, let alone contribute much of value to the proceedings when we played early concerts together in Earthworks. Both Botti and Simcock, in wholly different ways, were forces of nature, and I became very aware of the potency of both on Japanese stages.

In my 15 or so trips in as many years, I had worked and recorded for Japanese employers such as one of the nation's best known guitarists, Kazumi Watanabe, and played with another drummer behind two amplified koto players and keyboardist–producer Akira Inoue. I had delivered countless clinics and demonstrations on behalf of Simmons when their electronic drums were the instrument of the moment and attended the negotiations surrounding the proposed sale of the company to Akai when they were no longer in such demand. I had taken the night-train through the snow from Sapporo to Tokyo with Crimson, the bullet train with Earthworks, and the limos to the Budokan in Tokyo with Yes in 1992. I have no immediate plans to return, and it is one of the countries I shall miss the most.

I want to create music to soothe my soul. If an audience likes it, be they Japanese, Ugandan, or American, well and good; if not, that will still be the music I will create. The alternative view is essentially that you try to figure out what the market wants and then provide it. But it may be risky to focus-group your songs. That way you are dependent on the audience to validate the music. Followers of that theory believe the more people in the audience, or the greater the record sales, the better the music. Without audience approval, the music is, by definition, junk.

If, through market research perhaps, or analysing the most common North American female forename (it must surely be Debbie) and then writing a song called 'I Love You Debbie', I try to guess what it is you want, there is every chance that I will be simultaneously wrong, patronising, and dissatisfied when my target audience ignores my hollow offering. If, on the other hand, I'm Bob Dylan or John Lennon writing 'Like A Rolling Stone' or 'Imagine' in order to say something because it must be said, there is every chance that at least one person will be satisfied and a possibility that the candour and honesty will connect with millions. You write what you have to write, you play what you have to play, because you can't sleep at night. If you *can* sleep at night, you shouldn't be doing this anyway.

Few of the bands I've been in have actively courted the punter, and I've instinctively been more at ease with musicians and artists who believe that their first responsibility is to themselves. My obligation as an artist is to engage my highest sensibilities to their highest extent for as much of the time as possible. That's what I'm paid for, and anything less is a dereliction of duty rightly reducing me to the rank of a craftsman. The Marquis of Halifax had it about right four centuries ago: "Popularity is a crime from the moment it is sought; it is only a virtue when men have it whether they will or no."[2]

❏

It has been said that your first objective as a musician is to survive failure and your second is to survive success. Having had to sustain only a very short period of the former, and having received no permanent injuries from the latter, I consider myself in relatively good shape on both counts, and I remain a keen advocate of the middle way.

Success has many definitions, from the conventional 'selling a million' or 'being able to get vast amounts of everything I want, right now' to the more prosaic and careful 'having the respect of my peers'. I personally resonate with 'being able to leave the party when I want to', but there are probably as many definitions as there are musicians. My starry-eyed students have a notion of success that is slippery and verging on the unreasonable: to play the music they want to play and earn a respectable living. If only that were a little less impossible to realise in an industry of all-or-nothing.

It became very clear early in my career that what I would be paid would have no obvious connection to the work put in. Generally, remuneration moves in inverse proportion to the work involved. I've been grossly overpaid for doing very little and spectacularly underpaid for delivering a lot. Like film stars and actors, it is perfectly possible to do an extremely lucrative five minutes on the big screen in Hollywood, only to return to the Royal Shakespeare Company for a weekly stipend that wouldn't feed a dog. Those involved in putting rock groups together may be volunteering for a decade or more of penury while they dig a mountain of debt; conversely, the sight-reading acoustic jazz bass player, capitalising on his musical skills, may work six nights a week for much more reasonable pay than is commonly supposed, and which might well be the envy of his colleagues over on the rock side.

Success can be a minefield, to be negotiated with extreme caution. Mike Rutherford and Tony Banks, my former employers from Genesis, appear remarkably normal in the face of considerable success, but others have suffered at the hands of chemically-induced paranoia, a complete inability to handle money and its attendant responsibilities, delusions of grandeur, megalomania, crises of confidence ("I can't be that good"), an inability to be all things to all people, or a sometimes lethal cocktail of all of them.

I'm not sure Jon Anderson was ever quite normal, but his abnormalities have been undisturbed by the fruits of decades of labour, so I consider him also unscathed. The most 'successful' of all my friends has been Phil Collins, upon whose shoulders, I believe, the responsibility of the disposal of a vast fortune weighs heavy. Only he would know if the onset of global success in all its munificence has brought weariness above and beyond what we all feel after a few decades of this nomadic existence.

There are problems with popularity, too, on the larger scale. Equating popularity with market consumption is a twisty chimera. Sales charts, Nielsen ratings, music charts, bestseller lists (which are usually for sale), and circulation statistics are notoriously unreliable and open to manipulation by the very industry that initiates them. Perhaps more importantly, they provide no evidence as to why particular goods, or in our case CDs, are bought by the consumer and whether or not they're actually enjoyed or valued.

Musicians may be loathed or loved, and have influence and power, quite independently of their market share as measured by sales. It has been noted that *The Sound Of Music* topped the UK album charts for more weeks than The Beatles in the 60s, but no one in their right mind would claim it had a more radical influence and resonance in contemporary culture than the lads from Liverpool. The Sex Pistols sold infinitely less than Elton John in the mid 70s, but that doesn't mean we have to rethink cultural accounts of that particular period – it was obviously the Pistols who were doing the cultural damage, as it were, at that time.

To allow the market to determine the popularity and value of everything – if it's a hit it must be good – gets us to where we are today, with a chart full of hits, or what somebody tells me are hits, which nobody likes or will own up to liking. I didn't say it was a hit: someone else told me it was a hit, someone else made that judgment. To put the market above all is to deny the significance of value judgments in popular culture. The essence of popular cultural practice is making precisely these kind of judgments and assessing these kind of differences – there are talent contests, battles of the bands, arguments down the pub, and so forth – in which judgments, distinctions, and choice have to be justified. The industry would prefer to do the discriminating for us, the consumers – to reduce us to a faceless mass of credit cards while refusing to engage in the arguments that produce cultural values in the first place.

Hypocrisy is endemic. You will always come across the line from producer, record company, or booking agent: "If it were left up to me, of course I'd sign it, promote it, give it a tour, but sadly it's out of my hands," or: "There's no arguing with the charts: if it's in there it must be what the people want," or: "I'm just providing what people want." Loose talk like that has got us to the situation, to paraphrase Frank Zappa, where musicians record music they don't like for record companies who don't like it to give to DJs who don't want to play it to people who don't want to listen to it or buy it. EMI sales are dropping alarmingly; the single as a classic artefact of rock'n'roll – the three-minute slice of heaven – is dead on its feet; and the industry's physical sales have dropped about ten per cent a year for the last five years. But we don't love music ten per cent less than we did last year or the year before that. The proportionate rise in download sales is welcome testament to the democratisation of the business as power ebbs from the centre.

Generally, a popular musician is grateful to have achieved his moment in the sunshine and will happily regurgitate the hit as long as there is an audience to regurgitate it to. In the vaudeville and music-hall days back in the early 20th century, performers were often paid by music publishers to sing the tunes the publishers owned, in the hope of making them a hit and thereby increasing sheet-music sales. An artiste like Marie Lloyd or Albert Chevalier could tour the circuit for years with a 15-minute act comprising two or three novelty tunes before they came around again to the same venue and were forced to take on a new repertoire.

This being the default position for most popular musicians, singers, and instrumentalists most of the time, it may seem churlish of me, spoilt by a few years of artistic liberation in the post-Beatles era, when I insist that we can do better. If only to relieve boredom and stretch musical legs, we should combat the inertia that allows the paying customer to treat us as a jukebox. Put the money in: out comes the song you want. He could and should demand more, and we musicians should give more.

I noted with alarm a further sea change in 2007, as an acquaintance of mine, having forked out large sums for a ticket to a reunion concert of The Police, or perhaps Genesis, became very vocal on the subject of exactly what he was going to do to the band members if they failed to produce *all the old songs and none of that new stuff.* This wasn't a request, this was a demand, and it hadn't occurred to him that the old material was new material once. How far we've travelled since the days 30 years ago when exactly the opposite pertained. How we thirsted to hear the new works. We could hear the hit any old time.

❏

If you are indeed playing the music you have to play, irrespective of market requirements, there will be a price to pay, and success will likely be redefined as survival. I deliberately postponed the purchase of a computer until the last possible minute because I knew its arrival would enable me to do everything myself. I also knew that I'd feel obliged to do everything myself. Only when I had sunk elegantly below the mainstream radar did I reinvent myself as an online creature with a virtual record shop, virtual drum lessons, virtual everything. I'd been clinging on by my fingernails to my slot at HMV record stores up and down Britain with the manic strength of a climber on the face of the Eiger, but the ice-storm was coming and I would have to reinvent or freeze.

The computer brought mixed blessings, the consideration of which is purely academic, because it now governs my life and that of so many of my colleagues, and it is the key to my being able to bring any kind of music to an audience. Additional opportunities bring additional workloads, which may help or hinder our trudge to stardom.

On the positive side, email is certainly quick, but also quick to bring unnecessary traffic in unwanted or poorly thought-out responses. For the composer, Sibelius or other music software can be used to email a composition around the band, amend it endlessly, and reprint it quickly and easily. For the bandleader, contracts, press, and publicity and the multitude of other documents needed to conclude any kind of deal can be kept on file and sent around the world at a moment's notice. For the lecturer in critical and cultural perspectives on 20th century popular music – as I was recently – the web is an enormous source of information, available without having to park in Guildford. For the Arctic Monkeys, it has given them their ten minutes of fame by allowing them initially to bypass the few remaining record companies. To this list you may add any number of functions for which you will be needing computers and the net. There is the remarkable case of Marillion, a slightly shop-worn progressive rock group brought back from the dead by the internet in what may be a new business paradigm. Dropped by their label for being past their use-by date, the band had to cancel a US tour. Jeff Woods, a fan from Raleigh, North Carolina, who had been to 75 Marillion gigs, raised $337,000 online from other fans, and the tour went ahead. Then, underlining the power of the net to build a like-minded artistic community, 13,000 fans had within months each paid Marillion an average of $25 in advance – totalling $320,000 – to allow the band to make their next CD. Marillion had the biggest record advance of their career and complete artistic freedom. "What is so brilliant about the net," said singer Steve Hogarth, "is that we can ask 40,000 fans at the touch of a button what they think about a proposed release. It makes music incredibly democratic."[3]

What I like about this is the novel and imaginative use of the net to raise the money; what I don't like is the bit about asking the fans and making music democratic. Would Miles have made *Bitches Brew* as the result of a focus group? Would The Beatles have made *Sgt Pepper's* any better, or even at all, if they had tried to incorporate audience suggestions? That way for a democratic nightmare.

On the downside, there is the uncomfortable feeling, if you are an Arctic Monkey, that the same click of a mouse that elected you to be the recipient of a million sales can just as easily unelect you. For most musicians, the shop is now open 24 hours, and there is always an improvement to be made to that tune you are working on, always one more person in the world to whom you should be selling a CD. Every man is now his own record company, goes the new mantra, and direct (or niche) marketing means you will have to spend all hours getting to know your customer and being constantly available to him, to build the relationship on which not only the first sale but, more importantly, the return sale will be based.

It is possible to build a small market for your particular wares on the web, but the unknown band still needs to build a customer base by the old-fashioned methods of touring, advertising, and getting on the radio. No matter how small your market, it needs nurturing, amusing, catering for. Your customers will need to feel personally involved, so that they will look forward to coming to the next gig or buying the next CD. The questions about drumsticks never stop. Either I have to do this, or pay someone else to do it, and it all takes a toll on the creative side.

We are told that the real virtue of the net is that it offers genuine interaction between artist and fan. But as a fan, I don't want to 'interact' with the artist: I want to hear and buy his music, which I am sure will be better if I let him get on with it. And as an artist, I definitely don't want to interact with fans, or do any more hugely time-consuming and largely bogus online 'interviews', because I think my responsibility is to make the best music possible without constant interruption.

In turn, this comes down to what you think the transaction is between musician and fan. When I grew up, the idea was that the musician made the music, you bought it from a record shop, and he told you in the album liner notes as much or as little about it as he thought appropriate. Now the musician plays the concert for two hours, with another hour spent meeting the audience afterward. The CD tends to be bought at that point, not because of any music that may or may not be on it, but as a souvenir of that meeting. Having produced the record, the artist has typically to spend much time lying on hotel-room floors, with or without an ice-pack on his back, doing phoners and haranguing magazines just to bring to the public's attention the mere fact that the music exists. The relentless growth in the time spent on self-publicity doesn't look like getting any healthier in the near future, in part because of the net.

There is no such thing as a free lunch, as they say. It seems these days that everyone in a young band not only must play their instrument and assist in the creation of the music but also will probably have to assign themselves additional functions. One of them may be good at programming and music-writing software (usually the keyboard player); one may be reliable and methodical as a road manager – often the drummer, strangely. (The drummer's competence, reliability, and affability are often put down to the notion, real or perceived, that he needs the band more than the band needs him.) Perhaps there is an outgoing communicator who can hustle record company people? Must be the singer!

Everyone does double duty now. Record companies and managers were things you had back in the halcyon days of an expanding industry, and they seem to be the first things jettisoned as the industry contracts. And rightly, because they are expensive. But they also let you do your job, which is to make music. In fact, knowing when to hire in help – accountancy, business, tour managing, marketing, whatever – is another critical skill that you learn by trial and error. The trick remains, as always, to stay in business doing the thing we all want, which is being a musician, rather than to spend all our waking hours on ancillary services.

14 YES, BUT WHAT DO YOU DO IN THE DAYTIME?

"**L**ooking forward to Spain?" Carolyn had asked before I left, hoping for something better than the grudging, non-committal response. Another, more sullen, answer came to me when I was alone a day or two later, picking at a plate of grilled vegetables and garlic in the Cádiz hotel restaurant. "It's what I do. And what I do is what I am." That had a stronger, more definite ring to it.

My occupation seemed to have a decreasing connection with fun, happiness, or looking forward to things. Getting through the music business was beginning to require some sort of armour. Almost everyone I'd met had something, be it drugs, ferocious self-loathing, messianic arrogance, or a combination platter of these and many other coping mechanisms. You needed the discipline to stay focussed, otherwise you wouldn't make 40 weeks, let alone 40 years. I felt I had progressively, and probably inadvertently, become a hedgehog, and had curled myself up into a protective ball, as hedgehogs do at the onset of danger. I felt curled, but perhaps with reflective rather than prickly surfaces. I didn't want stuff to stick. Curled, with my eyes straight ahead – no looking back, and no looking at the distractions off to the side. But I'd been curled for a couple of decades, and I badly needed to straighten up.

Reconciling artistic and commercial pressure can result in what commentator Howard Becker has described as a particularly well-formed musicians' occupational culture, which has a number of features and even deviant values.[1]

First, there is the 'us-versus-them' culture. To dedicated jazzers, straight society is full of people who don't understand their gifts, who don't 'get it', and so the conventions and routines of normal society are mocked and satirised, often in a coded language devised for the purpose. At a particularly bad gig at Oxford Polytechnic, where the seated audience seemed to be enjoying what King Crimson had to offer about as much as a dose of salts, I was practically reduced to hysteria by our bass player Tony Levin. In the deafening silence at the end of every tune that greeted our efforts, he'd stroll back to me at the drums and whisper a series of ever more desperate one-liners.

"Whose funeral is it?"

"Stick to the charts!" (The band didn't have any written music.)

"It's either them or us!"

"Keep your head down!" The military metaphor is much used among musicians and features heavily in the lexicon of black humour that has helped keep infantryman and musician alike on an even keel. Like soldiers, musicians spend a lot of time hurrying up and waiting, sticking their heads above the parapets, and running flags up flagpoles to see if anyone salutes. Many musicians feel that endless touring is akin to being on active service in the trenches and long for retirement from duty while hearing is still intact and wits are relatively functional. Every time the musician's work is offered for public criticism, it's open season for being sniped at – so best keep your head down.

Second, musicians tend to develop a strong sense of loyalty to other musicians as insiders and a correlated resentment of the extent to which their work can be controlled by people whom they view as musically incompetent and socially contemptible – a group likely to include, for example, most critics and record company people. The experience of performance itself leads to a sense of alienation from the audience, which becomes, in turn, a kind of contempt for it. Simon Frith comments: "On the one hand, musicians learn to read and manipulate audiences, and to please them with the tricks and devices that they, the musicians, despise; on the other, the musicians experience rejection by audiences, often of the things with which they are most pleased. As [musician] Art Hodes puts it neatly, 'They don't always applaud what knocks me out; they applaud what knocks them out.'"[2]

If permitted, performance becomes a compromise, a compromise that is blamed on the audience. Musicians are also very quick to accuse each other of 'selling out' or prostituting themselves, whether by following the whims of an employer, an audience, or the marketplace. The implicit notion from the late-night jam session in a jazz club such as the 606 in Chelsea, London, is that the best music, the most valuable noise, is made without reference to an audience but with reference only to the needs of the music.

For commentators such as Robert Faulkner, a rigid contrast between art and commerce oversimplifies the complex patterns of musicians' aspirations. "It cannot be assumed, for example, that all musicians in the commercial sector are frustrated or failed jazz musicians: some regard their musical abilities primarily as a means of earning a living; others have a 'craft' orientation from the start, rather than develop it as a response to relative failure."[3]

Faulkner studied the highly skilled work of the Hollywood film sessions and found that the players there took considerable pride in their ability to play anything in any style at sight. The schedule left enough flexibility for the jazz-orientated musicians to play what their heart dictated at night, and the classical people likewise to maintain involvement with string quartets and so on.

Surprisingly to outsiders, even work in a famous band or prestigious orchestra can be unpleasant, poorly paid, personally disruptive, and intensely boring. One of Faulkner's interviewees explained it like this: "I guess I thought that being part of one of the world's great orchestras ... I should be proud to be in it. But this is false, actually. You're not going anywhere, you're not doing anything, and you're stuck with a small salary. You feel trapped."[4]

In general, then, it is an interdependence of musical and social factors that defines the way musicians feel about themselves, their situation, and their work. As with members of other social groups, they will be influenced by the reference groups with whom they compare their own situation and prospects – for example, colleagues from another musical discipline – and by the 'significant others' whose opinions really matter to them, whether for artistic or commercial reasons. 'Significant others' may be colleagues in your own musical discipline – in my case, for example, the opinion of other drummers whose work I admire, or that extremely perceptive critic at *The New York Times* who always seems to get it exactly right.

The way musicians behave can, over time, become internalised, so that their actions not only become habitual but also come to feel morally correct and defensible, as somehow right and proper. In commercial terms, musical activities are simply labour, which can be bought and sold on the market, in which music itself is a commodity to be produced, marketed, and consumed like any other. The forum in which that takes place is called the music industry, now interestingly and quite recently renamed as the music business (indicative of big change). Every musician's duty is, in the first instance, just to cope.

❏

After lunch, I lie flat on my back on the bed, clothed but with belt loosened, in a position that I've long since persuaded myself is the most likely to promote some sort of relaxation, and stare at the ceiling. I've done so much staring at hotel ceilings in my time, I'm beginning to the think the whole of North America and much of Europe is ceilinged in those white rectangular mineral-fibre tiles with dots. After a while, all hotel rooms come to signify the same thing. Physical characteristics may change, of course – although surprisingly little – but one main attribute supersedes all others: your hotel room is the only place you can be alone. Some rooms are better, some are worse, but all are sanctuary.

Musicians instinctively realise this and tend to avoid visiting each other in their rooms when they're on the road. The occasional knock to collect someone for breakfast, or the rare note shoved under the door: these are acceptable, but that's about it. Seldom are you invited in to view how a colleague arranges his private life in your absence, and seldom do you invite anyone in. My room is usually a tip. Damp and drying clothes are festooned over lamp standards and TV sets like a back street in Naples. All those leaflets about TV channels and leaving towels on the floor? Straight in the bin, to make way for my own elaborate paperwork. Naturally, the room needs to be personalised for the duration of the stay, and usually the mere rearranging of the furniture is enough to wrest the thing from the grasp of the hotel chain and make it mine.

I don't think I actually knew the price of anything connected with my trade for the first ten or fifteen years. I never paid for anything at the point of purchase. Paid for it in the end, of course, as all musicians do, probably twice over. But in the beginning, detailed accounts were as rare as the dodo. Bookkeeping was sloppy. Everyone was making more money this year than last, so, honestly, man – toss head, sharp inhale – what's the point? Road managers fiddled petrol receipts, managers fiddled hotel meals and commission, publishers fiddled royalty collection, and the record company fiddled everything.

Organist Keith Emerson's mother was the best-looked-after mother in the business, receiving, apparently, two or three glorious bouquets of flowers a week from her adoring son. Many were the carefully-noted entries in the expenses of Keith's roadie, Baz Ward: "Flowers for Keith's mum." Everyone was on the make, and everyone pretended not to notice. Only with the flattening-out of income in the 80s and the downturn in the 90s did it become profitable to employ a growing army of lawyers and accountants to do a spot of gentle auditing, to find out where all the money had gone.

For the first 20 years or so I assumed that the price on the back of the hotel door was in some way connected to the price you actually paid for the room. That was until I started to buy rooms myself and found that the whole thing was a haggle. Ultimately, all I wanted was thick walls, the very definition of a good hotel. All the chocolates on all the pillows in the world are insufficient compensation if you are nevertheless forced to listen to the nocturnal activity of the healthy young Brazilian couple next door or the insomniac's hot bath being run at three in the morning.

What I'm paying for in a hotel is a solid door and thick walls; what I'm paying for in a plane is distance from the next-door passenger. The tiredness endemic in travel stems from close proximity to strangers for unreasonable lengths of time. Like hotel rooms, the price of the ticket has nothing to do with better food or the rake of the seat and everything to do with those extra, precious few inches of separation from the woman determined to show you her bunions, all the way to Cape Town.

I set an alarm, as always, which is, as always, never required. I sit up refreshed and alert, but uncertain as to whether I've actually been asleep, five minutes before the alarm would have gone off anyway. The transport is waiting downstairs, and I have that pleasurable feeling of going off to work with a bounce in my step as I exit from the elevator into the lobby.

It's 4:30pm, and on stage at the concert hall a group of expectant faces surrounds a half-assembled drumset. I know immediately that the half that has been assembled has been assembled incorrectly. Other stage crew mill around with ladders and lights. It is one of the day's many hurdles: assemble and tune drum kit from scratch; mic it; liaise in pidgin English with Spanish-speaking engineer; get the whole thing to sound acceptable. You never get to 'good', let alone 'excellent'; on the road you settle for 'acceptable'. Time allowed: 75 minutes. That's when the other musicians will turn up and do something similar with their own instruments.

Half-assembled, clamped, and locked into the wrong position, new heads poorly seated on the drums, and the whole thing in the wrong place on stage. I am going to need every one of those minutes. I take off my coat and get to work on the hardware: adjusting, positioning, re-clamping. Then the drums: heads stretched to prevent further slippage, a quick tune to locate them all in a harmonious family of five; I've done it a thousand times before. So many times, in fact, that I'd developed Bruford's First Law of Drum Tuning, which simply states that no matter how many drums you have, one of them will always sound crap, and Bruford's Second Law of Drum Tuning, which states that it will always be a different one that sounds crap. The faces look on, intrigued, in part, to see how the Great Man does it, and in part, because they are surprised the Great Man has to do it at all.

After about 30 minutes, I take time to mic and position the grand piano, mic and position the bass amp, position the monitors and music stands, and complete the thousand-and-one other tasks that will make the stage ready for the arrival of my colleagues. This is, of course, the job of a production manager, for which I am now wearing the seventh of my nine hats. The drum kit is functional and soundchecked with minutes to spare; the others walk in. Unnecessarily sensitive to the collective mood, my radar scans the group and gratifyingly registers laughter, stories. Next up, then, for the next hour and everyone's amusement, is the bilingual soundcheck, with no translator.

"I want a bit of piano, and only myself in mine," says Iain Ballamy to no one in particular, referring to the monitor cabinets at his feet. "The tenor was a bit heavy in mine last night," adds bassist Laurie Cottle, and then, waving a DI box to the engineer at the back of the room: "Is this active or passive?" Ever helpful, the production manager, who dimly recalls that he used to be a drummer, prowls back and forth, the hapless promoter in tow. The promoter is the only man for miles who might have had a dog's chance of translating these comments to the right person, but he isn't doing very well so far. Lights also need adjusting and instructions given for their deployment. "Not too much flashing or movement – we're reading music," tries Iain again, but that is addressed, unwisely, to the piano tuner, who looks bored in the corner, awaiting his moment.

This pantomime of misunderstanding sorts itself out acceptably, on this occasion, in just about the hour allocated. Rule of thumb with these things is that you want to quit while you're ahead, before it all starts to fall apart, which, given the dangerously unstable look on the monitor engineer's face, it could easily do. Musicians, too, have been known to wander off in a huff, rehearsal disrupted, concert soured.

I have now been hard at work in this noisy, disordered environment for two-and-a-quarter hours, and the sweat is beginning to drip down my forehead. These infernal lights: you could fry in a small club with a low ceiling. "Must be hard work, hitting those drums," the punter will frequently suggest at the merchandising after the show. "It's not hard work at all, you idiot – does it look like hard work?" This is something the most effortless of drummers can only think but never voice.

Finally the band is mostly settled, and I move them respectfully but firmly to the third hour of this entertainment, the rehearsal. Last night's errors are checked, lumps removed, new material run down, and, if time, part compositions, bits of tune, and rhythmic ideas are run up the flagpole. The night's running order is produced and the list read in reverse order so the music will appear on the stand last tune at the bottom, first on top. All this is achieved with lighting ladders and PAR cans clattering and banging, strange instruments coming and going in the monitors, feedback and unwelcome piano frequencies being tracked down and expunged. Eventually the musicians begin to shuffle off stage trailing bits of baggage and always in the wrong clothing: a parka for the nice warm Mediterranean evening, because the day has started in Stockholm, or that colourful Hawaiian shirt in the chill mist of a November London evening.

A final misunderstanding with the Spanish engineer about muting various mics at various times, information which I know will be misconstrued the minute I open my mouth, and I leave the stage, three-and-a-quarter hours after I'd first set foot on it. It has gone smoothly as these thing go. Had it not, the penalty is you don't eat – and dinner is firmly in my sights: time allowed, 60 minutes. Just like being in the army. I left home in the UK this morning at 0530, reached the hotel in Cádiz at 1300, left for a three-hour soundcheck at 1630, and will play a little less than two hours. I will then sign CDs for an hour and pack up the drums, returning to the hotel at 0100 the following day.

"And what, exactly, do you musicians do during the daytime?" The innocent question from the dentist's wife at a Christmas drinks do back home floats into mind as I am given the wrong directions to the dressing room by the piano tuner. The ability to function well in less than promising circumstances is the supreme skill of the gigging musician. I am coping, just, but maybe that hedgehog posture doesn't sound so bad after all.

❏

It now seems to be the case that we listen to music as a fragmented and unstable object. Every entrepreneur uses music for his own ends, and the musical work has ceased to command respectful, structural attention. For old-timers like myself, the progression of musical pitch and melody with its accompanying harmonic logic only makes sense if you listen through to the conclusion of a piece of music. Ask a 14-year-old to play you something he likes, and he'll play about ten seconds and ask you what you thought. To me, it understandably sounds like constantly interrupted conversation – modern music-listening, like modern life, seems to be a series of interruptions.

For a whole new generation, listening to a piece of music from beginning to end seems unusual. Through TV advertising we hear slices of Beatles songs, Bach cantatas, jazz and blues pastiche, and – here is the point – *all of it incomplete*. No longer does the TV station wait in all decency for the end of the jingle-writer's effort – it is unceremoniously curtailed and butt-ended hard up, without a second to change mood, to the next jingle: bang! All our experiences of time are now this fragmented and multi-linear, and fragmented music is entirely realistic music – it represents experience grasped in moments. Hence the listener's attention is directed to the texture of the sound rather than the logical procedure of the notes in a formal structure to a logical conclusion. Tunes and melodies take too long to unfold. Melody goes. Harmony has to progress to exert tension and release – goodbye harmony. All that's left is rhythm and the timbre or texture of the sound – the important stuff, our 14-year-old would not unreasonably add. "Technology has liberated listeners from the completeness of musical form," concludes commentator Lawrence Kramer.[5]

"It's all about the sound" is something you hear a lot these days, and that's literally correct. The listener's attention must be directed to the sound, that which is heard immediately, rather than to the music, defined as a procession of pitches in a formal structure whose meaning is revealed on completion of the composition. Perception of the sound is now more important than consideration of the composition.

I conducted a class in improvisation recently at a local music school and asked for someone, anyone, to play a fragment of a melody on the guitar, any well-known melody. No one was forthcoming, even when the request was reduced to 'Happy Birthday To You', which I should have thought someone could have managed. But, silly me, that's the ordered procession of pitches in a formal structure, a melody whose sense is not clear until the last phrase is played – ancient history. But any one of those guitarists would have been able to supply information by the mile on the latest noise gizmo, effects processor, or aural exciter. Because it's all about the texture of the sound, not the notes.

Whether you think this development heralds the collapse of civilisation as we know it or the dawn of a bright new day, it is nevertheless logical for musical development to mirror our fragmented and unstable use of time and for the way we listen to music to adapt accordingly, as it is indeed doing. There used to be a spot in the terminally awful Friary shopping mall in Guildford where the in-house muzak would mingle with the music from the nearby HMV music store, and both would mingle with the radio from the clothes shop across the way. In the right spot, you could get a fairly even balance of all three, in a Varèse-like cacophony of sublime proportion. And no one passing appeared to notice any of it.

Most technological developments start within the given framework of the social practices of the day, or those anticipated for the near future, but seldom end up being used as intended. Early broadcasting, for example, was marked by a series of technical inventions driven first by military, propaganda, or commercial interests and only later by an awareness of a potential for entertainment. The specific form into which broadcasting technology was shaped in the 20s – that of centralised transmission and privatised reception – served specific functions in a new and specific social situation. It wasn't inherent in the technology, nor was it inevitable. It was the result of active intervention by governments and commercial interests.

Similarly with recording. The phonograph and gramophone were originally intended for office dictation and archiving rather than reproducing music. But once someone spotted the possibilities of mass dissemination, the necessary production technology, cheap playback equipment, and a global distribution network were quickly developed. By 1914, many urban and rural listeners could be supplied with the latest records and gramophones virtually anywhere in the world through the subsidiaries and agents of a small number of Western record companies and manufacturers. The long-playing record, originally introduced to avoid breaks in symphonic movements, was not meant for lengthy progressive-rock pieces that covered the whole side of an album, let alone the extended DJ remixes of more recent times.

Radio and records in the 20s and 30s allowed music to enter ordinary homes. Both, says Richard Middleton in *Studying Popular Music*, "were symbiotically connected to Tin Pan Alley, whose steady output of literate songs, drawing on bourgeois aspirations and traditions, and stressing individual sentiment, cemented the arrangement".[6] Gramophones were sold as, literally, part of the furniture, as pianos had been – they had to look nice in the parlour.

As electrical recording and the microphone were introduced, in response to the competition presented by radio's better sound quality, crooners appeared such as Bing Crosby, whose mellow, conversational, and intimate style tied in perfectly with the intimacy, privacy, and domesticity of home music-listening, crystallising the idea.

By the late 30s, there was a god in heaven and there was peace in the music industry. Powerful broadcasters and record companies peddled their wares to grateful and compliant listeners unable to seek alternatives. It looked as if it could last forever and the youthful music industry could sleep well at night, but the future was to be one of continuing struggle between this dominant model of benign authority and paternalism and the rise of alternative institutions using new technological developments. The invention of magnetic tape, for example, made recording cheaper and easier, decentralising it and creating the fertile soil for the hundreds of independent labels that shot up in the 50s and supported the noisy rock'n'rollers.

The rise of TV threatened much of radio's traditional programming and led to a search for new audiences, among them a pop audience. For a few years in the mid 50s, there was a real possibility of a whole new pattern in musical communication, but the window opened only briefly before the industry regulated and controlled the new changes to suit its own interests, epitomised by Top 40 radio, DJs, and playlists.

The music that surfaces at any given time is the end product of a complex interlocking web of activity, of which the technological aspect is an important part, but only one part. Recording certainly encouraged the switch to non-literary, or oral, composition methods. When this started in the States, it took place amid a restructuring of the record industry and a growth in the record market that gave musicians an increased freedom to use their own material – which was then marketed through the particular structure of the American record and radio industries to particular groups of people.

My own career started in similarly favourable circumstances, where the financial and political environment was set fair, the industry was growing, and three critical technological developments were all present: multi-track tape recording and editing; the long-playing record; and the American FM radio system. Had any one of these elements been missing, music would still have surfaced, but it would have been a different music.

Today, in a harsher environment, the problem is not primarily one of production – the means and the ideas are readily available – but one of marketing in a saturated marketplace. The technology has benefits (anyone can make a record) which immediately lead to drawbacks (everyone does make a record). The only music that can reliably be expected to surface is that which attaches itself to something else that is larger than the music, for example a political cause, such as civil rights or Vietnam in 60s America. "You gotta get a gimmick" urged the song from the 20s, or "something to hang it on" as is said today. It's more than just the music.

Technology and musical technique, content, and meaning generally develop together. Each makes demands on the other, but at every turn there is an area left over for those who want to inject something from the past or for the unforeseen possibilities of the future.

Let's take your standard run-of-the-mill guitar hero – please, take him. Legs apart, eyes closed, Spandex creaking, guitar cranked up – something I'm sure we've all practised in the mirror many times. He didn't just come from nowhere, and even though he seems to have been with us forever, he's a relatively new arrival as a rock icon. He was not simply a product of the technology of amplified guitars but of the way that technology was used within the social and aesthetic context of heavy and progressive rock.

Originally, amplification of the electric guitar began in response to a demand by big-band guitarists to be heard more clearly. Electrification then allowed an expansion of techniques, with fast runs, glissandi, inflections, vibrato. Then came a demand for sustain. Once you can sustain, there will be a demand for tonal modulation and processing, wah-wah, fuzz, and so on. Then the bass player wants bigger amps, so he too can be heard, and to and fro it goes.

The technology brings forth new techniques; the new techniques require new technologies. But in this decade, the 2000s, there is also a loving return to warmer analogue synthesizers from the 80s in a revolt against the digital 90s – a backward historical leap. The guitar hero's macho posturing as he delivers his solo dates back to the progressive rock days, which in turn brought in virtuoso legitimacy from instrumental jazz, where the solo was essentially the thing, the meat-and-potatoes of the matter. So the living, breathing Spinal Tap cliché that we have now is the end product of this interlocking web of activity on many levels: historical, political, aesthetic, technological, and ideological.

Once established, a particular musical–technological crystallisation like this can take on quite definite ideological references that can be very hard to shift. The electric guitar, because of its history, now means passion and sexuality, almost inescapably. Synthesizers, on the other hand, have acquired connotations of modernity, the future, rational control, exploration. Keyboards generally aren't welcome in guitar bands – the organist with Lenny Kravitz is stationed well to the rear of the stage behind a wall of amps, and the unfortunate guy who played keyboards with Oasis is offstage altogether, or used to be.

The contrast is now so embedded that it can be played upon. In contrast to the effete synth-pop bands of the 80s, the heavy sweating guitar bands of the day – Springsteen, U2, Big Country – were actively taken to signify commitment to rock's 'classic' values of honesty, hard work, and loyalty. In the 50s and 60s, the equation was acoustic equals folk authenticity and electric equals commercial sell-out, as Bob Dylan found out when he went electric at the Newport folk festival in 1965.

So your best hope of a hearing as a musician, young or old, is to offer radical work. Radical work can only succeed if it plays, by modification, inversion, re-articulation, or contrast, on the existing cultural forms, the existing musical status quo. When Dylan picked up the electric guitar that day at Newport, whether he knew it or not, he was about to do an extremely radical day's work.[7]

15 WHAT DO YOU CALL A GUY WHO HANGS AROUND WITH MUSICIANS?

I t is 35 years since the trip with Custer and the Braided Waif, and I've just got to a more comfortable bed after a percussion-quartet concert with the World Drummers Ensemble in the beautifully restored Theatre Carré in Amsterdam. About 3:00am, I put down my book, don my eyeshade, insert my industrial-strength earplugs, adjust my body to promote the swiftest possible onset of sleep, and turn out the light.

After a few minutes, it occurs to me that, actually, I am probably using the wrong sound on that Turkish drumming piece we'd just premiered and it might be better to revert to Plan B, with the right hand on the Swish Ride rather than the side of the floor tom. Come to think of it, there has to be a better sticking pattern for that whole passage. Maybe a different sticking could accommodate both timbres. Maybe the whole piece is sounding a bit lumpy, and we might be better off if we abandoned further work on it all together and moved on …

C'mon, snap out of it. I adjust my body to a second and hopefully more effective position: left side foetal, right leg extended straight to that nice cool patch at the bottom of the duvet. You have to sneak up on sleep. You have to outwit your conscious mind by a series of smart manoeuvres designed to distract it while oblivion slinks up on the outside. Haven't slept well since the arrival of kids. Above my head, a creak, and moving feet. In their infinite wisdom, the Dutch architect and designers of this post-modern egg-carton have decided, no doubt in the interest of their 'art', that there should be no soft furnishings in the rooms. No carpet, no curtains, no soft chair, no easy cushions. This ensures that no dampening would impede the direct transmission of the sound of the footsteps above – so thoughtful. The sound pauses. Where is he now? Going to the bathroom, coming back from it, or scratching his arse somewhere in between? This is ridiculous.

It's 3:17am. I consider a sleeping pill, but the problem there is that I will still be drowsy at 7:15 when I'll need all my faculties about me for the airport check-in and the inevitable excess baggage pas de deux. This is a sort of courtly dance of extreme delicacy, whether your partner is male or female. Sometimes the women at the airline check-in desk are a whole lot more stubborn than the men, with utterly inflexible Germans of either gender being the worst. So, first the selection of the most likely-looking agent, and then a whole lot of sweet-talking to reassure the agent that the four suitcases he has before him, collectively weighing at least a ton, won't prevent the plane from getting off the ground and are also essential to the cultural nature of the mission, namely to promote harmony and better understanding between peoples. As such, their owner should naturally be exempt from any possible charges arising, and would he or she like a signed CD? It doesn't often work.

I find a pill, split it in two, and swallow. I jam the earplugs further into my ears and roll over for another try. This time I'm more successful: in the grey half-light between waking and sleeping I find myself in surroundings familiar from my youth.

The room is large, stuffy, and strangely lurid, with pink psychedelic flowers painted on the wall. Instruments everywhere. Bubbles of colour, from what I guess is a liquid-pigment lightshow, expand slowly and burst into other oily bubbles – the whole place seems more like a nursery than a rehearsal room. Four or five musicians, elaborately clothed in velvet and tie-dye, drift around in a diffident fashion, noodling occasionally, but even that sounds curiously listless. I'm playing a drum kit that is heavy and sticky, as if made of treacle. Without saying much, a singer hunches himself over a microphone and parts long curtains of hair to reveal nose and beard. Somewhere in there I think I can see a mouth. Proceedings commence bravely, with a wordless one-note vocal over his own semi-pitched but rhythmic guitar scratching. No one stirs. Someone is obtrusively assembling a portable bicycle. The bassist's nose fails to rise up out of the technical magazine he is reading. Sitting at the drums, flipping aimlessly through the daily paper, I notice a fly on the bell of my ride cymbal. After what seems an age, the leader's sheer persistence elicits a feeble accompaniment from a couple of the others, which grinds to a halt after several long, repetitive minutes.

"Coffee, anyone?" I hear my enthusiastic voice. Anything to get out of the room. "Well, it's not very good, is it?" ventures the guitarist, a brave soul. "I mean it doesn't exactly go anywhere, does it?" Storm is a-brewing. "You bloody well do better then, if you're so smart. Took me all last night to write that," shoots back the composer of this modest achievement, challenging, aggressive, and aggrieved, all at the same time.

Pause. The fly has moved from my cymbal to the corner of the paper, and I'm ready to strike. This rehearsal room is in an old converted stable on a French country estate – no escape, no human existence for miles – and the flies live on in hope that the horses might come back. Bloody hell, this isn't like watching paint dry, it is watching paint dry.

Back in the 60s, when time was cheap, the whole band used to sit around in rehearsal rooms until the job got done – 'the job' being the construction, or what the musicians were pleased to call 'the writing', of the first 40 minutes or so of music that all parties could actually live with. That 40 minutes was the bare minimum that you could get away with on an album, and the sooner you found it, the sooner you could get the heck out of there.

For me, London and New York City have been reduced to a series of rehearsal rooms associated with one album or another, and all with a greater or lesser degree of torture, interspersed with long stretches of tedium. Quite commonly, the leader, which means the most opinionated of the assembled players, is the least equipped technically, and he depends upon a combination of threats and bribery to extract his preferred musical terrain from his better equipped and more docile colleagues.

"Well, I suppose you could make it a minor ninth, and sit on that for a bit," suggests one of the few people in the room who knows what a minor ninth is. We lumber into it again, but this time the musical sound of the harmony stirs something deep in the cranium of the torpid bass player, and his nose rises up slowly out of the magazine. He doesn't actually play, you understand, but he does give it serious thought. More long repetitive minutes, but this time with a minor ninth. "I think I might get a coffee," I try again. No one cares whether I do or not, and the lack of response explains that rather succinctly. The clock ticks, and the paint doesn't appear to be getting any drier.

"I wrote this thing the other day, and it sort of might go with it." This is proffered from an unexpected quarter: the keyboard player. New to the band, he has wisely kept his head below the parapet for our first few meetings but has become creatively emboldened since someone explained to him down the pub the value of publishing royalties. He has the confidence of the trained musician, and the others, especially me, are beginning to see him as someone who might make a silk purse out of a sow's ear, an invaluable skill when you are trying to get out of here, away from here, in the shortest possible time.

He launches into a fierce groove on his Hammond organ, with just enough chordal movement to allow it to cycle and build nicely. It is wholly unrelated to the previous thing we have been working on. "Perfect," says the singer. "Just what I was going to suggest. Do it again." The music comes again, but this time with his wordless howl on top, and the beginnings of a bass part from the bass department, by this time fully awake, or as fully awake as that department ever gets. I know that detailed instructions will soon be heading my way from our leader.

"No, not like that, like this. Split your hands. You want the right one doing 'chug, chug, chugga' on the tom – no, the other tom, that one there, look – and the left one hits the cymbal when I wave. Watch me."

Now it's definitely time for coffee. I stand and offer him the sticks. "What's that for?" says Our Leader. "You're so good at it, you do it," I hear myself say, cool as ice. The heat is stifling. That's the problem with these wretched places – no air. They all had to be 'soundproofed', which meant you were locked into the Black Hole of Clerkenwell for about eight hours a day with a diminishing supply of air. After about five hours everyone is either lounging about in a sullen torpor or at each other's throats, and it never seems to occur to anyone why.

Everyone has stopped playing – the first genuine musical silence of the day – and the only sound is the buzzing and humming of amplifiers. Quietly, and with ramrod self-control, I watch myself pick up the heavy snare drum stand from the trunk on my right, raise it as high above my head as I can, and, with every fibre of strength I can muster, bring it smashing down on the little man's head.

❑

With a sharp intake of breath, I sit bolt upright in bed. All around is blackness, not yet an inkling of dawn through the central join in the curtains. God, my whole forehead is running with sweat, my eyeshade soaked. My more common performance nightmare has developed a close cousin, the rehearsal-room nightmare – a dream made all the more terrifying by its proximity to the truth. Anything to escape from those long, supposedly democratic rehearsals, either frozen or boiled in airless basements, in which I had spent so much of my first 20 years.

Most of *The Yes Album* first saw the light of day in a mammoth writing and rehearsal session in a Devon farmhouse. *Fragile* gestated loudly in an upstairs room in Shepherd Market, Mayfair. The Una

Billings School of Dance in Shepherds Bush, walls unhappily covered in mirrors for a reflected and deafening high-end sound, gave birth to *Close To The Edge*. My earliest memory of rehearsing with Yes is in a carpet warehouse at the Holland Park roundabout, only about half a mile away from Una.

Robert Fripp and I pushed the previous night's beer glasses up the bar in the rugby clubhouse at Richmond AA ground, where Jamie Muir drove me, and probably Robert, to distraction as we laboured through *Larks' Tongues In Aspic*. A spectacular shortage of material and a simmering hostility between King Crimson's bass player and guitarist suffused the atmosphere as we tried to scrape something together for *Starless And Bible Black* in a room above a boathouse by the river in Kingston upon Thames. There was a draughty Dorset village hall for King Crimson's *Discipline*, the back room of a music store in Champaign, Illinois, for *Beat*, and *Three Of A Perfect Pair* was wrung out of us in a room four flights up in the Garment District of Manhattan and a barn in Woodstock, New York.

They were all forceps delivery. There were messy sheets, bowls of clean water, damp rags, tearful relatives, and blood on the floor. There were misunderstandings, wilful and accidental, unkind words, endless philosophising, horse-trading, power liaisons, late-night phone calls, and exasperation, all in equal measure. Mostly it was like getting blood out of a lettuce. Wisely, I don't think they do it like that any more. Somehow the work got done, but whatever they paid us, it wasn't enough.

❏

There is good reason why much of what we rockers and jazzers do is sniffed at by the chattering classes, musical academia, the cognoscenti. There are reasons why the drum kit has only recently become an instrument worthy of study in classical music academies, albeit only as part of the broader family of percussion. There was a reason that Dr Allan Bunney, the distinguished and very classical head of music at

Tonbridge School, should pronounce himself "sad" that, despite evidence of musical talent, I only wanted to play "the drums". And there was a reason that someone left that note on the piano when Django Bates was at the Royal College Of Music: "Not to be used for the playing of jazz music."

We can only hear music as valuable when we know what to listen to and how to listen for it. Our reception of it and our expectations of it are not inherent in the music itself. So the question becomes: what do people hear? The writer Simon Frith suggests that we value music according to our allegiance to, or proximity to, one of three different 'art worlds', or taste groups: the classical world, the folk world, and the pop world.

The classical world of art music has its roots in the world of 19th-century high culture and is organised around a particular notion of musical scholarship, a particular concept of musical talent, and a particular sort of musical event. This is the world of the academy, music departments, conservatories, formal arrangements, which promotes the idea that the music is handed down through the generations. "Central to this world," says Frith, "is the teacher–pupil relationship, the belief that musicians must serve an apprenticeship, must progress through fixed stages ... before they are 'qualified' to play. ... Only the right people with the right training can, in short, experience the real meaning of this 'great' music." To compose or play without having received the right credentials is to be labelled primitive or naive.

The ideology here is that the composer is answerable only to himself, creating purely what he wants without fear of acceptance in the marketplace, but, says Frith, he may well have "to please an audience – teachers, grant-givers, concert programmers, specialist record companies – which is in many respects more tightly in control of the 'acceptable composition' than the so-called mass public". Frith goes on to explain how the scholarly skills developed in musical academia are similar to those of the art historian or literary critic and have the same purpose, namely to establish and protect the classical works.

Think of this classical art world as a fortress, with gatekeepers, and with treasure inside. Ordinary people can gain access to this world, but it is strictly hierarchical: composer at the top, then conductor, performers, and audience, in that order. The treasures in the fortress are allowed out of the fortress for viewing under the close guard of a set of semi-academic authorities and practices, such as music critics, liner notes, classical radio stations, concert programmers, and so on, whose job is to bridge the gap between high music scholarship and the everyday music-listening punter.

Nineteenth-century American audiences did not at first grasp the seriousness of the classical concert, and they had to be taught the conventions, that the experience they were about to have in the concert hall was an almost religious one. Listening silently and respectfully, knowing when to applaud, no coughing – these are all conventions designed to underline the transcendent nature of the experience. Toilets, bars, and cloakrooms are all separated from the performance area. Carefully democratic and subdued lighting sets the right tone.

Compare this with the average jazz place, where totally different conventions apply. Talk is allowed under sufferance; the music is negotiated around people negotiating with waitresses; people walk about. This indicates an irreverence for the music, which is generally seen as the accompaniment to proceedings at some long-forgotten bordello. But in these circumstances the music must work, it must earn its keep, it must put expensive drinks down throats, and keep bums on seats. It must be more robust than the audience.

Following on from the classical world, says Frith, the second taste group is the folk world. Here there is "ideally no separation between art and life" and the music is valued as a cultural necessity. But in many ways, its emphasis on the natural, the authentic, the immediate, and the spontaneous is derived from the "perceived rules of commercial pop". Whatever pop is, folk doesn't want to be. Dressing up in stage clothes, overtly 'putting on a show', anything other than a shambolic amble to the stage and to a barely functioning microphone – all this would be dangerously close to glamour, to the glitz of artificial pop.

Like the classical taste group, folk has its own history, archives, and tradition, but it places most value on purity and the correct (read 'traditional') way of doing things. Folk music is thus evaluated or condemned – Bob Dylan going electric, for example – according to some concept of unchanging musical 'truth'. If pop is an impersonal technocratic culture, a culture of types, functions, jobs, and sales figures, then folk stands as the antithesis. The 50s folk revival, suggests Robert Cantwell, "drew on a vision of the old Free America, and made the romantic claim for folk culture as oral, immediate, communal; a culture of rights, obligations, and beliefs".[1]

Frith's third taste group is the commercial music world, "organised around the music industry, around the means and possibilities of turning sounds into commodities". Pop music 'events' offer an escape from the daily grind, as opposed to the high-art transcendental classical experience that, it is suggested, may make you a better person. A good classical performance is measured by the stillness it commands, evidence of the audience's concentration, and by the lack of all physical distraction, coughs, or shuffles. "A good rock concert, by contrast, is measured by the audience's physical response, by how quickly they get out of their seats, onto the dance floor, by how loudly they shout and scream." Rock stage-clothes and posturings are designed to show the musician's body as both sexual and instrumental, with plenty of sweat and tight trousers.

It's clear that, today, classical, folk, and pop music co-exist and compete. You know you are a folkie in part because you reject the values of the commercial world. And there is no admission to the classical forum if you don't have the right entry credentials. When the brilliant young Royal Academy pianist Rick Wakeman joined me in Yes in 1970, you could practically hear the wringing of the hands from the Academy across the Thames as its brilliant acolyte fell into the hands of the unbelievers.

This equation of serious with the mind, and thus high culture, and fun with the body, and thus low culture, can be traced back to the mid 19th century and the division of mental and manual labour built into the Industrial Revolution and the consequent organisation of education. The thinking was that feelings were best expressed spiritually and mentally, perhaps in church or in the contemplation of art, with a stiff upper lip, but best not in public. Frith says that "bodily responses became, by definition, mind-less" (now a term of disparagement). You can see this split admirably on display in the traditional Irish dancer, rigid upper body counterpointed with feverish footwork. Mind–body; brain–brainless.

The brain came to be associated with art music, and brainlessness with pop. Peter Stadler, in a 1962 essay *The Aesthetics Of Popular Music*, claimed that pop was "music requiring a minimum of brain activity". Jazz, too, was a music that "did not have to be thought about". When popular music crashed into black American music in the early part of the last century, a long history of Romanticism stood ready to define black African culture as the 'body', the other part of the European bourgeois 'mind'.

The 'primitive' pre-civilised world was viewed from the 'sophisticated' over-civilised world, which deemed these people to be innocent, uncorrupted by culture, and still close to some undefined human 'essence'.[2] This kind of racism was endemic through early jazz commentary and led to the cosying up of jazz to classical music, so that, for example, clarinettist Benny Goodman could commission work from composer Darius Milhaud.

But if African music is held to be more 'primitive' or 'natural' than European music (and I'm using all these adjectives in quotes), then African music must be more in touch with the body. And what's the difference between the two? Rhythm. So rhythm, goes the argument, must be the way in which the 'primitive', the sexual, is expressed.

Ted Gioia shows in his book *The Imperfect Art* that the French intellectual view of the primitive, the myth of the 'noble savage', meant that jazz was heard as a music "charged with emotion but largely devoid of intellectual content", while the jazz musician was taken to be an "inarticulate and unsophisticated practitioner of an art which he himself scarcely understands".[3]

Frith points out that "this matrix of race, rhythm, and sex through which white critics and fans made ideological sense of jazz was just as important in the interpretation of rock'n'roll".[4] As Charles Shaar Murray, the rock critic, writes about Jimi Hendrix: "The 'cultural dowry' Jimi Hendrix brought with him into the pop marketplace included not only his immense talent and the years of experience acquired in a particularly hard school of showbusiness, but the accumulated weight of the fantasies and mythologies constructed around black music and black people by whites, hipsters, and reactionaries alike. Both shared one common article of faith: that black people represent the personification of the untrammelled id – intrinsically wild, sensual, dangerous, 'untamed' in every sense of the word."[5]

It might be interesting to speculate just how far Hendrix felt he had to live up to his publicity as a bad-boy hedonist, and that he took it too far. That is the sense in which some say we killed him, or Michael Hutchence from INXS, or Diana, Princess of Wales – the sense in which they were attempting to live an externally imposed lifestyle.

Murray continues: "The ironies were murderous: a black man with a white guitar; a massive, almost exclusively white audience wallowing in a paddy field of its own making; the clear, pure, trumpet-like notes of the familiar melody struggling to pierce through the clouds of tear-gas, the explosions of cluster bombs, the screams of the dying, the crackle of the flames, the heavy palls of smoke stinking with human grease, the hovering chatter of helicopters. ... One man said more in three-and-a-half minutes about that peculiarly disgusting [Vietnam] war and its reverberations than all the novels and memoirs and movies put together."[6]

The racism endemic to rock'n'roll is not that the white musicians stole from black culture but that they exaggerated it. If Jerry Lee Lewis's 'Whole Lotta Shakin' Goin' On' was to succeed in advertising itself as white-boy-wildly-sings-black, then it had to do so quickly and simply – hence the coarse cartoon-like approach from Lewis as to what it means to sing black. It's a caricature. It's not that 'raw', 'earthy', and 'authentic' black sounds were diluted or whitened for mass consumption, but the opposite: gospel and early rhythm & blues were blacked up. Black performers could reach a rock'n'roll audience, but only if they started to behave as white people thought black people should behave.

Not only is the obsession with the mind–body split laughable – this insistence that notions of aesthetic, mind, harmony, intellect are superior to hedonistic, body, rhythm, natural – but it's also entirely artificial. It may be self evident to us now, but to many throughout the first part of the 20th century, the idea that musical rhythm is as much a mental as a physical matter was a real problem.

Any reasonable drummer will tell you that deciding when to play a note is as much a matter of thought as deciding what note to play. Any number of musicologists will assert that African music and dance are not performed as wild, ecstatic, emotional expression but rather as ways of expressing aesthetic and ethical structures. Sexuality has little, if anything, to do with it. As John Miller Chernoff says: "Ecstasy as we see it would imply for most Africans a separation from all that is good and beautiful, and generally, in fact, any such loss of control is viewed by them as tasteless, ridiculous, or possibly sinful."[7] So all those Edwardian music critics need not have worried: black music, no more than the flattened fifth in jazz, was not going to bring the house down.

Nor is African music more simple than European music, as is often suggested in the mistaken belief that something more complex is evidence of a more mature society. African music is just as complex as Western music, but complex according to its own conventions.

So the entire edifice of criticism of Afro-American music, and by extension the marginalisation of the jazz player, is based on a false ideology, not musicological fact. Respectable taste insisted, and to a degree continues to insist, that the Western invention of tonal harmony was evidence of an advanced form of civilised culture. Those who failed to develop it, or accorded it a lesser stature than rhythm, of all things, certainly had some explaining to do.

For me, getting all this straight has gone a long way toward explaining the perceived inferiority complex of jazz musicians, and particularly drummers, and their current working milieu. No wonder we're all a little crazy. Ever since coming from overpaid and over-praised rock to the tiny world of underpaid and under-praised jazz, I've been mulling over the explanations. In the UK, for every £1 of Arts Council money allotted to support jazz, roughly £30 is allotted to opera, which indicates that the balance may not be rectified any time soon.[8] But it may go some way toward explaining the longevity of all those drummer jokes. What *do* you call a guy who hangs around with musicians?

16 DO YOU JUST PLAY ANYTHING YOU LIKE?

I too am a listener but, like many musicians, something of a floating voter. Most types of music have percussion of some sort or another, and that tends to be the common denominator for my personal listening. As consumers of music, what we want tends to be determined by who we are. There is a strong connection between all our social and aesthetic values, and from this follows the idea that music may be interpreted as a coded expression of the social aims and values of the people to whom it appeals.

Music can offer comfort as it reaffirms your lifestyle. What we want is based on fantasy: we want a certain kind of pleasure; we have a certain set of psychological needs. Young people want music that fits those requirements. A pre-teen girl, for example, probably likes that mixed-gender pop group because, functionally, it shows her what to wear, how to dance, and how to behave at the club; psychologically, it provides material for her private sexual and maternal fantasies. At a few pennies for the download, that's a lot of bang for your buck. If the artist purports to be poor, abused white trash, and our young girl is in the mood to identify with that, then the poor-white-trash motif is being used as psychological fulfilment.

Music does so much more for us. It provides us with a sense of being sociable. Whether rap for the homies, goth for the goths, or

19th-century chamber music for the German Jews in Israel, it gives us the experience of collective identity. And in most popular music it's the words that give the song its social use. People may rarely appreciate the intended 'message' of a song, and the words themselves may be trivial and unrealistic, even if you can hear them, but that doesn't necessarily make them insignificant. Pop love songs "don't *cause* people to fall in love, but provide people with the means to articulate the feelings associated with being in love".[1] That, argues Simon Frith in his book *Performing Rites*, is the use that pop songs have for people, and in their use is their meaning.

In the admittedly extreme case of Jon Anderson's much-lampooned lyrics for Yes, I eventually decided that, for me, there was no problem. If, as has been suggested, 80 per cent of communication is non-verbal, I was perfectly happy with the rhythm and sound of the words alone, although millions of the band's fans evidently derived plenty of literal meaning from his efforts.

We advertise our chosen identities principally and most obviously through dress codes – leathers for the metal merchants and rockers, kaftans and tie-dye for the 60s hippies, studs and bondage for the enslaved punks, and so on. Some of our early attempts at finding an identity can be quite comical. When I read A.B. Spellman's book *Four Lives In The Bebop Business* as a 16-year-old jazz fanatic, I was convinced I had to walk around miserable in a show of solidarity for what I imagined were the downtrodden practitioners of that music. Popular music is inclusive, not exclusive. If I like a particular kind of music, it doesn't mean I necessarily have to identify with its political or cultural context.

Once we start looking at different musical genres, we can begin to document the different ways in which music works to give people different identities, to place them in different social groups. Whether we're talking about Finnish dance halls in Sweden, Irish pubs in London, or Indian film music in Trinidad, the music's aesthetic values are grasped by the host culture as the communal values of the incoming culture. What the Englishman thinks about the Irishman, and vice versa, is in part determined by each one's understanding of the other's music.

Music literally puts us in our place. For a little more than a century, popular music has been important in helping us learn to understand ourselves as middle class, black, feminine, British. But the sense of identity we derive from that music may or may not fit in with other powerful social forces from family, education, and background. We all know the punk with the Mohican who has been asked to leave home by his tedious middle-class parents because the identity that goes with his chosen type of pop music is hopelessly at odds with the identity he's been fitted up with since birth by his middle-class upbringing.

But music also suggests that change is possible: you can group together with other like-minded people in the musical genre of your choice and share dissatisfaction. In itself, the music is neither reactionary nor revolutionary, but it is a source of strong feeling that may lead to reaction or revolution – as seen, most spectacularly, with Bob Marley in Jamaica.

Musical pleasure is unique in that it is derived from fantasies and daydreams while simultaneously being extremely real. And it's just this fusion of fantasy and reality that integrates the aesthetic judgment that something *sounds* good with the ethical judgement that something *is* good. John Miller Chernoff's book *African Rhythm And African Sensibility* explains that among African musicians the aesthetic and the ethical need to be, and indeed are, balanced or unified.[2] If it sounds good, it is good. The issue is balance: a quality of rhythmic and musical relationships describes a quality of social life. Music making and music listening are bodily matters experienced directly and immediately. Music, for listeners as much as practitioners, gives us a real experience of what the ideal could be.

Finally, what also makes music special as a cultural form is that, in Simon Frith's terms, it "defines a space without boundaries".[3] It is the cultural form best able to cross borders – sounds carry across fences, walls, oceans, and across classes, races, and nations – and to define places. In clubs, scenes, raves, concert halls, we are only where the music takes us, where it transports us.

❏

But for me, as a performer, I am confronted by immediate and pressing concerns before my work is going to cross any borders. As record-company interest has dwindled in the areas of music that intrigue us, so we musicians have cast about with an increased urgency for any other possible source of support – financial, logistical, technical, or, if nothing else, moral. And it is the manufacturers of the tools of our trade who have, to a degree, stepped in to pick up the slack.

There is shared commercial interest here. The young musician is wedded to the idea that he must have the instrument that his hero uses. At least by buying that, there is some chance he will sound the same, isn't there? Well, maybe. But an army of advertisers is there to answer yes to that question, and glossy monthly magazines pour off the newsstands with shimmering pictures of drum kits that look good enough to eat.

The endorsing artist, pictured alongside this food-fest, may be usefully rewarded for his trouble. Free instrument provision, a guaranteed number of events at retail level ('drum clinics') for which he will be paid to demonstrate the attributes of his sponsor's kits, perhaps transportation and delivery of instruments to his specification at concert halls around the world, and national advertising that cross-promotes his own latest CDs – all or any combination of these will be well received by the endorsing musician. Generally, the industry seems to have a moratorium on out-and-out paying of the artist to play the instrument – unlike, I believe, our sporting colleagues. But for those willing to play the game, there can be rewards.

In common with tennis stars, there are, however, the slightly sinister rankings. The manufacturer naturally wants only the most popular artists on his roster of endorsers. In an edgy and unholy alliance between editor and manufacturer, music-magazine readers are asked annually to vote for their favourites. It can come as a relief to know you are number two in Holland, or the fourth best jazz drummer in the UK, or the third best studio musician as voted by the readers of *Bass Player* monthly, because without an appearance somewhere near the top ten of something or other, some executive from the company whose products you endorse will be on the phone in a jiffy asking what you propose to do to "raise your profile" so that his "people" will be able to continue supporting you this year.

For 30 years I've been fortunate to have had the support of the Japanese firm Hoshino Gakki Co Ltd. They manufacture Ibanez guitars and Tama drums and export this equipment all around the world. I've been in advertising campaigns for their drums for years, but recently their assistance has moved to a new level, in the sense that they are willing to provide drums to my specification in most cities. They stumbled recently in the case of Malta, but that's only because the cost of flying in a full drum kit was prohibitive. I speak to Atsushi Honjyo in their Dutch office and tell him which European city I'm playing next, and when I turn up two months later, the right drums and hardware are sitting on the stage. This has a cash value that in part enables Earthworks to function, and as such I applaud him and his company for supporting the arts. But now it's payback time for Hoshino's support, and I have, again, to earn my place in the rankings.

❏

There is an icy cut to the wind on a freezing November morning as I walk over to the Salle Pierre-Mercure for the Montreal Drum Fest. Aside from a solo performance or drum clinic in the back room of a store in Reading or Rimini, there is also a handful of these major drum festivals around the world, of which Montreal is one of the best. These events will typically have five or six drum stars a day over two or three days and pull in large crowds of anywhere between 1,000 and 3,000 drum and percussion-crazed customers.

Leading the pack, it is probably safe to say, is the Percussive Arts Society's annual convention. The four or five biggest hotels in a major American convention city, perhaps Columbus, Houston, or Nashville, will be taken over by an international community of hitters, bashers, scrapers, and slappers, all psyched and ready to hear an endless round of the world's leading percussionists in every aspect of the percussive arts, from military, through classical, drum corps, rock, jazz, country, Latin, electronics, tuned percussion, and all manner of ethnic styles and disciplines. Starting with some burning jazz quartet in the hotel lobby at 8:30am through to a display of classical tympani technique at 5:30pm, and spread over dozens of venues, it's noisy, exciting, and an unbelievably rich feast.

Perhaps the second most prestigious show would be the Modern Drummer Festival Weekend, run by the magazine of that name, the biggest and most widely distributed of the national drum magazines. And third on the list would be the Montreal Drum Fest, run for many years by the wonderful Ralph Angelillo and Serge Gamache, both true lovers of percussion in all its manifestations. You have only to lay eyes on these two to know they do it for the love of it. There will be 1,500 extremely knowledgeable drummers, other musicians, and listeners in the room, and they have all come to hear what it is you have to say. It had better be good.

I grab some coffee – black, no sugar – and make my way downstairs to the tune-up room. Each performer will be set up on a rolling riser so that he can be rolled out onto the stage with the minimum of delay following his predecessor. Unlike the more leisurely atmosphere at a drum clinic where you are the only artist, performing for as long or as short a time as you want, and at your own speed, these drum festivals are pressured situations where you are in unspoken but nevertheless tangible competition with your colleagues. I play equipment supplied by half a dozen manufacturers, including drums, cymbals, drumheads, sticks, microphones, and heaven knows what else, as do the other exceptionally talented drummers on the bill. Nervy sales reps from all these companies hover around the musicians in the tune-up room as they assemble, clamp, and tune their respective drumsets. If I'm asked one more time if there is anything else I need, I think I'll scream.

Upstairs, the show has started with an unbelievable display of dexterity from the new find, the currently fastest Wyatt Earp. I definitely don't have the chops that this guy has, so I'm going to have to use stealth. Maybe I could put some lead in his fuel tank. Anyway, I'm ahead on form, which should help. I have 40 years of recordings that have wheedled their way into these people's collective consciousness, so they will, with luck, be predisposed to like me. But I'm going to have to summon every last bit of musicianship I have.

In the tune-up room, the sensational Mexican–American Joey Heredia, from East Los Angeles, is being fitted snugly into his enormous kit, like a Formula 1 driver. He has the big shades and is wearing something that looks like fireproof overalls. Now all he needs is the helmet. I have only to look at these drummers and their kits to know how beautiful they are going to sound.

Unpacking his drums alongside me is the brilliant jazz drummer Bill Stewart, whom many say is leading the pack on sheer musicality on a drumset. He's quiet, taps the drums lightly with fingers to hear the pitch, tunes thoughtfully, taps some more. A small kit. Those guys are always the most dangerous.

Someone risks his life by asking me again if I have everything I need. A quick escape route might be nice, but there is not much getting out of this. Executives chat distractedly with magazine people or try to look busy dusting invisible specks from their gleaming new equipment. My instruments work all right, but suddenly everything I do as I warm up seems lumpen, tired, and graceless. I shouldn't be here; I don't deserve this; I'm a fraud: all the old skeletons come out of the closet at once and do a dance in front of me.

After what seems like an eternity of backstage industry chit-chat, my drums are moved upstairs, put on a riser, and fitted with mics and a small sound-system, because I'll be playing along to backing tracks.

Drum karaoke. It's quite common for drum stars to play along to tracks of their latest CD, or freshly prepared music, with the original drums stripped off. Sounds just like the real thing, and the drum-crazed audience not only don't care that there is no one else on stage, they prefer it.

I have a horrible cold, and my hearing is 50 per cent down in my right ear. This morning the doctor has made me feel worse and does precious little about it. Hell, I should be in bed. My drums sound dull, muffled, terrible; but that's me, not them. Another eternity, the drums are moved onto a very big stage, and I'm called up. I'm greeted with a surprise standing ovation as Ralph presents me with a plaque for my efforts over the years, but all I can think is that I forgot to tell the lighting man "five per cent on the house". I stare from the stage into a jet-black void that I know contains – only because I can hear them – 1,500 knowledgeable, passionate, and hungry drum freaks. Somehow if you can actually see the punters, and work to a face, you realise they are probably more terrified of you than you are of them. But too late for that now.

Lord only knows what my performance was like: the instruments sounded like distant cardboard boxes. Obviously I said and did something, but I don't remember much about it. Everyone makes the right noises as I leave the stage, so I assume honour has been satisfied. An enormous sense of relief descends, to be mixed with a poignancy as I hear the sublime Bill Stewart's elegant and unhurried opening phrases some 15 minutes later. His playing is imaginative beyond my wildest comprehension, and I remind myself that there are some 350 million North Americans, of whom about three million play a percussion instrument regularly, and none of them can play like Bill.

The evening is rounded out by a performance of Roy Haynes's group. By now I've regained some composure and join Stewart by the side of the stage to watch the Grand Master at work. He's not smooth and elegant like Bill – more a rough diamond, an old-school bundle of energy who, at age 83, ought to know better. He dresses sharp, cowboy boots and a big Stetson, moves like a man half his age, and calls his group The Fountain Of Youth. Hasn't anyone told him this is no way for a senior citizen to behave? Haynes remains a mystery to me. How come he can do all this with such little apparent wear and tear? His music-making must be absorbed so deeply into the fabric of his being that he and it have become one and the same thing.

My background, by contrast, is of a deliberate but near-fatal separation between the two – musical life (bad) from domestic life (good) – in an effort to cope. That strategy may have served me well in the past, but now it's come back to bite me in the rear. I'm paying the price for that separation in an exhausting attempt to juggle the two. So much of my career seems to have had this central theme of illegitimacy: it shouldn't really be *me* doing this at all. It's for someone in a black skin, from another country, another caste, or someone miserable, or someone on drugs, or with an American accent – anyone but me, surely, not good ol' Sevenoaks and Tonbridge me. I've still not come to terms with my professional life and I'm leaving it rather on the late side to do so. Furthermore, there is no future until I do.

Later, back at the hotel, and restless after an industry dinner, my mind runs over the events of the day. My self-awareness at the drumset is reaching epic proportions. I can see every beat I'm about to play, and in the nanosecond it takes for the stick to descend to the drum or cymbal, my conscious mind sticks its oar in and says something distinctly discouraging. No sequence of notes now seems playable without an agony of self-doubt and self-recrimination. Forty years worth of baggage is rendering me all but incapable of fresh thought. Every stroke is compromised, every choice studied, chewed over; everything has to be exhaustively rethought.

I compare this to the blissful ignorance of youth. At 18, I knew I was terrific. The best. The direction and purpose of the music was self-evident – everybody liked it, so I hardly gave it a second thought. My position was secure, but I wouldn't have recognised it as such because I had no knowledge of insecurity. What, exactly, was that? I had the confidence of the young man before he meets self-doubt. It is a window opened to a few for a short time, unless self-doubt is unexpectedly delayed at baggage claim.

In my case, it arrived in no uncertain terms in the shape of Jamie Muir, who, you'll remember, took about five minutes out of his day to explain to an over-confident, noisy, and arrogant young Bruford that, actually, *I exist to serve the music. The music does not exist to serve me.* The fact that this had not occurred to me is a measure of the arrogance under which I was labouring, and it was a wake-up jolt of a profound nature. I am uncomfortably aware that my journey has been from a position of knowing everything, at age 18, to knowing that I know nothing now. All certainties about the music industry, my musical ability, my place within music, and the meaning of the musical life itself have gradually evaporated to the point where I seem to struggle to play a note.

But if there are sticks, there are also carrots. The carrots don't come often, and their appearance may be fleeting, but when they do, they are undeniable, the real thing, orange and earthy, producing a warm feeling of certainty, of rightness, of confirmation. I need to get drunk on this feeling about four times a year. In between, everything else is just beer and skittles, froth and posture. This confirmation needs no outside validation and cannot be created externally. The occasional record that worked out really OK; the text-book rendition of this piece in that town where you could *feel* the audience just getting it; the moments when the stuff is just easy to play. At the instrument, you look down, as if outside yourself. Legs and arms move smoothly, effortlessly. There is no delay between thought and action: the thought generates the appropriate action. The music feels good so it must be good.

I am tempted to say that playing a musical instrument 'can' and 'does' provide enormous heartache matched only by an equally strong sense of wellbeing, but I prefer perhaps the words 'may' and 'should'. Increasingly, we're told that the impatient fame-and-iPod generation have no time for such an old-fashioned occupation, one that may require several years before meaningful results appear. That, of course, flies in the face of the evidence of the baby-faced prodigies lined up behind drumsets and other musical instruments the world over – young men and, increasingly, women who seem to have musical maturity beyond their years and a scarcely believable technical capacity for which they have sacrificed many teenage hours.

Thirty minutes spent in honest labour trying to pacify a reluctant combination of string, wood, gut, hammers, and metal are thirty minutes never wasted, as I repeatedly reassure anxious Surrey women, mothers of aspiring young drummers. The sustained effort to control small movements of wrist and fingers, to judge and correct any combination of pitch, timbre, and tempo, to learn to walk before you run, to fail and to try again – all of this will bear fruit. All the great drummers I know are still trying to play four decent beats in a row with greater control than they did yesterday.

Pablo Casals, the great Spanish cellist, is said to have practised the simplest of major scales for 30 minutes or so every day of his life. Weeks turn into months, months into years. With more or less effort you may struggle to a sunlit place where at last the music is there, pouring out, easy, conversational, technical concerns now sublimated to the greater good of music-making, the hours of practice producing the phrases that you want, when you want them, now. All else forgotten, these are the moments that every musician longs to inhabit, exists to create. I've had more than my fair share, for which I shall give thanks unto eternity. I've seen the sunlit place, but my visits are fleeting, and it is a greater mortal than I who is able to conjure the sunlit place at will.

Food and language may provide useful metaphors when it comes to attempting to explain what it is that drummers do. The casual observer, like Yes's old manager Brian Lane, bless him, considers that the average drummer hits pretty much anything he wants at any time as hard as possible. That analysis is wrong on several counts and is derived from the fact that our casual observer tends only to come across the drummers who are fairly far down the food chain – your average rock or pop group worker on telly. In my country, for years and until recently that meant a single programme called *Top Of The Pops*.

In fact, most drummers do broadly and increasingly the same thing. Far from hitting anything they want, they stick to a simple and effective four-note rhythmic pattern, with the bass drum on beats one and three and the snare drum, or backbeat, on two and four, and played within in a very narrow tempo range of about 90 to 130 beats per minute. Almost all rock and pop drummers do something like this, as if this rhythm descended from a government department and deviation requires a special licence. Considering what is possible, it is the drumming equivalent of a steady diet of dry toast, and with no knowledge of beef Wellington, let alone foie gras. You won't die from it, but if you ever try the beef, you'll want to change.

There is little dynamic variation in this basic rhythm – the demands of FM radio have seen to that. I remember purring down La Cienega Boulevard, Los Angeles, in a limo with a senior vice-president of Atlantic Records. It's June 1973. King Crimson is in town for a gig at Long Beach Auditorium, and we are here promoting our new offering *Larks' Tongues In Aspic*. The record is hot off the press, and this fellow hasn't heard it yet. A voice from the radio announces the upcoming show and, by way of a taster, here's the new album's first track. The car is picking up speed, and the familiar opening 'tinkleberries' – Jamie Muir's extremely light percussion – are barely audible. We've contrived to make a record that takes 3:40 to get from virtual silence to the first riff that sounds anything like rock music, the sort you might be able to hear above the road noise of the average car or sell to Atlantic Records. The executive moves from an attentive anticipation to a nervous glance out of the window – is this Art? – to an uncomfortable boredom. Interminable minutes of hesitant violin playing from David Cross finally give way to the juggernaut riff that we are both extremely relieved to hear.

Once again, the Mighty Crim has shot itself badly in the foot. We'd forgotten about – or wilfully ignored – the demands of FM radio, a desert wilderness of flat dynamics, a place where you need a licence to play quietly and then another one to play a bit more loudly. The frequency range of modern pop music is compressed, or squashed, prior to broadcast so that the quiet bits get louder and the loud bits get quieter, thus ensuring a flat dynamic range and continued attention from the listener.

Rock drummers, then, don't really play louder or more quietly any more – no call for it – so variation is usually supplied by adding something (extra guitar or ride cymbal) or taking something away. The effect, to those of us aware of more sophisticated possibilities, is rather like being shouted at in words of one syllable, in a monotone, without phrasing or breath. Further up the food chain, the more advanced player can deliver toast all right, but he also knows how to prepare and enjoy his beef Wellington and foie gras.

We drummers may eschew dynamics, but we can't afford to be so cavalier with tempo. On pain of death, the finished 'product', and even the live performance, must be metronomically, mathematically in time. In the studio, a few clicks of the mouse is all that's needed to put the human's wayward performance into the straightjacket of computer 'clock' time, in the mistaken belief that if it is metronomically accurate the rhythm track is 'right' and may be safely ignored. The early and wholesale seduction of record producer by computer as the 80s wore on produced cardboard-stiff performances by people such as Spandau Ballet and The Thompson Twins, which sounded like rigor mortis had set in. The computer relieved the producer or musicians of having to listen and make a value judgment. The business of making hits was too serious to be left to musicians and producers. Better let the computer help.

Drummers didn't always play along to machines or a click track. In the same 'less developed' parts of the world that failed to espouse the cause of tonal harmony and stubbornly kept rhythm at the centre of all things musical, they still don't. I spent my first 13 years blissfully unaware that I was supposed to be keeping measurable, metronomic time. But then somewhere in the late 70s, Roger Linn invented his

Linn drum machine, and a chill went down the drummer's spine as he realised he would be required to stay in tempo with this thing, down to an accuracy of but a handful of milliseconds. Suddenly the only drumming that was considered 'right' was that which was precisely with the machine.

In an era when producers were increasingly uncertain about what was or was not 'right' in drumming, here was scientific proof, measurable, visible on a screen, with which the poor drummer could be berated as his hapless bass drum flammed with the click from the machine, an unforgivable seven milliseconds late (or early). Recording sessions in the 80s were peopled with drummers terrified of being humiliated in front of their colleagues because they couldn't play 'in time'. The producer's lip would curl into a sneer as he stopped the take after about two measures, pointed to the drummer, and suggested he "tighten it up with the click". Take 2, of course, only got worse.

In a recent and belated discovery that the heart and soul of music isn't always to be found in automated clock-time, more sophisticated producers are beginning to resurrect the heresies of the past, and there is much talk of the music feeling natural and being allowed to breathe – both the kind of thing it was doing all the way from Motown to Liverpool and London to Los Angeles in the 60s and 70s. The more things change ...

The parallels between music and language are perhaps even more acute than those of music and food. Speaking well requires a faultless technical connection between the thought and its physical manifestation in language through the correct movement of lips, tongue, and teeth. A good speaker will need a rich vocabulary to provide words with which to say something interesting. He will also need expression in order to attract and retain the listener's attention. A nice sounding voice will help, too. And he'll need some sense of pacing and timing for dramatic effect. Every time we speak we have most of these in place to a greater or lesser degree, and every time they play, so do the top musicians.

The student drummer learns first to be able to control the sticks so he can play a note, and then a series of notes, steadily and at all dynamic levels, from a whisper to a roar. Assuming he's using the matched grip, in which both sticks are held the same way, he strives to give each stick an identical movement, the better to achieve an even sound from each hand. He learns then to evenly space these notes at all possible tempos, from very slow to extremely fast. He learns to co-ordinate various limbs to play complementary patterns simultaneously. And then the tricky stuff starts.

Now he has his right hand get louder and louder with fewer notes, while his right foot gets progressively quieter while adding more and more notes. Now he trains his feet to play three notes in the time it takes his hands to play four, or five. Now he has added a seemingly endless cycle of triplet variations between his left foot on the hi-hat and his left hand on the snare drum, rising and falling in dynamic waves across and around the beat, like the wind and waves howling up the beach in Cornwall, and retreating almost to silence before they come again.

At the highest level, the conversation within and between the jazz drummer's limbs and the rest of the ensemble is fluent, gripping, and an exercise in tension and release. Another man's phrases are set up, underscored, highlighted for effect, downplayed as if dismissed, doubled for emphasis. The more notes he plays, maybe the sparser the drummer will become, and vice versa. No use all talking at once. Maybe a high-speed squabble breaks out, or the music lapses into melancholy, or the other guy can't get a word in edgeways. The master of the drumset has no time delay between feeling the feeling or thinking the thought and the correct series of notes, on the right instruments, appearing at an appropriate dynamic level. And you can hear all this, or something close to it, nightly, in jazz clubs around the world, for the price of a beer and some peanuts.

And make no mistake about it, the young ones are good. They think fast and study hard. The teenage years will fly past in a blur of ever more graceful flam triplets in all inversions, duple and triple time. Sport, girls, food, and probably homework all go on hold. YouTube is full of clips of pre-teens performing amazing feats on the drumset, blissfully unaware of the obvious fly in the ointment: that rock, the conduit to fame, is a simple music that has little requirement for such dexterity on the kit. Its rhythms are straight, oscilloscoped, airbrushed, government-prescribed, neutered, and no foolin' around. You want to play that weird stuff: go and form your own group. And they do – and the best wind up playing to 1,500 other drummers at the Montreal Drum Fest.

I've sat at a drum kit most working days of my life, trying to acquire enough technique so I can forget about it. Some players make the fatal error of acquiring technique for the sake of it and then imposing it on the music. "I'm going to display my blazing quintuplets if it's the last thing I do." *The music does not exist to serve you; you exist to serve the music.* Better, I think, to hear something in your head that the music requires. If you can't play it, then go find a technique that will allow you to do so.

When I first pick up the sticks, I feel stodgy and slow. I need to warm up. Simple, powerful strokes eventually get some blood circulating in wrists and fingers, and soon the strokes come more easily. Drummers usually practise the rudiments, a codified set of sticking patterns with colourful onomatopoeic names such as flamadiddle and ratamacue. There are traditionally some 26 of these, mostly derived from military drumming, and it's like practising the correct fingering for your piano scales. These are the building blocks of the language, the basic words, from which I will compile rhythmic phrases and then sentences. They need to be mastered at all speeds and all dynamics, and in both duple and triple-pulse forms. Then you can forget about them.

A good snare drum specialist, like Jan Pustjens from the Amsterdam Concertgebouw Orchestra, can articulate these things so fast and so quietly that you have to stand about an inch away from the drum to make sure the sticks are actually touching it. If a mouse belched, it would drown out the sound. He can then play them so loudly, with the sticks descending gracefully from shoulder height and describing a beautiful arc, that he'd kill most people in a heavy metal group and the noise-abatement people would be over in a jiffy. Most of us just slog along trying to play them reasonably competently, slowly, a little improvement at a time.

Then there is the co-ordination bit. Three notes with this foot, four notes with this hand, both in the time of five notes with the other hand. For hours you can't play it, and then there comes a moment when suddenly you can. You feel a synapse buzz in your brain as two wires fuse, connect, bind, and make a circuit. For weeks you couldn't ride your bike, and then you got it. You wobbled a bit, but eventually you got it. Next day, you pick up the bike, and you don't even wobble. A good drummer is going through that a lot in his daily practice. The mere acquisition of technique, however, doesn't mean you're a musician of any calibre at all. It's the appropriate, effective, and subtle deployment of this stuff on the bandstand, in the heat of the moment, that proves you can play. We are all fantastic in our own front rooms.

Finally, as a mature, accomplished player, you will sew these more elaborate and sophisticated phrases and patterns into a fluent vernacular. As in conversation, one thought will flow seamlessly into another, now arcing back to reiterate a point in a different way, now leaping forward in a rush of excitement and adrenalin. Sometimes the musical point is alluded to, or understated, sometimes heavily defined or overstated.

Now that you have the technical capacity, the interest lies in what you choose to say and the way you choose to say it. Ask any four great drummers to play four simple measures on a standard kit, and each one's style and touch will be immediately identifiable and recognisably different from the next man. Ask them to improvise for a few measures, and their choice of notes and depth of expression will mark them out as superior raconteurs, unique storytellers. And the stories they are telling are the stories of the thousands of choices and options resulting from the millions of micro-decisions they've made over a lifetime at the instrument. They are the music, and the music is them. Like Roy Haynes.

❑

Another city awakes. Vancouver? Taipei? Chicago? A reflected dawn on office glass accompanies the gathering roar of traffic and the gathering complaints from behind my sleepless eyes. Could be anywhere. Even before breakfast – especially before breakfast – I have too much time to ruminate on my souring relationship. Recently we've fallen out, the drums and me. They demand too much. I used to believe they were inert until played upon. I used to believe it was I that breathed life into them, extracted life from them, while they remained, timeless and grateful. My reflection, once young, eager, handsome, and, above all, self-assured now appears as a shadow of its former self.

Oh sure, when we go out together in public, everything seems as though it couldn't be better. We are the perfect couple, me and my top-of-the-range Starclassic bubingas. They look beautiful in a deep piano black with a gold inlay, dressed to the nines. Thousands admire us as we dance prettily for the cameras. Ava Gardner to my Frank Sinatra. I play: my drums sing sweetly. But underneath, the relationship is rotten to the core. Fifteen-hundred unsuspecting Montrealians for whom we have just put on a dazzling display would be astonished to hear that, privately, our love affair is sapping me, its continual demands too much to bear. Something'll have to give.

17 YES, BUT WHAT DO YOU *REALLY* DO?

I t was 2004, and it seemed like a good idea at the time, as so many of these things did. My partner, the saxophonist Tim Garland, suggested expanding Earthworks up to nine pieces. He offered to write some fresh charts, and we could go to New York and hire some top-flight American players that Tim knew. (Tim knew everybody.) You'd only need one afternoon's rehearsal; it'd be cracking.

All the timings and availability pointed to Christmas or just before: images of a pristine, chilly New York City with happy shoppers carrying those huge, rectangular (always rectangular) red (had to be red) parcels floated through my mind as I listened to my booking agent Laurel's proposition on the other end of the phone. She was suggesting a return to the Iridium Jazz Club at 51st and Broadway. It had gone well last time, she cajoled me, and besides, this time it would be a week before Christmas. The city would be alive with out-of-towners doing shows and spending like crazy. There was bound to be a healthy passing trade.

Large ensembles are traditionally way too expensive to tour, so this was looking like a one-time event. One-time events, I knew from long experience, were things you needed to record. This would fill a nice gap in the CD release-schedule around the band's 20th anniversary. The weeks and months passed, visas were acquired, hotel rooms booked, recording equipment and engineer hired, charts written, the rehearsal room and musicians negotiated with and booked. There seemed to be some minor hiccup with the club booker, Ron Sturm, as to which nights we were required to play, but Laurel appeared to be taking care of that. It was going to be a five-night run, Tuesday through Sunday, with the Thursday off as the club had a private function. Perfect. We would record the Friday and Saturday.

The first night in New York I don't sleep much. The following morning I present myself at the agreed time at the agreed rehearsal room as the rain lashes down outside. Everyone has been well prepared with charts and audio beforehand, and the agreeable camaraderie gives way to some serious work for the first few hours. We take a break and wade over to the deli on the corner. Just as we are returning, one of the players corners me in the elevator.

"Bill, I've got a problem. I'm going to have to split and fly down to Miami. Got some family problems to take care of – need you to help me out." My blood runs cold. Rain water drips from this guy's hat, which he is fingering awkwardly as the elevator creaks slowly up to the 13th floor. "What kind of problem?"

"My brother's wife has smothered her baby and hanged herself." My mouth says one thing while my brain desperately rummages around for damage limitation. Is this guy crazy? Hard to tell: I only met him four hours ago, but we are both in the world's capital for crazed musicians, so I don't rule it out. Protestations of sympathy: " … horrific … of course you must go … spend time with your brother … as much time as you need … ." But I *need* this guy. There are only a handful of people in this city who can do this gig and they're bound to be busy. Players of this standard don't have whole weeks free in the middle of the holiday season.

Back up in the rehearsal room, it seems that I am about the last to know of this crisis, because the musicians' emergency network has started to kick in. A couple of calls later, a replacement has been located, in world rankings possibly an even better player than the departing musician. Unbelievably, he is not only available but already on his way down to the studio. Breathtaking. Only in Manhattan can you get internationally known players of such skill to help you out at a moment's notice, and this isn't even for big bucks, either.

We do the gig, without recording, on the Tuesday – with Thursday the agreed night off before moving in the recording gear for the weekend shows. The music is great in patches, but not yet showing the consistency you need in order to generate a whole CD's worth of cracking material. I am not unduly worried – these guys are extremely talented and professional, and I know I am in safe hands. But at the end of the evening lightning strikes again, this time in the form of the club-owner's father-in-law. This old buzzard lurks around upstairs, above the organisation's second property, The Starlight Diner, a singing-waitress-on-roller-skates kind of place. Although I didn't know it at the time, he is on strong medication to calm his aggression. Problem is, tonight he's forgotten to take the medication.

Turns out that the club has had the private function cancelled for the Thursday and needs me to bring the band in on its pre-arranged night off. Everyone has made other plans, accepted other gigs. There is no way we can come in, and the first few requests, and then demands, are easily batted away. This festers through the whole Wednesday gig like an open wound. The buzzard is accustomed to getting his way, and this limey he's never heard of is refusing, point blank, to play when so ordered. Ten minutes before the second show, I walk back into the dressing room to find eight musicians cowering in the corner while this bristle-headed lunatic is prowling up and down like a demented Marine Corps Sergeant telling them what he's going to do to me when I come back. I walk in, and he goes ballistic.

Standing inches from me, his face a little lower than mine and apoplectic red, he starts screaming at me. Who do I think I am? Don't I know this is fucking Broadway we're talking about, not fucking New Jersey? Over his shoulder I see the cowering band, jammed into the corner of this miniature dressing room, wondering how I'm going to wriggle out of this one. He's screaming that if I don't agree to do tomorrow, Thursday, not only will he cancel the rest of the gig through the weekend, but – and this is the bit I really like – "YOU'LL NEVER WORK IN THIS TOWN AGAIN." Really, he said that. I'd waited much of my career for one of these assholes to come up with the cliché to end all clichés, and here it is. I savour the moment.

But his face is still inches from mine, and he's not going to let this go. My problem is, if he's not bluffing and pulls the gig, my next album goes down the tubes. The upfront costs will hurt, and all these guys will need to be paid, whatever. How I don't hit him, I'll never know. I gamble, decide he is full of shit, and call his bluff. I remain unfailingly polite – regret that won't be possible … extremely sorry – in an exaggeratedly English kind of way, my voice getting quieter while his gets louder. He doesn't know what to do with a wimp that won't fight, one who's whispering in a foreign language. For him it is like screaming at a French blancmange. Eventually he storms out, saying that's it, the gig is cancelled, to pack our bags, and so forth.

We don't play the Thursday, as long ago agreed, and after many unreturned phone calls, an apologetic Ron Sturm explains the bit about the medication as we wheel in the recording gear for the Friday. Hey, happens all the time, he laughs. Doncha just *lurve* Noo Yawk? I could love it a whole lot more without this weasely apologist and his manic father-in-law. When I was 15 or 16, I probably dreamed of playing in an organisation like The Jazz Messengers one day. Had I the imagination, I would have considered that the highest possible objective would have been to one day play my own music with a big-band of crack NYC players for a week in a great club and record the results. After that I could imagine no more. I could die happy. That is where I have arrived at, this week, some 35 years later, and I'm damned if I'm going to let a local lunatic destroy it for me.

❏

What we musicians really do tends to be elusive, variable, and under constant redefinition. The computer and digital storage have again shifted the perimeters of the ballpark, bringing into question a whole host of previous assumptions. As American composer Milton Babbitt has pointed out, the computer has shifted the boundaries of music away from the limitations of the acoustic instrument, or the performer's ability to play it, to the almost limitless possibilities of the electronic instrument. For Babbitt, the new limitations are the human ones of perception.[1]

This raises questions of musical origin. All digital sources can now be digitally reassembled, reversed, inverted. There is no necessary expressive weight or realism; there is instead a flattening out of the differences between human and non-human sound, natural and non-natural sound, intended and found sound, music and noise. No sound, in short, can guarantee trust.

I remember lying in bed early one morning listening to the radio in the UK, sometime in the early 80s, and hearing one of my first experiences of sampling. The sustain and decay of a bell at Winchester Cathedral turned imperceptibly into a choirboy's treble voice, and back again. How did my perception of the value of the sound change, when I knew it was a bell, and when I knew it was a human voice? New ways of listening are being devised as we speak, in a new world where we no longer know, nor seek to know, the origin of the sound. Who, then, is the author of the music: the computer operator, the software designer, or the recording engineer? Whose 'self' is being expressed?

There seems to be a growing feeling in today's musical environment that the words jazz and rock, along with the other creaking musical nomenclature of the mid 20th century – rhythm section, gig (a one-night engagement, or more generally, employment), charts (the written music), and so on – are not only meaningless but also patently misleading.

The question now, surely, is not "Is it rock?" or "Is it jazz?" but "Is it alive? Is it dead? Is it Memorex?" Were any human beings involved in the making of this music? If so, were they in the same place at the same time, and thus able to adjust their performances in accordance with what they were hearing from someone else in the room? Was it a recording of their performance, or was it a recording of their performance as 'source material' for later manipulation, otherwise known as post-production?

If human beings interact musically on some basis in real time, and the recording of that event is, broadly speaking, deemed to be the main point of the exercise, let us, for the sake of argument, describe the resulting music as 'performance-based'. By this definition, the performing musician has a heritage of millennia, going back to the first time somebody rattled some bones in a cave and someone else looked up and said: "Yeah! Do it again!" Encouraged by this, our prototypical cave musician is amused by the ease with which he had managed to get a smile, friendship, warmth, and love. He repeats it, and finds that the magic could be made to work twice.

The performer lives or dies – and neither outcome is certain – in a performance space in front of other human beings. He must earn their love, possibly on a rainy Thursday night in Swindon. His audience have probably had babysitter problems, certainly had transport and parking problems, and have just been relieved of about £80/$150 by the time they've sat down and had some drinks and a bite to eat. In the next two hours, the performer's livelihood depends on his being able to charm them into the belief that what they have just heard was not only worth it but would – this is the important bit – be worth braving all the babysitters and car parks again for the same ticket price plus a bit for inflation when the performer returns here in 18 months time. If he can do that, he has a career on a stage, which is dependent on no middleman, except possibly the promoter, but certainly not a record company, nor tour support, nor sponsorship, nor any of those unhealthy things.

The performer must communicate in such a way as to transport the listener to another world, a world of dreams if you like, that is inhabitable only by going to that performance by that particular band or artist. Different fantasies are on sale. The listener can identify with the power and control of an artist over the audience, whether it is the brazen instrumental heroics of a Nigel Kennedy, a Buddy Rich, or a Jimi Hendrix, or the more intimate lyrical seduction of, say, a singer-songwriter, a James Taylor, a Tracy Chapman, or an Amy Winehouse, or any number of variations in between. The concertgoer joins a like-minded club of people, the audience, all of whom, by the nature of their considerable outlay on the event, have a vested interest in the performance succeeding to everyone's satisfaction, artist included.

The well-known and much loved English troubadour Roy Harper still, remarkably, has an audience, despite his well-documented ability to shoot himself in the foot. I played in his band for a while and would be as entranced from behind the drums as the audience were in the room as he came to the close of a heartbreaking rendition of one of his beautiful songs. He was seated at the front of the stage, bathed in a slowly tightening pool of light, and you could practically hear the sobs and sighs from the female members of the crowd as the last guitar chord hung in the air, to fade like stardust. With the audience in the palm of his hand, this is a moment many artists strive for, and which Roy could create effortlessly. After the applause, he'd look up, sneer, and say something like: "I would have enjoyed it too if it wasn't for these fucking monitors." You could hear the air escaping from the balloon, mortally punctured. You could hear the sound of the Ming vase hitting the floor. As if to say to the listener: I can make it, and I can just as easily smash it.

The instrumentalist will know hours of lonely practice time, relieved only by marginally more sociable rehearsal time. He'll know terminal boredom, transport delays (because of course no one has as yet managed to find a way to bring the audience to him), sweaty palms, and performance nightmares. He'll know the elation of success and the unnerving feeling that everything he is doing might just be irrelevant. He'll live in the fear that his ability to weave this magic that we call music may one day desert him and that the people will come no more.

This could be distinguished from another kind of music, whose essential characteristics are governed by the computer and in which the

303

sound sources are predominantly pre-recorded samples. If human performance is required at all, it is usually provided sequentially from one or more performers rather than simultaneously, provided in ignorance of what future or past contributors may or may not have played, and provided as musical 'raw material' for later editing, manipulation, and insertion into the fabric of the artefact, as deemed appropriate by the programmer – who may well begin, continue, and complete the entire project at his computer.

The key word here is control, and it tends to be used often. The programmer, who may well be the record's producer, indeed has complete control over all aspects of the recording, which will be polished, enhanced, and 'improved' until it is 'perfect'. Minor 'blemishes' are airbrushed out over months of painstaking work until the 'product', polished and manicured, is wheeled out to the waiting public. He may well play no musical instrument, as we know it, at all. He may play several. He may have no ability to read or write music and be equipped with only the barest of understanding of any musical theory. Or he may be able to do both. No matter: he sits at his computer in silence, usually alone, the digital orchestra-in-a-box awaits his command, the cursor flickers on his Sibelius music software, and he inputs the first note, on silence. It's the beginning of a long process toward some sense of completion, a process that if you are Peter Gabriel may take ten years.

Like a sculptor, notes and sounds are added and removed, the whole shaped in the programmer's own time without the response of an audience: plenty of time, maybe too much time, to reconsider, change, and amend. Finally, the day comes when he can say it's finished, or it's finished until he starts again, or the client will wait no longer, and the long march begins to sell the music to whomever: record company, publisher, TV station. Not for the programmer the sweaty palms, the performance anxiety, the hours training the body in the small muscular movements of the violinist or the coordination and stick control of the drummer.

Instead, he's like the novelist, secluded with orchestra-in-a-box and computer, able to work anywhere in the world until the product of his labours must be taken to market, like the fattened pig, and sold for the best price, if he can find a customer. He may perform his music live, but more likely it will be sunk into the audio track of our lives as background, library, TV, movie, or advertising music, the demand for and supply of which is huge. He may often remain anonymous, hermetically sealed from the fickleness of audience-demand, which is translated to him only indirectly through the demand from his clients.

Both programmer and performer reside under the large umbrella called 'musicians', but the process and mechanics of their respective production couldn't be more different, and the key difference is real time versus programming time. We are at a point in a continuing process that started with the invention by medieval monks of musical notation, which for the first time allowed music to be made without the composer present. Right up to the 60s, you needed at least a few instrumentalists to realise what was on the paper, or in the demo, or in the writer's head. With the subsequent inventions of multi-track recording, of early string-synthesizers that could give an approximation of a string section (and which incidentally gave the Musicians Union a near heart-attack), and of MIDI, there was a decline in the use of and need for instrumentalists. As digital samples have improved and become completely acceptable, the programmer need hire no musicians at all for his full-scale movie score. The one activity – programming – seeks to remove any doubt or mystery from the process; it seeks a kind of perfection.

The performer, on the other hand, implicitly or explicitly acknowledges that music is wholly imperfect from the start, even at the level of the imperfection of the Western scales he uses. He acknowledges that for his performance to be a success, both he and the audience must, to some degree, lose control rather than exert it. He is on a tightrope, and he can only go forward, never back. The programmer acquires control so that he may know the outcome; the performer relinquishes control because he knows he cannot know the outcome. The person who wants to make what we've agreed to call, imperfectly, 'performance-based' music has no interest in perfection, believing that music in general and he himself (as both musician and human being) are so riddled with imperfection that pursuit of the perfect becomes not so much foolish as irrelevant. His interest lies in the outcome when he and two or three or a hundred of his colleagues play something simultaneously. Unpredictable thousands of mis-intonations, uncontrollable hundreds of combinations of sound-colours, and uncountable variations in rhythmic phrasing are collectively known as expression. From this he derives meaning – and, hence, pleasure – from the music.

The beast to which he and his real-time colleagues give birth might surprise them, as they meet it for the first time on playback speakers. It may well have ugly bits. It may not be quite as planned, if they had attempted to plan the music at all. But it will also have a kind of truth that cannot be denied, expunged, or enhanced. It is, simply put, what it is. You want something else? Do another take or get a computer.

If the one kind of music is characterised by acquiring and retaining control, and the other by surrendering it, then I am, by inclination, in the second camp. There is nothing pejorative in this analysis: anyone is at liberty to find meaning in music in whichever way he or she can. 'Performance music' is neither better nor worse than 'computer music', but the aims and outcomes involved in and derived from making it are qualitatively different. For me, the computer path, in the broadest use of the term, is the one where I can make no musical sense, where I can derive little meaning while nevertheless standing astonished at the practitioners' technical skill. I have no frame of reference by which to distinguish indifferent from imperfect, truth from half truth, the artfully cosmetic from the downright dishonest. It's probably just too new, or I'm too thick.

'Performance' music, on the other hand, an idea that is thousands of years old, seems to have a simpler frame of reference. After several hundred years, we have a rough idea of what can be done on a piano and violin and, more recently, drumset and saxophone. Others have gone before, and we feel connected to their earlier endeavours. One of the many attractions in a return to acoustic in-the-moment jazz recordings is that the authorship is clearly audible. I and my drumset are clearly identifiable on the other side of the recording medium. The world of live or recorded performance is one that resonates with unforced error, human accident, happy coincidence, missed chances, astonishing good luck, hidden intentions, oblique references, and the full catalogue of happenstance that is mirrored in all human existence. It sounds like a place in which I can live and breathe and have my being.

All music was performance-based music until the very recent technical innovations of editing and multi-track recording. The brave new world of the current digital manipulators is perhaps too young to have produced its *Rite Of Spring*, its *Love Supreme*, its *Are You Experienced*. So just before we all give up learning musical instruments in favour of buying a computer-based recording system, let's take a moment to reconsider the remarkable mystery of music and the way it imparts its multiple meanings to both practitioner and listener. When we look each other in the eyes, count to four, and start hammering, we have more than simply you and I playing. We have the two of us playing *together* and, if we are lucky, a third element will appear, and we'll make something called music – or at least the only kind of music I'm ever likely to inhabit. Three of a perfect pair. Call it jazz, rock, or anything else you like.

❑

With the rise in digital post-production and remastering has come the parallel demystification of the composer and his art. He now seems to be someone who provides raw materials on which the serious business of digital surgery and processing will be performed. The war of the artist and the scientist in the recording studio has been going on for years, neatly paralleled in what is going on either side of the glass. Time was when, as the providers of the sound source, the musicians had a very big space in which to operate, while the manipulators of the sound – the scientists or engineers – had a sort of small hut full of razor blades and editing tape that no self-respecting musician would go near.

Gradually the positions have been reversed, so that now the scientists' place, full of gleaming knobs and hi-tech gear, is four times the size of the tiny performance space, where a human might, on occasion, overdub, one at a time, onto some previously prepared tracks. The message is clear: most of the composition will be created from sounds residing in or digitally transferable to the computer, and the fellow with the trombone is an increasingly unusual sight.

Similar and vital arguments continue about the purpose of music, the freedom of artistic intention, the freedom of listener response, and so on. Technological development has irrevocably changed the context – the sense of musical time and space – in which the debate takes place. In the abstract, it is true that musical technology has made possible new, liberated ways of composing, performing, and listening. But it is also true that it doesn't operate in the abstract, but as a commodity force, a matter of equipment to be bought and sold, hi-tech magazines to be read, bits of equipment to be owned that will give you the edge over the other guy but also enslave you to an unwinnable arms race eagerly fostered by the consumer electronics and pro-audio industries. The detailed effects of new technology are always unpredictable, because nothing seems to get used exclusively, or even at all, in the way it was intended, but at the end of the day the conservative manufacturers of technology are unlikely to lose, no matter what we musicians do with it.

This is the context in which tomorrow's fresh-faced and bright-eyed instrumentalist, or 'musician', will begin work. This is the shop floor on which his efforts will be judged and found to have more or less meaning and value. If it isn't already, talk of rock and jazz will soon be effectively meaningless. The debate for the drummer, much the same as any musician, will be to do with the way in which, and to what extent, the human interacts with electronics, or if he or she chooses to interact at all. Live or programmed? Electronic drum gear will need to become more user-friendly in terms of expressive power, through easily accessible, real-time controller functions such as sustain, portamento, and pitchbend, and stop pretending it's an acoustic set.

The phenomenal technical ability of some of today's drummers is being developed in the service of the manufacturers away from the music – any music – in the hothouse atmosphere of drum clinics and extravaganzas, and there is a potential problem here. There will always be a guy who can spin plates faster than the previous guy, but the imaginative leaps necessary to refine, define, and redefine the role and purpose of a drummer in a musical context may be harder to come by, and will only come from within the music. The more subtle virtuosity of a Bill Stewart or a Jack DeJohnette is rooted in the subsoil of the music from which it came: it's connected to something other than athletics. In that context, some really interesting young players to watch are Mark Guiliana from Avishai Cohen's group, in the USA, and Martin France and Asaf Sirkis, in the UK.

Immediate future developments in the musical landscape for the drummer seem relatively predictable. Generally, the cannibalistic and jaded Western mass music market will continue to refresh itself with the more vibrant musics from elsewhere, as it has done with great effect already with the music of Cuba, Jamaica, Senegal, Brazil, and elsewhere. More drummers will need to know more about more music, so if you have experience of the art of other cultures you'll already have a head start. More djembes and darabukkas on stage!

The rapid decline in payment for recorded music is matched only by the rapid ascent in payment for live music. For those of us who remember only yesterday making impressive tour losses on the road in the name of 'promoting' the big cash cow, the album, this is a reversal of practically indecent haste. If you can play, live, in the moment, if you can hold an audience's attention with a display of control, then abandon, if you can seduce and tease with your instrument, if you can make it up on the spot, or even appear to make it up, you'll always have a gig. If it's a different and unique performance from night to night, from city to city, and you can give the customer that feeling that it is a one-night-only ticket-buy, an un-downloadable experience never to be repeated, you'll always have a great gig.

At the beginner's end of the scale, the future is very exciting. More people of all ages are starting out with better instruction on continually improving equipment, daily discovering the joys and heartaches of trying to play four decent notes in a row. Good teaching has a pivotal function in all of this: it must signpost new ideas, techniques, styles, and cultures and it must facilitate the coming together of the like-minded across continents.

Broader interpretations of the effects of technology on popular music have tended to reflect either an optimistic point of view or a more pessimistic one. Optimists see in the new technology, almost any new technology, the means of democratisation and empowerment. We can all make CDs in the bedroom, sell them on the internet, and put on a live show in the pub – certainly democratic and empowering. The pessimist – and the 30s Frankfurt School cultural theorist Theodor Adorno was the original music-industry pessimist – tends to regard the consumer in mass society as little more than a walking credit card who, docile and compliant, buys the music he is given by a cynical record industry. For people like Adorno, technology is dominant, beyond human control, and popular music is only one of the ways in which a docile labour force can be kept in mindless contentment. For the optimist, technological innovation has given ordinary people the potential to exert some control over their cultural environment, and choosing their own music is one of the ways in which they can affirm and celebrate their newfound sense of identity.

Most likely the truth lies somewhere in the middle: that the modern music business exhibits the characteristics of a dual economy in which dominant hi-tech industry and mass-production can co-exist with small-scale participatory projects. They may even exist within the same company. Richard Middleton, contrasting the views of Adorno and colleague Walter Benjamin, put it this way: "The main types of development taking place in the 30s, and extended much further since, are both an immense strengthening of the possibilities of uniformity and control, and a broadening and democratizing of opportunities."[2]

In his book *Big Bangs*, Howard Goodall tells us how American composer Steve Reich talks of electronic music as the urban folk music of our time. "He believes that music is returning to its original condition – one in which the divisions between 'classical' and 'popular' did not exist. In recent years, record companies have paid lip service to the notion of 'crossover' music. What they mean, though, is one artist symbolically crossing the floor of the record store to plunder the audience of another artist. [Nigel] Kennedy playing Hendrix, Vanessa-Mae playing Bach with a drum machine, symphony orchestras playing Queen songs, [operatic] tenors pretending to be football stars, and so on. They do not mean crossover in the Steve Reich sense, that is, the true collaboration of idea A with style B to create form C."[3] Reich seeks an urban music through an infinitely richer cross-fertilisation between musical genres, between the acoustic and electronic, the analogue and digital, real time and virtual time, that technology can now afford us.

❑

I've had 40 years to make my modest contribution to the percussive arts, and I've been exceedingly well heard. Not for me the sour grapes, the if-onlys, the constant whining that it could have been different. If anything, I've had too much public attention, and I've paid too much attention to it. My music – I can hardly bring myself to call these inadequate scraps compositions – has been well played and beautifully recorded. It has been disseminated globally, listened to, considered, and reviewed internationally, and I've been well rewarded with a comfortable living. I'm not in the least bit stage-struck. Unlike the song, I believe there are plenty of other businesses like showbusiness, only most are considerably less corrupt and corrupting, and I certainly don't believe the show must go on.

But I still have the passion. No doubt about it. Looking out at a hundred or a thousand or ten-thousand smiling faces at the end of a couple of hours of music-making, and receiving the applause with grace and dignity, is the real payback. The financial reward is the end-product of external negotiation about the music's monetary value, but at that moment in the evening, right then and there, there exists, for a few moments, a simple incorruptible relationship between you and that sea of smiling faces, between entertainer and entertained, between performer and audience, that is beyond compare.

The following morning, though, I may reflect on the quieter laboratory-world of some of my other friends in the arts – the sculptors and painters in their studios, the writers and composers picking away at their laptops – and envy the way their work can develop slowly, and far from the madding crowd. The creative musician in a commercial world must push and shove, market and network, and grow and flourish in a jostling, noisy, overheated, and highly competitive forum, miles from home, and in circumstances not, usually, of his own making. We do our best to contribute and push things forward, and afterwards we clear up the mess and lick our wounds. That's what we do in the daytime. That's what we *really* do.

18 ARE YOU MAKING THIS UP?

When you try to give up nicotine, you're treating with the Devil. I thought the deal was that if you gave up, the desire to smoke would also leave you, so that you wouldn't have to give up again every day. Somehow you took it as read that if you gave up, so did the craving. But the Devil saw me coming and sucked me right in. Oh, I gave up, but the delicious smell, feel, and touch of a cigarette remained as firmly embedded as ever.

My relationship with the drums is similarly bedevilled. The deal that I believed was on the table was this: as the days of intense practice turned into months and years, you were entitled to believe, or even expect, that such labour would bear fruit in the shape of a calm, relaxed certainty in performance, that it would deliver all the tools necessary for such a performance, and that those tools would never fail you. Surely, I reasoned, if you worked hard enough, that gnawing anxiety at the back of your head that you might be improperly prepared, that you might stumble in front of colleagues and listeners, with the inevitable greater or lesser humiliation, that anxiety would lift like the morning mist and you would operate only in the warm sunlight of confidence.

Like, say, Earthworks' demon young pianist, Gwilym Simcock. As a boy, he had laboured for years at Chetham's School Of Music, with teachers patrolling outside practice rooms to ensure correct schedules were adhered to. This apparently Dickensian treatment has equipped him with an enviable surety of touch. He doesn't make mistakes.

In my case, it's evidently going to take more than mere diligence. I work and wait, and wait and work, but the anxiety never quite lifts. Most of the time I keep it under control, and at the very best of times, when I feel at the top of my game, I can delude myself that the beast is conquered. Turns out it is merely skulking in its lair, waiting for me to age and whither so it can redouble its efforts and bind me into helpless inertia, as it wreathes my body and wracks my mind with the paralysis of self-doubt. That, surely, was not the deal at all.

After all those albums, phone-calls, upsets, tantrums, and tears, I seem to have arrived at a place I hadn't quite bargained for. The undeniable elemental force that had forced my adolescent arms straight down to the floor, that had electrified my soul (never mind the hairs on the back of my neck), that had proved to me that I *had* a soul, dammit – all that is now reduced to an uncomfortable feeling in the pit of my stomach every time I hear the latest whizz kid on record or on stage. People young enough to be my children have a technical facility and a depth of expression on the instrument that men, and increasingly women, of that age have no right to possess. How do they get to be that good?

I am being pushed aside inexorably into irrelevance. It's perfectly natural, chirpier friends reassure me: you've got to make way sometime. But an indignant half of me doesn't feel ready to make way. I still possess a quick tread up the staircase; I have quick wrists, a straight back, and volumes of experience, don't I? Anyway, look at Roy Haynes; he's not making way. The difference between the two of us is that there is no separation between him and the music: he *is* the music. There is a price to be paid for that. For me, the music is still external. I could, and did, separate from it to be a father and husband. I have had a life outside music. There was a price to be paid for that too.

Turns out everything of value has a price. Somewhere – I can't exactly locate the epicentre, but it is deep in the back and rear of my skull, a little more than half way down – there lies a deep and overwhelming tiredness. Like a soggy blanket, it must first be thrown aside to kindle the sparks, which themselves become daily weaker. Time was when the briefest of puffs would turn the glowing embers of musical effort into a raging fire of creativity, so hot that it was difficult to dampen down at the end of the day. But now the blanket is getting heavier, the embers duller, the effort nearly insurmountable.

Keep going, I berate myself; but every time I lift a foot, it comes down in the same place, without progress. I am not quite inert, but forward movement has stopped. With a skeleton staff, and only one working light-bulb, the factory will be kept open for a few more months in the event of new orders from a wholly unexpected source. But, I have to admit, that is unlikely.

As a youngster, I couldn't stop playing. Now, it seems, I cannot start. Then, every note was perfect, polished, wreathed, garlanded, and bedecked with self-confidence; now every note is riddled with the maggots of self-doubt. My earlier recordings were the sound of surprise, the sound of opportunities being taken, the sound of recklessness. Now, as an infinitely superior player, I don't hear what you hear. All I can hear when someone presses playback is a digital litany of caution, inconsistencies, and missed opportunities. And it has only taken me years of practice, study, and touring to get from one to the other. This is the baggage effect at work.

A hundred recordings, three-thousand concerts, the sheer number of times I've heard it done, by myself and many others better and worse than me, the staggering amount of critical consideration resting in thirty-five volumes of scrapbooks, the baggage – the history, god, the history – all conspire to render me impotent. Weighed down with that lot around my neck, it is a miracle I can still function at all. Practicing is an effort of memory, and it has been several years since I managed a couple of hours without watching the clock.

At the end of my fourth decade, I now play in public infrequently and continually have to relearn the vernacular of some long lost language in which I was once so fluent. I remember individual phrases and several bons mots, but that's far from inhabiting it. This predicament is an inch away from intolerable, and I can scarcely wait to set the burden down. I know too much and can think of nothing to play. Best be silent, then.

❑

The essence of the relationship between musician and instrument is monastic, timeless, and unchanging. It may be a relationship as close as and as exclusive as man and wife, or even more so, as many a spouse will attest. The instrument is passive, the musician acting upon it. He comes to understand himself as the imperfection of his daily endeavours upon it are scrutinised for the slightest hint of progress. His life's work becomes the distance travelled from that first day so many years earlier when he first attempted to extract a pretty sound from an unobliging combination of wood, gut, metal, and reed laced together with piping, pads, hammers, and tension rods. He tried on that first day, when no one was listening, found his efforts wanting, and tried again. Twenty minutes or twenty years later, he may or may not have achieved more musical results – and twenty-thousand may be listening.

The instrument appears to offer up its delights more readily as it recognises the hand and touch of an improved player, or perhaps a master. After long hours, the young acolyte's rewards become more palpable: now he really can play that fugue with the feeling it demands or that ride cymbal with a defined, personal touch. It is a journey without end and without competition, a journey of gradual enlightenment, during which he may come to understand himself better. It may be a journey of almost religious intensity, as it is for me, and I believe the distance travelled on that journey to be the only worthwhile measure of my life's work.

Society, however, may try to persuade me otherwise. For many years now we have measured a musician's success by how much money he earns from his efforts. 'The richer the musician the better the musician' goes the fallacy in this age of commodification. Unless the young aspirant understands, clearly and from the beginning, the essence of the private relationship he is about to have, how this relationship will be the source of all his strength and stamina, how it will be this relationship to which he will turn when the public listens elsewhere, as surely it will, how this relationship must remain unsullied, inviolate, if he is to have the slightest chance of achieving peace of mind and balance without which further right work and therefore happiness will be impossible – unless he understands all these things, he may easily be blown off course and stranded on the rocky and desolate shores of bitterness and regret. Only if the core relationship with the instrument remains sacrosanct will the original early joy of the child musician be protected and sealed from the slings and arrows of outrageous commerce.

I reflect on all this as I sip the first strong black coffee of the day and wait for my computer to fire up. It's a concert day, and I'm trying hard not to think why I do this. At the bottom of it all, driving events for the last four decades, there has existed in me a need, a desire, to contribute. To contribute to the drummer's art, and then to be publicly acknowledged for that contribution. To leave things, after you go, just a little bit different from how they were before you appeared on the scene. From that simple idea stems all the gig-hustling, the cold-calls, the weird rehearsals, the pushing, the shoving, the phoning and emailing. It seems only obliquely connected to being famous, a notion that doesn't exert one tenth of the pull of a much more important prize to be won – that of the respect of my colleagues.

Back at the start, I liked to subscribe to the idea that if you locked me in my music room with a snare drum, a pair of sticks, and some snare-drum etudes, I'd be blissfully happy to never come out again. We musicians maintained that the audience was a distraction, an easily-led flock of sheep that never 'got it'. This was mostly humbug. In fact, I was playing to an audience of significant others – my colleagues and peers in the music industry. Sure, it wasn't a very big audience, but it was very influential. I came to need their approval as much as I needed oxygen. It was an approval indicated not by record sales nor audience attendance but by a genuinely warm handshake backstage in the VIP bar, when visiting colleagues would drop by on their night off, in Rome, or New York City, or Tokyo. It was the ferocious camaraderie of this elite group that was the object of much of my strivings. These people knew what you had to go through to be that good, and if I was going to do it, I damn well wanted them to recognise it.

The drum and percussion community is large and may be the fastest-growing sub-group of musicians. Internal opinion-forming tends to be dominated on the commercial side by a few large magazines, and on the academic side by the Percussive Arts Society. Here a small clique of benefactors, stellar players, academics, and corporate bigwigs, almost exclusively American, have it within their power to confer on a lucky recipient the kind of public acknowledgement of a lifetime's contribution that many drummers quietly thirst for. The heck with trying to persuade the proles that they needed a 50-minute digital slice of state-of–the-art improvised music – boiling, fresh, audio libido. In an age of 'free' music and the declining CD, that's a mug's game. They'll never 'get it', anyway. But to be elected to, say, the Percussive Arts Society's Hall Of Fame – a glittering dinner with the assembled nabobs, a few words from the Master, a toast, congratulations, a short demonstration with the big-band, more toasts – after that, a man could die happy.

But in another lair lurks the nightmare, and the nightmare is Irrelevance. For the creative musician in a commercial world, relevance is confirmed in the only way it can be: by profit. I love profit and detest its absence. Profit is evidence of connection with real people who, having considered your work, find that diverting scarce resources from, say, that takeout Indian to your latest CD is a wholly worthwhile gesture. And in that gesture lies confirmation for the artist; that way lies sanity. The vanity publisher is toying with, at best, the irrelevant and, at worst, the delusional. Therefore, if you don't make a reasonable profit, you are either irrelevant or delusional, or possibly both.

Vanity publishing may be defined as the 'publishing abroad' of the writer's efforts by dint of his own private expenditure, irrespective of any market demand for the endeavour. By extension, any artistic effort brought to reality and the public's attention at a financial loss to its creator may draw the withering accusation of vanity publishing. If you, the artist, persist in cluttering the marketplace with objects, irrespective of monumental public indifference, evidenced by an unwillingness or outright refusal to pay for them in sufficient quantities to cover the cost of bringing them to market with a modest profit, then we, the public, may safely accuse you of vanity publishing.

It follows that those of us involved in the creative act who wish to elicit from the market a modest return, which may, at the lower end, be translated as a permission to continue, if not exactly an encouragement to do so, will inevitably spend a disproportionate amount of time on marketing and self-promotion. The market being now so crowded with all-comers, there is beginning to reside in this artist the cold fear that his efforts may cease to bathe in the warm and validating glow of public approval, as indicated by said modest profit, unless he spends every waking hour on relentless self-promotion. Tell the world you and your efforts exist. Get down on the hotel floor with an icepack and a strong coffee and do six mind-numbingly banal phoners before lunch.

The more edgy the fruit of your musical labours, the harder you will have to fight: not for its survival, but simply for its appearance in the market. And it hasn't even got into the (virtual) shop-window yet. Making a CD used to be 80 per cent music and 20 per cent logistics and marketing. Now the figures are probably reversed – 20 per cent music and 80 per cent logistics and marketing. Sales at Summerfold and Winterfold Records, my two small labels, are gratifyingly robust, but will continue to be so only with constant care and attention to the customer base. To employ assistance tends to raise costs without a commensurate increase in sales, thereby bringing you ever closer to the two-headed monster – she who must be avoided at all costs – Irrelevance and Delusion.

To be talked about, to be noticed for your work, is life. To be ignored – the unthinkable makes me shudder – that way lies death. "Did you hear Bruford's last CD?" (The one that took 184 emails to arrange, and a C-section without anaesthetic to give birth to.) "No … ?" (This rising at the end, with a question mark, a hollow interest desperately summoned.) "Didn't hear anything about it. Wow. That came and went pretty fast. Got another one soon, has he?" The lack of interest is palpable: both participants in this conversation are happy to be able to write off another contender as burnt out, harmless, no longer a threat to their own ambitions.

And every year, more good ideas are required to keep the chatterers chattering, to keep the industry's opinion-forming organs and journals well-oiled with dazzling articles on metric modulation, interesting ideas for two drummers, the possibilities of electronics for the improvising player, rhythmic displacement – that sort of thing. I've been in the forefront for years and made sure others knew about it, but there is no guaranteeing anything more than a two-paragraph obituary in a record industry magazine when I pop my clogs.

You see, this pop entertainment lark is all very well, but we musicians, we muddy foot soldiers – and there are plenty like me – thirst to generate a music worthy of serious consideration. We envy professionals with professional salaries: the bicycling, bearded university lecturer, a leading authority on nano-physics commanding commensurate respect; the veterinary surgeon like my father to whom the cattleman doffed his cap in the cowshed on a misty Kentish morning; the engineer who can throw a bridge across a mile-wide span of shifting estuary sands. These people do things, or know things, or both, and the letters after their names proclaim it loud and clear. Maybe I should have been one of them. Either you have some fun as a self-abusing, pouting rock star, or you have some letters after your name as a Fellow of the Royal College of Music. But don't faff around in the middle, neither rock nor jazz, with neither fun nor letters. In my 'popular' field of music, positioned well outside any academic ivory tower, there is precious little professional recognition to be had. My sort get their hands dirty in the tawdry commercial world, scrabbling around looking for coin in the most unsavoury of places and then tripping over their colleagues and workmates as they race toward an extra few thousand CDs, a marginally better gig, a BBC broadcast (much prized for the reasonable pay attached).

There is much lip service to the idea that my kind – the untrained, the unwashed, the unread – are of course every bit as good as that lot from the Royal Academy or the Juilliard School. The two problems being that nobody at the Academy or Juilliard seems to believe it and no one has told the great British public. So the disdainful look on the face of the Wimbledon estate agent as it becomes evident during the small-talk at his Christmas party that actually one has – horror of horrors – *no qualifications* in this music business, and is therefore barred by the authorities from teaching a child doh-ray-me, will be around for a little while longer.

❑

With three-thousand concerts and a hundred CDs since the start line, I find the landscape between me and the finish line not quite how I had imagined it. Instead of the smooth fertile plain of endless imagination stretching to the far horizon, I now find further progress blocked both by the rocky mountains of inadequate technical ability and the gulf of imaginative shortcomings. I cannot quite summon the ability necessary to create, absorb, interpret, and contribute to new music in new circumstances quickly enough; in short, I'm lacking sufficient quantity of the jazz musician's skills.

To survive, the jazz musician adapts. What makes him so economical, and hireable, is his ability to perform anything with anyone anytime, and still sound good. My background, by contrast, is the controlled regulated environment where music comes slowly and is laboured over collectively for weeks before being 'unveiled'. Nothing is likely to be required in a hurry. This is the comfortable environment I'm used to and that which I've subconsciously tried to impose on jazz, and it doesn't really work. The pivotal technique is sight-reading, and I'd certainly have to work it up were I to progress further. I am musically uneducated in the formal sense: a musician who neither reads nor writes music fluently. I tend therefore to thrive in a slower, more controlled musical habitat than my jazz colleagues. That, in turn, inhibits physical and artistic mobility. The ability to mutate on a whim, to function creatively in an environment of perpetual change – this is the great skill of the artistically imaginative and technically more secure jazz musician. Stubbornly, it remains beyond me.

Recent success at the Cheltenham Jazz Festival is followed by a letter of thanks saying how much the committee liked my work and would love to have me back "with another group ... or a special project". There you have it. I don't, unfortunately, do special projects. Or I don't produce them fast enough. The absence of these adaptive skills now, at this rather late stage in my career, points to my following the dodo. Opportunities to build platforms for my abilities and offer them to promoters diminish. Work dries up to 40 gigs a year, and progress slows, starved as it is of the oxygen of performance, the key to forward movement in jazz. Loss of confidence follows, and, like all malignant growths, feeds on itself.

Appearances with Russian pianist Olga Konkova, Swiss pianist Patrick Moraz, my American friends in B.L.U.E., and my Dutch partner Michiel Borstlap, with whom I'm appearing tonight – all these represent attempts to break out of this vicious circle. This scenario may have been disguised, or offset, in a happier economic climate but is exacerbated by the current commercial mayhem of declining CD sales, diminishing recording opportunities, and increasing performance and travel costs. My colleagues are running to take shelter in academia, and I need reasons to continue battling the mountain of emails and the desert of performer's block.

For a start, I'll need a fresh attitude to the very idea of what it is to be a musician. I look around at the other late-fifties executives at baggage claim at Heathrow T4. We've done well, absorbed a lot of change, contributed conscientiously, but we're looking and sounding perhaps a little long in the tooth. A comfortable retirement awaits. We surely cannot be expected to contribute forever at this pace. Besides – I cast around looking for excuses – others are waiting in the wings. Let others have a go. Every stage I occupy is one a younger player does not. Tim Garland would probably have a different, more enabling and positive view, something to do with relaxing into being what you are.

Every note I play, every choice I make on the instrument, is now the product of so much incremental thinking – so much baggage – that it is invidious to expect that next Thursday, or anytime soon, I shall suddenly have the vigour, youth, and confidence that I recognise in younger players, like the talented Mark Guiliana. And that's OK, apparently. Being who I am, and not finding what I am to be lacking, would be a good start, if I could only twist myself around to that way of thinking. How can I develop this fresh attitude? Presumably the same way Roy Haynes developed it. Roy is a product of his times as we all are, and that's of value in itself. I don't doubt that others accept my efforts as valuable: it's just that I don't. Anyway, tonight I have a London concert, and I don't know whether I want it or not.

❑

It may be possible to improvise my way out of this particular cul-de-sac. Certainly worth a shot. The word improvise has clear roots from the Latin for unforeseen. Improvising is what a musician does when the paper runs out, and it's great for developing new attitudes. When we improvise we're dealing with the unforeseen, and the rules of the game change markedly. It is a highly subjective process, long since banished from the world of corporate rock, which must reliably provide a standardised product. It won't do for the concertgoers of Wigan or Westchester to get a listless, sub-standard, and short set of music while the people a little further down the road, in Bolton or Boston, get a bonus 30 minutes because the gig was going so well, and the improvising so good, that the musicians couldn't be levered off the bandstand.

At its simplest, back in the days of rhythm & blues and early pop, improvising called for the instrumentalist to invent a new melody on the chord structure of the song. The term 'solo' is misleading, because usually everyone else kept playing, although now with added abandon. As soon as the singer stopped, the instrumentalist boys in the band could have a little fun. The tempo might pick up a bit (the volume certainly would) and everyone would dig into the music a bit harder now that they didn't have to keep shop for the singer. In the 50s and 60s, all this fun might last for a couple of choruses or so, and certainly 'stretch out' on the bandstand, but all good things have to come to an end, and with a smug "Bring the band on down behind me, boys!" the singer would announce his or her return to the mic, to be supported by a neat and tidy backing. There were plenty of 'boys' who didn't want to be 'behind' the singer and didn't think much of singers in general.

A more sophisticated form of improvising grew from this, invented for and flourishing in small-group instrumental jazz after World War II. A prescient Lennie Tristano, the blind Chicago-born pianist said: "All great jazz will come from improvising, not writing."[1] While the lead voice, typically a tenor saxophone, embarked upon a solo or reinvention of the melody, it became de rigueur to replace the basic chords of the song with richer alternatives, known as 'substitutions'. This process of reharmonisation lifted proceedings to a new level of skill.

A canny accompanying pianist provided a fresh harmonic terrain for the soloist that better complemented the line he was playing and suggested where it might go next, all the while sticking to the skeleton, or form, of the song. The continually evolving harmony had implications for the bass player, and with the drummer starting to stress different and ever-changing accents in the rhythmic phrases, it wasn't long before the modern jazz quartet was established as an ever-mutating organism of equals. This style reached a fearsome level of artistry with Charlie Parker, Dizzy Gillespie, Max Roach, and the John Coltrane quartet or Miles Davis small groups of the mid to late 60s – a level that many say took improvisation about as far as it could go.

As the psychedelics of the 60s merged into the progressive rockers of the 70s, this culture of expression through improvisation was espoused to a greater or lesser degree and to greater or lesser effect by musicians who commonly lacked the technical facility necessary to improvise anything other than a one-chord wall of sound. Fifteen-minute 'solo improvisations' by Jimmy Page of Led Zeppelin, Chris Squire of Yes, and Keith Emerson of ELP dispensed with any kind of a dialogue and moved the notion of improvisation into the circus, where it was roundly and rightly laughed at by the incoming punks.

By the mid 70s, the instrumentalist, and instrumental interludes in the music, had broadly become suspect. Gone were the two or more choruses of tenor sax on a Fats Domino or Jacky Benson recording, the fiery choruses from Scotty Moore on Elvis Presley's 'Hound Dog' that had so transfixed me as a youngster, the eight or twelve-bar guitar breaks on later metal records, the instrumental hooks of records like Gerry Rafferty's hit 'Baker Street' or Paul Simon's drum-led '50 Ways To Leave Your Lover'. Gone too was the progressive rocker's tour-de-force showpiece solo. Increasingly terrified by the possibility of 'tune-out', the record industry deemed it essential that the voice – the great connector on the radio – continue uninterrupted through the song, and the instrumentalist again became marginalised in the recording studio, needed only for the diminishing number of increasingly mundane jobs that could be done in less time by a human than it would take to program a computer.

Improvisers returned to their lairs whence they came, lairs sometimes called 'jazz' and sometimes 'contemporary improvised music', or just 'new music' if the i-word was deemed too scary for audiences or there wasn't a strong enough component of it in the proceedings. A hardcore of the committed wanted to remove the harmonic skeleton altogether and let the music grow without reference to correct or incorrect harmony and without linear melodic development. With the removal of forward planning, it was presumed that the music might have a greater chance of growing from small beginnings into unexpected areas, guided only by the intuition and instinctive interaction of the participants.

Jazz improvising implies listening and participating in a conversation, as opposed to reciting a written text. A good improvising jazz quartet, with or without a harmonic structure, is participating in a four-way discussion at lightning speed on the highest level. Paramount for success will be the ability to listen, to know when to contribute and when to be silent. I was well rewarded in the publishing and performance credits for a King Crimson improvisation called 'Trio' of 1973, and rightly so, although my only contribution had been silence. Had I played, I would have materially altered the composition, so my silence spoke eloquently enough to warrant a royalty share.

Depending on the musical skill of the participants, a spontaneous four-way discussion may produce passages of stunning beauty or terminal boredom, but certainly results that could not or would not have been realised on paper beforehand. Like any conversation between friends, improvisations may get heated, boring, amusing, poetic, argumentative, aggressive, and sullen in varying amounts and at different times, and in musician Glenn Sweeney's eloquent phrase they may be "as alike or unalike as trees".[2]

Britain has produced many musicians who have inhabited this music for years with honour and precious little succour: Derek Bailey (the late guitarist and friend of Jamie Muir); saxophonist Trevor Watts; trombonist Paul Rutherford; the venerable pianist Keith Tippett, who offered a marvellously spiky and largely atonal contribution to an early King Crimson piece, 'Cat Food' – all have ploughed a sometimes lonely furrow in the field of instant composition. There wasn't much succour either for earlier US improvisers Ornette Coleman, Archie Shepp, and Cecil Taylor, and I shouldn't think there is any more now for brilliant younger American players such as guitarist David Torn, pianist Matthew Shipp, and saxophonists Tim Berne and John Zorn.

Detractors suggest that this form of music-making may be of more interest to participant than listener, and they are distrustful of music that has not been 'worked on' with due diligence for hours on manuscript paper and in the rehearsal room. That ignores, of course, the fact that the music has indeed been worked on for the musicians' whole lives. Much of the point of adopting this method is to locate and occupy the space between the bar lines, the pitch between the pitches. If it could have been written, there would have been no point in improvising it. This is spontaneous composition, unpredictable (the participants may be as astonished and bemused by the results as the listener), honest, and raw. Unmanicured, it will convey a truth about the musicians that may be hard to arrive at in any other way.

As a keen improviser, I have come to learn much about my musical self in this particular forum. Improvising collectively with a noisy King Crimson in the 70s and again in the 80s, or in my conversational duos with pianists Patrick Moraz or Michiel Borstlap, I've been able to reach the parts that other methods of music making do not permit me to reach. One of my favourite Crimson tracks is the totally improvised, brooding 'No Warning' from *Three Of A Perfect Pair*. The unsettling, dark timbre of the drums from my hybrid acoustic–electronic kit defined an area that drew appropriate gestures from Robert Fripp, Tony Levin, and Adrian Belew – the whole as much a surprise to us as anyone else. Surprise is a common outcome in improvisation: intellect suspended, I listen to the audio of my hidden intentions. I watch arms and legs striking unlikely combinations of sound for no other reason than that is what my years of experience led me to strike.

Arnold Schoenberg allegedly maintained that "all composition is just very slow improvisation", and we accept the corollary, that improvisation is extremely fast composition, to be equally true.[3] Ideally, the listener cannot hear the join between the two – the composed sounds improvised and the improvised sounds composed.

For the improviser, there is no good or bad and few recommended 'techniques' other than to try to stay out of the way of the music, to react in the moment and only when you can no longer resist reaction, and to trust your 'inner man'. The absence of rules can make it a hostile arena for our classical colleagues who are not given to trusting anything that is not written down on paper and, thus, safely someone else's responsibility. The classical musician's contract seldom extends to the choice of note, merely its production. During the making of one of King Crimson's best-known albums, *Red*, the assembled cast was engrossed in the completion of the album's mini-epic, the 12-minute 'Starless'. The celebrated classical oboist Robin Miller offered a compelling reading of the main theme toward the end of the piece, to much approval from behind the control-room glass. We all wanted more, so he was asked to extemporise a short 30-second passage over a couple of chords for a fade out at the conclusion – with no written music provided. Robin felt unable to comply.

❏

These thoughts and others are occupying my mind as I drive up to the Purcell Room at the South Bank complex on the Thames. This is concert-hall territory, and round here serious is spelled with a capital S. In fact, the promoter of tonight's performance for the London Jazz Festival is John Cumming of Serious Music Producers. No larking about, then. I am playing tonight with my occasional Dutch partner, Michiel Borstlap, the other half of the Bruford–Borstlap Duo. Michiel is a classically-trained pianist with the mind of a jazz musician and knows these waters well. Accustomed to solo concerts, doubling the number of people on stage to two is, for him, practically a vacation. Halving the number I'm used to, from four down to two, doubles my anxiety.

Tonight, we will improvise. This is something we've done on a number of occasions around Europe and Japan, but going on stage without any prepared source material at all still gives me vertigo. As I approach the drum stool, my stomach turns over at the sheer reckless abandon of the enterprise. After several gigs with Michiel, I'm getting used to how he's likely to react in a given musical situation, and presumably he is becoming similarly attuned to my reactions. The absence of a bass player allows a keyboard player to produce his own bass parts, and the music can go anywhere without fear of harmonic contradiction, at least. I don't really know what he does or does not like, because I've barely been with him long enough to ask. At meals we skirt around the subject and steer the conversation toward the safer topics of luggage, telecommunications, and musicianly gossip. Like illicit lovers, we meet off planes, say little about the inevitable physical, acoustic union, do it, and depart without further analysis. And clearly we both like it that way. What's there to talk about?

Tonight, it is to be a pleasure like no other. The room is packed, and a sea of smiling faces is visible because this time I remembered to ask for five per cent house light – it's easier to play to humans than a black void. A hugely supportive audience seems to 'get it', and knowing they're on board can only help. One idea flows smoothly to another, within and between each instrument and player. For some peculiar reason, whatever I do sounds good, and I assume it therefore *is* good. From the drum kit, I monitor the architecture of each piece as it grows under our hands. This powerful instrument can imply, dominate, nudge, and control in matters of pacing, tempo, metre, dynamics, and timbre. Woods, metals, heavy, sparse, light, dense, quick, gentle, slow, violent – whatever space one has ventured toward is complemented and enhanced by the other in a courtly conversation without words.

There is the recurring sensation that I, or we, are not doing enough, that this is too easy – a wonderful feeling that is to be preserved, and one that is easily dispelled, as I have learnt to my cost, by doing more and making it more difficult. I steer around that particular trap. Tonight my accomplished and receptive partner and I are highly tuned – if not of one mind, then closing the gap between us rapidly. Eighty minutes seem like twenty. Drained, spent, soaked, we eventually conclude, and stand for a couple of minutes acknowledging the applause in a moment of deep satisfaction. This most delicious of feelings, the sense of having pulled something unique out of the hat, something that lives briefly but will surely die, whose short life gave pleasure to so many in the room: this is what I do it for. But what do you *really* do? I make music like this in real time with a feeling that can be as intense as any feeling I've known.

We musicians labour and endure, as does everyone. The only difference between us and plumbers is that, after labouring and enduring, we must produce a moment of magic at the Guildhall, Preston at eight o'clock on a rainy Monday night, whether we want to or not. Many others have produced magic for me. The Graham Bond Organisation at The 100 Club in Oxford Street in 1966 made time disappear. At another time and in another place, when Sting had stopped singing and moved to the back of the stage, pianist Kenny Kirkland took a solo of such intensity and energy that I thought the roof of the Royal Albert Hall might actually start to lift off if he did another chorus. At an industry convention in Los Angeles in 2004, Soulive played a set in a chandeliered hotel ballroom that was so committed it could not be denied – it was the only music in the world for them at that time. Weather Report produced a beauty and stillness of such quality you could practically touch it in a packed and sweating tin-roofed club outside Dallas, Texas.

Michiel and I had to do something similar tonight, and I'm not ashamed to say that, for several people in the audience, we probably did. For tonight at least, the beast is conquered.

19 LETTING GO

There is much clamour in the music industry about the pace of change, but at a deeper level, where the normal human instincts of greed and lust for power exist, life continues much as usual. The business of popular music is by nature deeply conservative, and there are several areas in which life for the instrumentalist has changed little in almost a century.

Foremost among these is our obsession with novelty, alive and well in the industry now, as it was around World War I. Then, the musical-hall act was in search of the novelty song that the milkman could whistle. Now, fame-show contestants are looking for that edge that will give them a 'new' feel. But novelty has a sliding floor. The only thing harder than attracting the public's attention is retaining it for more than Warhol's 15 minutes. Generally, genuine newness would not be welcome, were it to occur, because there would be no frame of reference against which to measure it, and a whole army of critics, theorists, and tastemakers would be instantly speechless. It is inadvisable to take a risk on something that seems too new. Too much newness attracts instant critical disapproval – Stravinsky, Miles Davis, the minimalists. Anyway, new to whom? Newness in the artwork or in the reaction to it?

Punk was not a new music: it was basic three-chord guitar rock, but a bit louder and a little faster. What may be considered novel was the reaction to it as it was dispensed by those particular people at that particular time following that particular Grundy TV show. Almost all popular music is judged in reference to the 'other' – it's not that, so it must be this. To be too far ahead, to offer a music that is incomparable to another, would be unwise. In practice, we settle for a rearrangement of ideas that previously have been accepted: a joining of this to that, folk to punk with the music of Billy Bragg, rap to rock with Aerosmith doing 'Walk This Way', and the ultimate post-modern way of making music where sample-based records have bits of this stuck to bits of that, as in the work of DJ Shadow. We throw the ingredients up in the air and see what lands – white reggae, gangsta rap, or the particularly organic kind of singer-songwriter-based rock bands we've had recently in the shape of Coldplay, Travis, David Gray. Not much new there.

Secondly, the corruption endemic in the system almost a century ago is still very much in evidence now, despite the efforts of platoons of inspectors from industry trade bodies. Remember the attractive figure of Allen Klein and his thumbnail description of business practices surrounding the Stones and The Beatles? Or the music publisher who paid the music-hall act to sing his songs, an older version of the American payola scandal of the 50s? Or the manager in the reception at Advision studios with his artiste's 'biography'? Yes got started in return for a small consideration, as did (according to manager Brian Lane) Pink Floyd, Jimi Hendrix, The Animals, and countless other household names.

Our favourite records have been spun by our favourite disc jockeys since time immemorial in gratitude for the cut of publishing royalties, the favourite white powder in an envelope, or the invitation to guest on holiday with record executive or artist manager. The picking of hits is too important a matter to be left to the public, in an industry that continues to border on the barely legal. The obsession with power, too, remains very much as it always has been. The big fish continue to swallow the little ones. The perpetual struggle for the establishment and protection of copyright by record companies, publishers, and composers continues unabated, if now largely in cyberspace, and this remains the battlefield on which the musician must perform and survive.

Finally, the occupation of being a musician continues to be muddled up with celebrity, in part because the creation of pop music today seems more concerned with the problems of design, packaging, and marketing than anything to do with the specifically musical. Once you have decided what it is to be, once it has been designed, the actual production of the artefact seems relatively easy. Most musical building blocks are now available pre-formed, ready cooked, on preset 1, with built-in reverb for all occasions. With the absence of harmony, counterpoint, instrumental skill, and notation there is no need for all that traditional knowledge, and looped drum samples will take care of the rhythm – a bit like painting by numbers.

Anyone can do it, and is doing it, in his or her bedroom. The specifically musical skills of, say, arrangement, if you were Benny Goodman or Nelson Riddle, or melody if you were Cole Porter or Paul McCartney, appear to belong to an earlier era, now deemed irrelevant. In the cold, brave, post-modern world, the creation of music for the popular market is down to designing the sequence of audio events and the accompanying visual, be it video or live on stage, in a way that attracts maximum attention. The right synthesis of musical gestures and audio events is required to trigger the investment required to bring it to public notice.

There were a couple of interesting developments that came to light a few years back, perhaps in reaction to this situation. The first takes us back to the analogy of the horse race, with the difference now being that the one horse that does win no longer pays for the nine losers. Industry insiders will confirm that the hits no longer pay for the misses.

Secondly, and more interestingly, pop is becoming more local. According to British critic and commentator Robert Sandall, "seven out of ten CDs bought in the world now are by locally-based acts unknown outside their country of origin. Acts like our own Ms

Dynamite, who go down a storm in London, but don't sell all that well in Edinburgh, much less in Detroit".[1]

I take this as a welcome sign that control is once again swinging back to the musicians, which is where I instinctively believe it should lie. That recalls the post-modern mantra: "Think locally, act globally." Any music benefits enormously from being derived from some specific local context or sub-soil, for example Bob Marley, John Lydon, the music of whole cities like Detroit, Charlie Parker, Pete Seeger, Ms. Dynamite, a French chanteur, an Italian 'voice' unknown outside his own country but selling out stadia within. It is from the local context, from real connection to real people, that any music – your music, my music – will get its longevity. The art of the songwriter is to take the specific and make it general, make it touch us all, even across cultures.

So the music is fine, or will be fine, if we just leave the musicians alone to get on with it. It is the business that is sick. The good news is that even the men in suits now appear to realise this, and change is possible. Industry commentators say it will take two to three years for the companies to put their houses in order, and they are worried that a generation of customers is being lost. This may be described as an understatement of gargantuan proportion.

❑

SUMMERFOLD RECORDS PRESS RELEASE
Bruford to retire from active service.

Yes, King Crimson, and Earthworks drummer and bandleader Bill Bruford will no longer perform in public effective January 1 2009. After an exemplary 40-year career that has moved through progressive rock to electronic jazz and on to acoustic jazz, Bruford will hang up his sticks and concentrate on 'related activities'.

"It's been an exciting four decades, but now it's someone else's turn," said

Bruford. "I'd like to thank my friends and colleagues and the greater listening public for giving me a more-than-fair hearing. My ambition was always to try to contribute to drumming and music in the broader sense – to try to imagine a better way of doing things today, or the sort of things we might expect drummers to be doing tomorrow. If I've managed to push things forward an inch or two over the years, then that is a source of satisfaction."

Bruford will continue to talk and write on the subject of his career and the percussion scene in general, and will archive and manage his voluminous back catalogue of recordings on Summerfold and Winterfold Records.

I called Carolyn into my room for a second opinion. She said something about it not seeming much after all those years of graft and went back to the kitchen licking the spoon. This was the worst thing – there was no gold watch in this game. I should have liked one of those. Presented with that bauble, the mothballed colliery worker, the creaky security guard, and the dusty academic with the elbow patches on his Lovett tweed jacket could all put a line underneath their lives' work and move on. But that seems beyond us in the music business, which requires that, like Sir Cliff Richard and Donny Osmond, we are all Peter Pans, forbidden to grow old. I had to write a book before I could move on.

I swore I was going to cease activities when one or the other of these three arrived: 3,000 concerts, 50 North American tours, or the new wide-body Airbus A380 superjumbo. Arrival of the big plane wins by a short head. If you think I'm standing at baggage claim with 600 people waiting an hour for my suitcase, think again. I'm not going to choke to death in my sleep like Tommy Dorsey, or Hendrix, or die in a hotel room. Heck no. I'm going to put the damn thing down before it kills me.

My personal journey through music started as an ignorant 18-year-old who knew everything and became, after decades of honest toil, the marginally wiser 59-year-old who at least knew he knew nothing. A modest achievement, I hear you say, but any change is better than no change, and change by its nature is unpredictable. Most musicians don't even manage that – and here's the rub – because we don't really want them to. I change only the word 'writing' into the words 'playing music' in the first line of this quote from Alan Bennett's *Writing Home*: "I know so little that [playing music] is like crossing a patch of swampy ground, jumping from one tussock to another trying not to get my feet wet (or egg on my face). Of course, at a distance no one can see the ground is swampy, and at a distance, too, one's movements are smoothed out, the hesitations diminished. Fifty years on, the anguished leaps may seem like confident strides. Except who will be looking?"[2]

I am lost in the pleasure-grounds of grand despair. Daily I look for evidence that my heart may be in it still, and daily I look in vain. The miracle is that my heart has been in it for so long. Scarcely a day goes past without me thinking how I can wriggle out of this. I consider the meaning of retirement, and the meaning for me is retirement from public performance. Staying on top of the instrument is the hard bit, and daily I seem to lose confidence, exacerbated, no doubt, by the fact that I'm grinding into yet another dry patch. When my foreign trips do finally arrive, I face each one with greater trepidation and sweatier palms than the one before: each generates more tiredness and each gets me home even faster than the one before.

What gets up my nose is these people who seem to think that you "just love playing, doncha? You'll never quit, you're a musician. You love it really". What makes them think I don't want to put down the drumsticks as much as the accountant his calculator, the surgeon his knife, the politician his portfolio, the lawyer his brief? Is music in some way less onerous? Oh yeah, right, I forgot … it's a gift.

It is late April 2007, and I have one foot out of the door for a thirteen-day ten-city clinic tour across Canada. I am riddled with apprehension.

After a long lay-off, this daily two-hour solo show will administer an impressive electric jolt to the system. Just to get on the plane, to get from private to public, domestic to professional, I now must go through a psychological separation that requires physical manifestation. I will even have to separate from Carolyn and the calm routine she represents by sleeping in another room the night before departure. In the same way as it seems to be taking longer to recover from tours, shows, and late nights in general, it also seems to be taking longer to separate from domesticity and espouse the platform. Sleep remains elusive. I panic: what if I don't go to sleep at all? The feeling of doing all the long-haul tours (and, increasingly, closer gigs) with a paper-bag of tiredness over my head is becoming irksome.

I'll hang up one pair of sticks on the wall, put the tubs in their cases, and do it cold turkey, like that clarinettist – what's his name? Artie Shaw. That's the guy. Retired to California as the 40s equivalent of a megastar: golden clarinet, the whole works. On his 44th birthday, had a little play, put the instrument back in its case, clicked the lid shut, never touched it again. Said his perfectionism would have killed him, that compulsive perfectionists finish last. I like this guy. Couldn't wait to lay down the burden. Amen to that.

The feeling of the end of something is unshakeable. Maybe it will be death by a thousand cuts. Eventually the sheer scale of the petty irritations may outweigh the fear of having to answer the obvious question: "So what else would you be doing?" So long as that one remains unanswerable, I guess the petty irritations will remain tolerable. The crippling self-absorption, the shameful navel-gazing, the sleep deprivation, the recurrent self-loathing, the debilitating jetlag, the endless soundchecks, the relentless self-promotion, the email 'interviews', the patient dovetailing of domestic and professional, the feeling in the pit of my stomach as I hear Harry's puttering Peugeot in the driveway, the never being there, the haggle at check-in, the pushing and shoving – all of it, the whole shooting-match, the whole nine yards could be dumped if I could just mouth six little words: "I no longer perform in public."

The drum industry revolves around the guys with tattoos, now, and World's Fastest Drummer competitions. This stuff is pumped up by the drum magazines and by retail, who need to shift kits. There is a whole industry egging on a battalion of over-qualified drummers who think music is some kind of athletic enterprise, and who have mistaken drumming to be an Olympic sport. And they're all so damn well behaved, clutching their latest DVD on '32-Way Independent Co-ordination over 1,001 Ostinati', complete with a seven-hour instructional bonus DVD on how to set up the drums. I ask you. Oh, but they've never played in a band, let alone one that's produced any music worth a damn. Get outta here.

What is the origin of this dull aching-to-stop, this desire to lay down the load? I've become the wet dream of every 40-something white male with a receding hairline and a drum kit he put in the closet when he got a mortgage. I'm doing what they would have done, they think, if they'd had the balls. "Don't ever stop," they order. "Keep doing what you are doing," they instruct. Until when? Until they let me stop? Until I drop? And all this aching while I have the best band with the best musicians with whom I've ever worked, and the best review from Neil Tesser I'm ever likely to get. It is one of God's little jokes that, after diligent labour and focused improvement over this long a stretch, I am, despite the accumulation of the experience and technical ability of a lifetime spent at the instrument, unable to imagine the future.

There is motor reflex involved in this, for chrissakes. Gimme a break – I can't be expected to have all those patterns at the tip of my sticks at 60 same as I could when I was 20. Conductors may go on developing into late middle age, like claret, but with the possible exception of Roy Haynes, drummers go flat. Like beer. Anyway, I don't want to end up like grandmaster Max Roach, the American living legend, he of the MacArthur Foundation Grant. Last time I heard him, and it was shortly before he passed away, there was daylight between him and the bass player. Not even close. How are the mighty fallen. You don't want to see Muhammad Ali in the ring again, do you? Get outta here. Give the young cats a turn. Every time I've got my fat old rear-end on a stage, some other kid hasn't.

On a cultural level, I wonder why I seem to have been born into one of the most determinedly arrhythmic nations on Earth. I blame the Protestants: we were quite a merry lot until they turned up. After 40 years, I suppose myself to be a bit of an expert in rhythm. After all, I've spent my life studying it, dissecting it, prodding it, seeing if it is alive, wondering why it's inert when it shouldn't be. And not just the mechanics, but its metaphysical nature. Few days have gone past since the age of 15 when I have not had a pair of sticks in my hand and a rhythm running in my head. I've lived a working life in increments of a millisecond, the time it takes for the stick on the cymbal to move from playing ahead of the beat to playing behind it.

I've spent countless thousands of hours, often with Casals in mind, trying to space the notes evenly. I don't think I'm much good at it, but there are certain tempos at which I've become reasonably accomplished and within which I'm pretty unshakeable. At those tempos, I can play ahead, behind, or smack through the middle of the beat, can produce illusions of the pulse getting faster while the tempo remains the same, and can blur or shade the rhythm with fancy rudimental embroideries such as flams and drags and little rolls that inhabit the inside of that rhythm. I now play the best music I can with the best musicians I can find to a higher standard than I have ever played before – and it's time to stop. Another of God's jokes.

In rock music's terms, I'm an extremist – practically a terrorist. I occupy a position slightly to the right of Attila The Hun. I look like Marks & Spencer Man. I subscribe to an English middle-class 50s blueprint for lifestyle and morals, and I like to be in bed by 11 o'clock if at all possible. I have one wife and one family, all of whom are entirely functional. I am unable to brandish a broken home, an unhappy childhood, poverty, addiction, malnourishment, or a child-beating father as evidence of my street credibility. I don't drop my aitches or affect a different social status to the one into which I was born, and yet I have more in common with Johnny Rotten or Patti Smith than I do with the tattooed and spandex'd 'alternative' corporate rockers – Megadeth, Metallica, Motorhead – tediously peddling their Daily Mail version of the 'rock'n'roll lifestyle' from the Jacuzzi-laden shag-carpeted private 747s so beloved of the tabloids. I have a different version. And what is this revolutionary creed to which I subscribe? I practise a musical instrument assiduously in order that I might come to know myself, and I don't think it's a joke. I think of new ways to deploy it, and I don't think that's a joke. I write music and join and lead bands to demonstrate that deployment. I try to get better at all things musical. And I don't think your opinion on whether I am successful or not in these modest endeavours is particularly relevant. I mean, c'mon, how anti-establishment is that?

Bill Bruford Productions Limited was incorporated in 1972 to provide percussive services to the music industry, on the advice of my then manager Sam Alder, and since then has done a good job of accumulating paper. There are the draft contracts, the revised drafts, and the final contracts customary when hiring the services of a publishing house, a record company, or a management firm in one of about 30 countries.

There are four decades of correspondence with accountants and lawyers, British, German, and American, VAT Inspectors and tax authorities, collection agencies such as the Performing Right Society, industry organisations such as the Percussive Arts Society or the Musicians Union, musical instrument manufacturers and distributors, insurance companies, phone companies, and financial advisers. There are the accounts, the audits, and the audits of the audits. From tour accounts, ongoing disputes, and withholding tax, to petty cash disbursements and petrol receipts, the company's global efforts generate a mountain of discussion and the ensuing paperwork.

Then there is the constant hum of legal affairs, the negotiating of the contract and its subsequent renegotiation as soon as the ink is dry. Rule of thumb for a musician is that if you receive something around 75 per cent of what you are owed, you're doing well. There is always the manager of an Argentinean radio station or the owner of a Bulgarian jukebox who has mislaid the playlist return. US independent record distributors have a habit of scuttling like crabs in the sunlight toward Chapter 11 of the Bankruptcy Code when the going gets tough. Jem Records of Plainfield, New Jersey, neglected to pay EG Records in the UK for 14,000 copies sold of my first Earthworks title. This was more effrontery than financial disaster – how could these people do this? – and caused considerably less pain than the $200,000 hit taken by Robert Fripp's admirable DGM Records when American distributor Indy-Alliance went down without paying for some 15,000 King Crimson boxed sets. That was a severe knock to the solar plexus of a small company. At the time, they were distributing my music, too, and for a minute we thought the ship might not recover. Yes, but what do you do in the *daytime*?

Haven't been in a recording studio in ages. Are there any left? The home-recording phenomenon is now so engrained that I can't imagine wheedling a budget out of someone and watching the clock again, like back in the Livingston Studios days with Earthworks. All my most recent records have been recorded live on stage, and that has a rightness about it. It returns the artefact – the recording – to its proper place, where it should be. Its artificially elevated stature over these many years has given all us instrumentalists an unnecessary amount of grief. Let's get back to the proper relationship: the one between an audience and the performer. If you must record the event, well, OK, but I'd really rather you didn't.

Beneath this administrative mountain, I struggle to play. How energising it would be to know what I know now, yet be released of the historical baggage, both commercial and musical. One small drum kit and my playing ability remain, everything else wiped clean. There is the remarkable case of jazz guitarist Pat Martino who, in 1980, underwent surgery as the result of a nearly fatal brain aneurysm. The surgery left him with amnesia and, among other things, without any memory of the guitar and his musical career. With the help of friends, computers, and his old recordings, Pat made a remarkable recovery and learned to play the guitar again. There is, he claims, "some irony in this. You may have lost what you thought was valuable, but in the [healing] process itself, you gain so much value, primarily because you are a clean slate; the board has been wiped".[3] It might be nice to have your board wiped.

Most musicians, like most people, will tell you all the things they are going to do when they win the National Lottery. There is the first symphony, the jazz suite with strings, the second instrument they always wanted to play. Luckily, they never win the Lottery. I won a lottery when I was 22 and have been able to indulge my wildest musical fantasies ever since. Satiated, I fantasise no more.

For better or worse, I seem to have acquired the notion that life constitutes a hurdle race. It began when I was young and will finish, maybe, upon retirement. At the beginning of the race, the hurdles were low, the spacing wide, my energy indefatigable. As the race has progressed, the hurdles have become higher, the spacing closer, my energy diminished. The most recent hurdles – live albums in New York, cross-Canada clinic tours – are practically insurmountable. I have paused by the side of the road to catch my breath. If life is to be an endurance test, then the only way out is to allow patience to give purpose and meaning to the endurance. Carolyn has endured with me and been a witness to that endurance. To live in the present and to pay attention: these appear to be two among many life skills at which I have not excelled. If I go back to anything from Robert Fripp's reading list of 1972, it is always to P.D. Ouspensky's two-word reminder to "remember yourself".

The system is constipated and clogged, with little room for the fresh and new to appear. And it's me, my history, and I that are doing the clogging. Rock has moved up through the demographic, and the stadiums are filled with grandparents listening to pensioners like The Rolling Stones. We can all do better.

I'm spending a lot of time these days with my pride and joy, Summerfold and Winterfold Records. I got all my recorded material back from something that was EG Records, who sold my music to Virgin, who were swallowed by EMI, who now are probably Universal, but I can't be sure of any of this. The big boys are probably punch-drunk from having to deal with Robert Fripp, a feeling I know well. If you've gone ten rounds with Robert, you'll likely throw your hands in the air and concede defeat.

My lawyer wrote one letter to the legal man at Virgin/EMI with the words King Crimson, Robert Fripp, and Restraint Of Trade in close proximity, and that was it. Surrender. Some 30 titles have now been reissued and repackaged, and I'm proud of all of it. Those snapshots are my babies. In the early days, every note was laboured over and fought for, but jazz has a more confident swagger and a little more maturity, so the later records were made more in the moment.

There are readers of this memoir who are probably lamenting the absence of a track-by-track breakdown of my recorded efforts – which cymbal was played where and when, who produced what track, and why did the Japanese version contain three fewer edits than the European standard version? I can't remember most of it – detail on that level fills me with ennui. Only the bigger picture holds any interest now.

After this length of time, you, I, and Led Zeppelin are in the heritage business, whether we want to be or not. I'm curator of the All-Things-Bruford Museum. "This way to the first Yes bass drum head, if you please."
"Early electronic drums, sir? This way, over to the right."
"Yes, sonny, that really is the snare drum he used on 'Roundabout'."
I'm a theme park. Was it really like that in 1969? "Why, sure." A time

before microphones on the drum kits, monitor systems on stage, security at airports – a time now so indescribably ancient that young people can barely place it in any kind of timeframe. If I had looked back 40 years when I was a beginner, it would have put me in about 1925, staring at sepia pictures of Zutty Singleton or Baby Dodds, with a funny little drum kit comprising a Chinese cymbal, some woodblocks, and an enormous bass drum as big as his grin.

Having left the 70s largely undocumented, we hit the road running by the time we got to the 80s. We recorded the gigs, the rehearsals, the rehearsals of the rehearsals, and walking to the rehearsal room. Twenty years hence, someone, somewhere, will pay for this: that was the unspoken motivation. Now we've all got movie cameras, so we can add and retain the visual element, too. *Sorry, I apologise.* It used to be that someone checked with you before you 'released' a recording to the public, so the customer was spared the warm-up, the almost, the nearly, and the not-quite. Those were binned, never to see the light of day. Now, any old ejaculate from the rehearsal room is prettified into a boxed set, for someone to buy – and he will. The small attaching cheque usually quietens any moral or artistic qualms. We've learned to look the other way. *Sorry, I apologise.*

Anyway, not much of this bothers me now. I can see the finishing tape. It's white, twisted, and fluttering in the breeze just up ahead. I feel good, coasting to a victory lap of honour. I did it, goddamit, I did it. The records got made, the gigs got played, the bills got paid, and no one found out. I've run this thing as long as I can. Gotta get outta here before someone calls me a 'heritage act'.

I tried to count up – it gets a bit bleary if you include short trips for sessions and so on – but I did, for sure, undertake and complete at least 46 American tours. I can remember meeting Alvin Lee, the widdly-widdly-widdly blues guitarist of Woodstock fame, on an American Airlines flight to New York shortly after that event, around 1971. He told me he had been on three whole American tours. Couldn't believe it.

Anyway, this victory lap … what I'll do is I'll take Carolyn, and we'll do a two-month tour of North America. We'll go to all the cities, in the same order we used to, from Boston to San Diego, only – and here's the sting – I won't have to play a gig! I'll just have the dinner afterward with the promoter and my friends and loyal supporters and maybe a radio guy, and we'll talk old times all night long and have way too much to drink. Then back to the hotel, and a flight the next day, on to the next town, for more reminiscing. Maybe the same thing in Europe, too. And after that I'll never look back.

❏

It is late 2007, and after twenty years and hundreds of thousands of miles, Earthworks is parked. I switch off the ignition, make sure it's got some petrol in case we need a quick restart, and leave it without looking back. As I come through Heathrow Terminal 1 on a grey December evening, I find myself lingering, dawdling. For the first time I can remember, I am in no hurry to leave the 'office', because it might be the last time. I look around to make sure I haven't left anything behind. I look at the departures hall where I had met Earthworkers so many times before with pre-dawn bleariness, switch out the lights, and walk slowly to the bus for long-term parking.

Apprehensive as heck about the future, but just now I need a rest. I feel like I'm very slowly shedding a skin and gaining a new one. This process is very slow, and seems so far to have a couple of characteristics. First, happily, this is out of my control. For all these years I've been in control, and there is a warm feeling from the fact that I am unable to regulate this skin-shedding or its speed. Second, it seems to be about diminution of self. The old self-centred skin of the performing artist, protective, thick, and prickly, is giving way to a thinner, shinier, more reflective, more selfless skin, with less need of protective qualities.

Perhaps what happens is that you give up playing for a few years, find that you cannot settle in any other walk of life, and then return to it, finally fully committed and knowing you'll do it until you cannot, because there is nothing else you can do. Maybe like Miles. Or like one of those released prisoners who tries civilian life but ends up wishing he were back in his cell. You might want to leave it, but it might not want to let you leave. You can check out but you can never leave. Maybe that's my future.

At 15, with A.B. Spellman's *Four Lives In The Bebop Business* in my school rucksack, I thought I too had to live the jazz life – drugs, unhappiness, poverty, premature death, the works.

I did my best to be miserable and doodled the fabled names of American nightclubs inside my schoolbooks. In these places I would carry out my whole life. I'd invent a new way of drumming at Small's Paradise in New York City like Max. I'd change the direction of music with my new band at the Plugged Nickel in Chicago like Miles. I'd record live at the Lighthouse on Hermosa Beach in Los Angeles like Cannonball, and probably be shot to death by my girlfriend between sets at Slug's in New York like Lee. And I'd be on first-name-only terms with everyone.

But it wasn't quite me, and at 22 years old I thought I could do better than that.

With a little compartmentalisation, I figured I could have it all. I could be music star in the music world and a normal guy in the normal world. Balanced, considerate Marks & Spencer Ordinary Guy would slot effortlessly into the ordered world of school runs and parents evenings, before changing in a phone booth and launching back out on the road as self-obsessed, all-consumed, all-consuming rocker.

Mostly it worked, and I fooled some of the people some of the time. But four decades later the chickens have come to home to roost, and now I'm not so sure. My schizophrenic methods have twisted me into silence, unable to be quite sure who or what I am. Maybe my first instinct was the best instinct, and everything should have been sacrificed on the journey. Was there another musical life I could have lived? Was there another whole series of parallel options, untaken, that would have led ... where?

Truth be told, I haven't really enjoyed my music-making for a while, even from my position of untold riches. There, I've said it, but don't be mad at me. It is given to some to enjoy this activity; the rest of us just keep our noses down and get on with it. The latter group, I believe, far outweighs the former in number. There are bits of the procedure that are intensely agreeable: the watching as arms and legs produce genuine surprise; the applause at the end of the concert; the camaraderie of fellow musicians; the fleeting moments when everything comes into focus live or on record and you know there is a God in heaven. Like all occupations, there also exists the intensely disagreeable. But neither the agreeable nor disagreeable circumstances surrounding the music-making should be confused with the pure enjoyment of the music-making itself. We musicians go a long way, literally, in search of that most intense of feelings. Until recently, I've always found just enough petrol to keep going, but not a drop more. Now I'm running on empty.

I keep a diary now, in the hope that it will enable me to look back over the years to the aspirations, hopes, and fears of months and years gone by, and to see how much was born into reality. Reality will not be so easily tamed. The present, and its relationship to its cousins the past and the future, is tenuous, slippery. Everything is in flux, including those hopes, fears, and aspirations. Yesterday's nightmare is downgraded to mere anxiety; tomorrow's fears are as yet unrevealed; today's aspirations may be forgotten tomorrow as new evidence comes to light as how best to plot the course of a life.

Who am I fighting? Me, of course. Could've been the drums I suppose, but it's me. And me's winning.

For the intrepid soul who wishes to perform on a musical instrument in public, and for whom we should have the greatest respect, everything bends and changes, but in different rhythms.

ENDNOTES

2. WHY DID YOU LEAVE YES?
1   *Jazz UK*, undated.

3. WHO MANAGED THE MANAGER?
1   Sid Smith *In The Court Of King Crimson* p.186 (Helter Skelter 2001)
2   www.bill-parkinson.co.uk/tom%20jones.html

4.HOW DO YOU GET THAT FANTASTIC SOUND?
1   The author is indebted to Simon Frith *Performing Rites: Evaluating Popular Music* pp.226, 227 (Oxford University Press 1996) and Richard Middleton *Studying Popular Music* (Open University Press 1990) for much of the argument here.
2   Kenneth S. Goldstein *A Future Folklorist In The Record Business* in Neil V. Rosenberg (ed) *Transforming Tradition: Folk Music Revivals Examined* pp.118–21 (University Of Illinois Press 1993).
3   Simon Frith *Performing Rites: Evaluating Popular Music* pp.333 (Oxford University Press 1996).
4   Howard Goodall *Big Bangs: Five Musical Revolutions* (Chatto & Windus 2000).
5   Chris Cutler *Technology, Politics And Contemporary Music: Necessity And Choice In Musical Forms* in *Popular Music* 4 1984, pp.279–300

6. DO YOU STILL LIKE PROGRESSIVE ROCK?
1   David Tame *The Secret Power Of Music: The Transformation Of Self And Society Through Musical Energy* (Turnstone 1984).
2   T.S. Eliot preface to Harry Crosby *Transit Of Venus: Poems* (Black Sun 1929).
3   Hollie I. West *Black Tune* in *The Washington Post* March 13 1969.
4   Lester Bangs *Energy Atrocities* quoted in Edward Macan *Rocking The Classics: English Progressive Rock And The Counterculture* (Oxford University Press 1997).
5   Robert Christgau *Christgau's Record Guide: The 80s* p.232 (Pantheon 1990).
6   Edward Macan *Rocking The Classics: English Progressive Rock And The Counterculture* (Oxford University Press 1997) and Paul Stump *The Music's All That Matters: A History Of*

Progressive Rock (Quartet 1997) informed much of the analysis of progressive rock here.
7   Allan F. Moore *Rock: The Primary Text – Developing A Musicology Of Rock* (Open University Press 1992).
8   Irwin Stambler *The Encyclopedia Of Pop, Rock, And Soul* p.374 (St. Martin's Press 1989).

7. DO YOU LIKE DOING INTERVIEWS?
1   Matthew Brennan *Down Beats And Rolling Stones: An Historical Comparison Of American Jazz And Rock Journalism* (Ph.D thesis, University Of Stirling, 2007).
2   Theo van Leeuwen *Music And Ideology: Notes Towards A Socio-semiotics Of Mass Media Music* in Terry Threadgold (ed) *Sydney Association For Studies In Society And Culture Working Papers* 2(1) 1988, pp.29–30.
3   Igor Stravinsky & Robert Craft *Expositions And Developments* pp.147–8 (Faber 1962).
4   Anthony Storr *Music And The Mind* pp.187–8 (Ballantine 1992).

8. WHAT'S IT LIKE WORKING WITH ROBERT FRIPP?
1   John Miller Chernoff *African Rhythm And African Sensibility: Aesthetics And Social Action In African Musical Idioms* p.112 (Chicago University Press 1979).
2   Sid Smith *In The Court Of King Crimson* p.248 (Helter Skelter 2001).

9. WHAT DO YOU MEAN, YOUR 'SPIRITUAL HOME WITH A BED OF NAILS'?
1   Andrew Evans *The Secrets Of Musical Confidence; How To Maximise Your Performance Potential* (Collins 1994).
2   *Telos*, spring 1991, interview by Florindo Volpacchio.
3   *Playboy* November 1971.
4   Russell Sanjeck *American Popular Music And Its Business: Volume 3: From 1900 To 1984* p.593 (Oxford University Press 1988).

11. IS IT DIFFICULT, WITH A FAMILY?
1   *The Sunday Times* January 28 2007.

12. DO YOU SOMETIMES PLAY WITH OTHER PEOPLE?
1   The author is indebted to David Tame *The Secret Power Of Music: The Transformation Of Self And Society Through Musical Energy* (Turnstone 1984) for the gist of the argument here.
2   Yehudi Menuhin *Theme And Variations* p.9 (Heinemann 1972).

3   David Tame *The Secret Power Of Music: The Transformation Of Self And Society Through Musical Energy* pp.18–19 (Turnstone 1984).
4   Simon Frith *Performing Rites: Evaluating Popular Music* pp.236 (Oxford University Press 1996).
5   Philip Brophy *You Are There: Notes On 'Live' Music* p.2 (Unpublished paper 1987) quoted in Simon Frith *Performing Rites: Evaluating Popular Music* p.239 (Oxford University Press 1996).
6   Philip Brophy *The Architecsonic Object* pp.109–110 quoted in Simon Frith *Performing Rites: Evaluating Popular Music* pp.240–241 (Oxford University Press 1996).

13. DO YOU STILL SEE ANY OF THE OLD GUYS?
1   Ruth Artmonsky *Musicworks* p.105 (Artmonsky Arts 1992).
2   George Savile, Marquis of Halifax *Moral Thoughts And Reflections* (Tonson & Draper 1750).
3   Teri Saccone *New Perspectives: Guide To The Music Industry* (Emerald 2003).

14. YES, BUT WHAT DO YOU DO IN THE DAYTIME?
1   Howard S. Becker (1963) *Outsiders: Studies In The Sociology Of Deviance* (Free Press 1963), *Art Worlds* (University of California Press 1982), *Art As Collective Action* in *American Sociological Review* p.39 (1974), and *Art Worlds And Social Types* in *American Behavioural Scientist* p.19 (1976) for the general thrust of the argument here.
2   Simon Frith *Performing Rites: Evaluating Popular Music* p.53 (Oxford University Press 1996).
3   Peter J. Martin *Sounds And Society: Themes In The Sociology Of Music* p.213 (Manchester University Press 1995).
4   Robert R. Faulkner *Hollywood Studio Musicians: Their Work And Careers In The Recording Industry* p.75 (Aldine 1971).
5   Lawrence Kramer *Music As Cultural Practice 1800–1900* p.45 (University of California Press 1990).
6   Richard Middleton *Studying Popular Music* p.85 (Open University Press 1990).
7   Richard Middleton *Studying Popular Music* p.85–90 (OUP 1990) for the general thrust of the argument here.

15. WHAT DO YOU CALL A GUY WHO HANGS AROUND WITH MUSICIANS?
1   Robert Cantwell *When We Were Good: The Folk Revival* p.57 (Harvard University Press 1996).
2   Simon Frith *Performing Rites: Evaluating Popular Music* pp.36–41, 124, 125, 127 (Oxford University Press 1996) for much of the argument here.

3   Ted Gioia *The Imperfect Art: Reflections On Jazz And Modern Culture* (Oxford University Press 1988).
4   Simon Frith *Performing Rites: Evaluating Popular Music* p.129 (Oxford University Press 1996)
5   Charles Shaar Murray *Crosstown Traffic: Jimi Hendrix And Post-War Pop* (Faber 1989).
6   Charles Shaar Murray *Crosstown Traffic: Jimi Hendrix And Post-War Pop* (Faber 1989).
7   John Miller Chernoff *African Rhythm And African Sensibility: Aesthetics And Social Action In African Musical Idioms* p.141 (Chicago University Press 1979).
8   *First Person Singular: why does opera get all the cash?* by Maureen Paton, Telegraph.co.uk, August 4 2007.

16. DO YOU JUST PLAY ANYTHING YOU LIKE?
1   Simon Frith *Performing Rites: Evaluating Popular Music* p.164 (Oxford University Press 1996) author's italics.
2   John Miller Chernoff *African Rhythm And African Sensibility: Aesthetics And Social Action In African Musical Idioms* (Chicago University Press 1979).
3   Simon Frith *Performing Rites: Evaluating Popular Music* pp.274, 275, 276 (Oxford University Press 1996) for much of the argument here.

17. YES, BUT WHAT DO YOU REALLY DO?
1   Glenn Gould *The Prospects Of Recording* in *High Fidelity* April 1966, p.58.
2   Richard Middleton *Studying Popular Music* p.67 (Open University Press 1990).
3   Howard Goodall *Big Bangs: Five Musical Revolutions* pp.210–211 (Chatto & Windus 2000).

18. ARE YOU MAKING THIS UP?
1   Ruth Artmonsky *Musicworks* p.100 (Artmonsky Arts 1992).
2   Glenn Sweeney of Third Ear Band www.users.globalnet.co.uk/~rneckmag/thirdear.html
3   www.watershed-arts.com/walker.html

19. LETTING GO
1   *The Sunday Times* February 16 2003
2   Alan Bennett *Writing Home* (Faber 1994).
3   http://www.allaboutjazz.com/php/article_print.php?id =764#health

INDEX

Page numbers in *italics* indicate illustrations.

ACKNOWLEDGEMENTS

AUTHOR'S THANKS

I would like gratefully to acknowledge the advice and input of Maurice Hamilton, Louise Haile, and David Luxton without whom this book would never have got started, and Tony Bacon, my eagle-eyed and ever helpful editor, and Nigel Osborne, both at Jawbone, without whom it would never have been finished.

In between, sundry members of the Bruford family, whether or not mentioned herein, have been more than patient in requests for suggestions and corroboration. Acknowledgement is also very much due to authors Howard Goodall, Richard Middleton, Edward Macan, Paul Stump, Anthony Storr, John Miller Chernoff, Simon Frith, David Tame, Howard Becker, Peter Martin, and Sid Smith, from whose expertise I have drawn, and to my sister Jane de Haven who unwittingly initiated my career in music – be careful what you give your little brother, he might just use it! Tony Levin is well known as the best photographer King Crimson ever had, and I am indebted to him for the use of his work. Hugh O'Donnell at DGM Archive has been helpful beyond and above the call of duty.

The book will have done little if it fails to draw attention to the sometimes brilliant work of the colourful cast of characters mentioned within, all of whom have ensured there was never to be a dull moment. Their ability to put up with me and my ever-shifting understanding of what it means to be a musician is gratefully acknowledged.

This book is dedicated to Carolyn, who was there.

PUBLISHER'S THANKS

Jawbone Press would like to thank Paul Cooper, Roy Flynn, Jim Halley, Peter Hodgson, John Morrish, David Simons, and Michael Wright.

PICTURE CREDITS

The photographs in this book came from the following sources, and the publishers are grateful for their help. Location or page number in bold is followed by an identifier and the name of the source. **Jacket front** (with King Crimson, Felt Forum NYC 1974) Peter Hodgson/DGM Archive. **Jacket rear** (at London Jazz Festival, 2007) Victor Franko. **1** Bruford Archive. **2** Tony Levin. **6–7** Bruford family, Bruford Archive; Yes portrait, Bruford Archive; Lane, Jim Halley Collection; Flynn/Hendrix, Roy Flynn Collection; Yes stage, Bruford Archive; beach Bruford Archive. **8–9** Muir, Robert Ellis/DGM Archive; UK, Bruford Archive; Ertegun etc, Bruford Archive; Alder/Fenwick, Bruford Archive; Genesis, Waring Abbott/Genesis Archive; Crimson studio, Barrie Wentzell. **10–11** Greek Theatre, Tony Levin; Simmons, Bruford Archive; *Feels Good* session, Dick Wallis; rehearsal, Tony Levin; ABC TV, Tony Levin. **12–13** ABWH, Bruford Archive; Gomez/Towner, Tony Levin; Crimson 94, Tony Levin/DGM Archive; Fripp, Ken Sharp/DGM Archive; Earthworks Mk I, Bruford Archive; Crimson 82, Bruford Archive. **14–15** World Drummers Ensemble, Fred van Diem; Earthworks Mk II, Bruford Archive; B.L.U.E., Yuka Fujii; Earthworks 2000, Matthias Ketz; Earthworks Underground Orchestra, David Sokol; Bortslap, Bruford Archive. The publisher has made every effort to contact the copyright holders of photographs used in this book, but if you think there's a mistake then please contact us and we'll correct future editions where necessary.

"The important thing is not what the author, or any artist, had in mind to begin with but at what point he decided to stop."
D.W. Harding *Experience In Words* 1963